Adult Education and Nation-Building

Adult Education and Nation-Building. A Symposium on Adult Education in Developing Countries.

Edited by John Lowe. Edinburgh, at the University Press

© EDINBURGH UNIVERSITY PRESS 1970
22 George Square, Edinburgh
North America
Aldine Publishing Company
529 South Wabash Avenue, Chicago
ISBN 0 85224 073 2
Library of Congress
Catalog Card Number 71-129105
Printed in Great Britain by
R. & R. Clark Ltd, Edinburgh

Contents

To all who
seek to promote
the cause of adult education
in developing countries

Introduction

J. LOWE

The States of Western Europe and North America have seldom attached much importance to the education of adults; Denmark in the nineteenth century furnishes a rare exception. Things have been otherwise in Soviet Russia and China, and they are otherwise in many of the so-called developing countries, where adult education is commonly a major concern of public policy and may well assume the proportions of a mass movement. The reason why governments in developing countries have to treat adult education seriously is plain enough. Resolved to achieve rapid economic and social development and to promote national unity they must somehow produce a skilled and informed adult population. Capital investment alone will avail them nothing if human skills are wanting; President Kaunda of Zambia might have been echoing the conviction of many heads of state when he recently affirmed that 'skilled and educated manpower is Zambia's scarcest resource'. In developing countries 'education for nation-building' is no idle slogan but a recipe for political survival. Yet it is salutary to note that a politician's recognition of the central importance of adult education does not mean that in practice he is either able or willing to match words with deeds.

The amount of published material about the theory and practice of adult education has suddenly begun to accumulate, especially in North America, and leading adult educationists in many countries travel widely in search of inspiration and assistance; among themselves they also speak a common professional language and subscribe to the concept of 'integrated life-long learning' now enunciated by UNESCO. Recent years have also witnessed the birth of several regional and international associations, supported by such new professional journals as those of the African Adult Education Association and the South-East Asian and South Pacific Bureau of Adult Education. Nevertheless, deep ignorance continues to prevail about adult education in particular countries and there has been virtually no attempt to draw cross-cultural contrasts and comparisons. Such efforts as have been made tend to be sketchy and unscholarly. For example, in 1964 UNESCO sponsored a comparative study of literacy that consisted in

the main of an indigestible compilation of data both difficult to interpret and almost certainly thoroughly untrustworthy.[1] After all, how
can you establish an international bench-mark for comparing levels of
literacy ?

The truth is that it is too soon to initiate detailed comparative analyses since little hard information is available about individual countries.
Moreover, statistics about adult education are almost universally un-
reliable for several reasons. First, agencies producing facts and figures
interpret its scope in a variety of ways; for some it refers to any educational activity that adults engage in whereas for others it means exclusively literacy programmes or remedial instruction or formal education. Secondly, methods of collecting data tend to be conspicuously
unscientific and there is evidence that some institutions are addicted to
padding enrolment figures. Thirdly, there is in general an awesome
gap between aspiration and reality, between what policy-makers like
to pretend or honestly believe is happening and what is in fact taking
place in the field. In more than one developing country, imposing
charts and tables are produced indicating how adult education programmes are staffed and organized from the metropolitan centre right
down to the village level, but on close inspection they turn out to be
imaginary. Moreover, whenever foreign investigators appear on the
scene such misleading evidence is often reinforced by more or less
elaborate window-dressing since few officials want outsiders to know
how painfully inadequate are many of their facilities. In any case, at the
central government level, and all too often at the local level, there are
few objective criteria by which to assess quality of performance. Any
achievement is often considered better than none at all and consequently magnified beyond its true deserts.

It is rapidly becoming essential to devise internationally approved
models for describing the aims and functions of adult education in
different countries. Meanwhile we are necessarily restricted to qualitative and descriptive surveys of selected countries. Thus the present
volume seeks to make no more than a modest contribution to the beginnings of comparative studies by presenting several papers, all prepared by professional educators with first-hand knowledge, on a number of developing countries now engaged in designing systems of
adult education. The only tentative attempts at direct comparison are
made in this introduction and in the concluding chapter, in which Dr
Alan Thomas enjoins us to reconsider the meaning of the concept of
'development' and advances the argument that some of the problems
besetting the developing countries equally beset Canada, his own
country. This symposium does not, then, purport to put forward even
the semblance of a comparative analysis. Single country or regional

studies necessarily mark the baseline from which comparative studies can begin, and this is what we seek to provide.

Terminology

A few preliminary comments about terminology are unavoidable. The meaning of the two key terms 'adult education' and 'developing countries' especially calls for elucidation.

Confusion still reigns about the meaning of adult education both within each country and in international exchanges of ideas and information. What appear to be more or less similar phenomena are described by a perplexing welter of names such as Fundamental Education, Social Education, Mass Education, Continuing Education, Lifelong Learning and *Education Populaire*. Even the term 'Community Development' is often used as though it were interchangeable with 'Adult Education'. The semantic muddle is further complicated by the fact that many activities palpably concerned with the education of adults are neither acknowledged as such nor carried out under the auspices of a Ministry of Education – in Spanish-speaking South America, for instance, as Dr Wenrich points out : 'the ministry or department officially responsible for education...has little to do with most of what will be here classified as adult education programmes'.

The International Congress of University Adult Education is currently trying to dissipate the fog of confusion by defining the field of adult education in such a way as to permit valid comparisons between one country and another. To date it has put forward a universal definition and a formula for describing subject matter. The Congress offers the following definition:

> 'Adult Education is a process whereby persons who no longer attend school on a regular and full-time basis (unless full-time programmes are especially designed for adults) undertake sequential and organized activities with the conscious intention of bringing about changes in information, knowledge, understanding or skills, appreciation and attitudes; or for the purpose of identifying and solving personal or community problems.'[2]

Missing from that carefully worded definition is the strong emphasis upon collective as opposed to personal development found in developing countries. Mr Roy Prosser, one of the present contributors, has taken this factor into account in proposing his own definition:

> 'The real nature of adult education can be exposed by defining it as that force which in its ideal application helps society to determine its ends, brings about a maximum of readjustment of attitude within society to any new and changed situation in the shortest possible time, and which evolves and imparts new skills and techniques re-

quired for the change.'[3]

In a recent paper, Mr Paul Bertelsen also stressed the implications for adult education of revolutionary social changes:

'The ideal of adult education is enhanced because in Africa development is not only a question of quantitative growth accompanied by minor structural changes. After their political revolutions most African countries have now embarked on a process of social revolution. Very many of the changes needed to enable growth to take place are of a qualitative nature, and important policy decisions are continually called for both at central and local levels; and if people shall not become mere objects of change, they must understand what is going on around them, and as far as possible participate in the decision-taking.'[4]

Between them, these three definitions or statements embody the idea of adult education as it is conceived in this symposium.

In order to differentiate subject-matter or content the International Congress of Adult Education has adopted a classification reflecting the specific adult needs that education seeks to satisfy:

1. Remedial (that is, Fundamental and Literacy Education).
2. Vocational, Technical and Professional.
3. Health, Welfare and Family Living.
4. Civic, Political and Community Competence.
5. Self-Fulfilment.[5]

It would be hard to improve upon that classification.[6]

The phrase 'developing countries' is normally used to denote a country that is generally thought to be economically 'backward'. A more precise definition is required for the present purpose. In a recent work F. Harbison and C. Myers[7] divided the nations of the world into four groups according to their economic use of human resources. Their groups are:

Level 1 Underdeveloped Countries
Level 2 Partially Developed Countries
Level 3 Semi-Advanced Countries
Level 4 Advanced Countries.

As their criterion for classification the authors took such factors as the number of teachers per 10,000 population and 'enrolment in third level (higher) education as a percentage of the age group 20 to 24'.[8]

The countries nowadays styled 'developing countries' appear to embrace levels 1 and 2. Of those herein considered the following would appear to be located at Level 1:

Ethiopia
Ivory Coast
Kenya

Senegal
South Pacific Territories
Zambia.
The following are located at Level 2:
Bolivia
Equador
Ghana
Peru
The Philippines
The West Indies.
Although in many respects economically worse off than any of the above countries, India is classified as 'semi-advanced' and so appears at Level 3. The explanation is, of course, that while economic progress in India is wildly uneven, the country nevertheless contains a large number of educated people, many of whom are university graduates.

The typical developing country tends to exhibit all, or nearly all, of the following characteristics: poor nutrition, overpopulation, a lack of capital, low real income *per capita*, low agricultural yields, low industrial output, low expectation of life, a shortage of hospitals, and poor communications. Within one country there may be a wide disparity in the rate and level of progress between one region and another. Having won their independence only since the Second World War a majority of developing countries must also face a variety of transitional problems such as tribal divisions, linguistic conflicts and hostility from their neighbours. In specific relation to education there are usually very few university graduates, not many people with a secondary education, and a shortage of primary school places. As a result most of the adult population will not have attended school at all or at best have spent a few years in an ill-equipped primary school. The illiteracy rate will be high.

Countries and contributors

The rationale for the choice of countries in the present work was dictated by a combination of related criteria. These criteria were: a representative regional spread; a reflection of the differences between countries arising from the particular colonial influences to which they had been subjected – namely, American, British, French and Spanish; each country should have a reputation for doing something positive about adult education, however little it might be; an adult educator in a key position should be available who would be able and willing to contribute an original and authoritative survey. It is perhaps unnecessary to point out that many countries other than those selected have done much to foster the growth of adult education: Hong Kong readily springs to mind as also do Tanzania and Nigeria. In other words, there is no suggestion that the selected countries have been uniquely successful.

The assumption underlying the regional selection was that the countries known as 'developing' are congregated in South-east Asia; the Indian sub-continent; the Middle East; Africa; Central America; Latin America; and the various Ocean Territories. Selection then proceeded as follows:

South-East Asia	The Philippines
Indian Sub-Continent	India
Africa	Ethiopia
	Senegal
	The Ivory Coast
	West Africa – English-speaking
	East Africa – Kenya
	Central and Southern Africa – Zambia
Central America	The West Indies
Latin America	Bolivia, Peru and Equador
Ocean Territories	The South Pacific.

One region is unrepresented, namely, the Arab-speaking area of the Middle East. The reason for this was that none of the Arab countries, with the possible exception of Egypt, which in any case is also an African country, appears to have a sufficiently developed system of adult education to warrant description. In the case of Africa it was of course essential to select examples of both English-speaking and French-speaking countries.

In addition, Dr Alan Thomas, Director of the Canadian Association for Adult Education, was invited to make some cross-cultural comparisons. One reason for inviting him was that he has argued that the demarcation line commonly fixed between the developed and developing countries is both artificial and potentially misleading. As he points out, judged overall by accepted economic norms, Canada is highly developed, yet at the same time much of its great land mass is underdeveloped. Furthermore, development should not be measured in economic terms alone but in relation to the quality of life. A second reason for inviting Dr Thomas to be a contributor was that in 1968 he spent four months as a visiting consultant in several African countries. It seemed desirable to ask him, in view of his distinguished reputation and strategically central official position in North America, to comment upon the similarities and dissimilarities between the situation he faces in his own country and that which he observed on his African journey.

Two of the contributors, Professor Jones-Quartey on West Africa and Mr Rex Nettleford on the West Indies, have written almost exclusively about the role of universities in adult education. This is not because they are élitists but because in their countries, as in several countries once under British rule, the universities have shown more concern for adult education than any other agency and because, as in the West Indies, they are sometimes the only agencies with far-flung responsibilities. Moreover, it is useful to know what two such well-established and forward-looking university extra-mural departments as those of Ghana and the West Indies are trying to achieve, since as a rule it is the universities who are expected almost everywhere to provide not only high-level courses but also professional advice and leadership.

A glance at the official positions held by the contributors should be sufficient testimony of their professional competence. The need for a symposium was demonstrated by the fact that when approached each of them instantly accepted the invitation and that during the period when the material was being assembled only one person asked to withdraw.

The sole restriction placed upon contributors was in respect of the number of words they should write. For the rest they were asked but not directed to deal with the following subjects : the indigenous definition of adult education; the historical background; the declared objects of the public adult education system; financial control and administrative organization; personnel; special problems. They were asked to refer to linguistic, religious, economic, and geographical factors in so far as they appeared relevant, and to conclude with an assessment of the effectiveness of the present provision and future prospects for expansion. Beyond that general recommendation no attempt was made to impose a standard pattern of presentation or a standard definition of adult education. Apart from recognizing the prerogative of such experienced people to tackle the topic as they saw fit, the editor was also aware that priorities and emphases vary from country to country. For example, unrealistic accounts would have been evoked had the formula prescribed by the International Congress of Adult Education been taken as a mandatory model. Thus in Spanish-speaking South America heavy stress is laid upon social action engendered by methods characteristic of community development. To have circumscribed the range of adult education would have obliged Dr Wenrich to leave out of the reckoning what he regards as the most dynamic and productive kind of educational effort. It so happened anyway that the contributors shared much common ground thanks to the care they take to keep up to date with international trends and the literature of adult education.

Common themes and distinctive approaches

What are the common themes that emerge from these accounts? All the contributors are pragmatists, seeing adult education as indispensable to and principally within the context of national development. For them it is no fringe activity but a social force which governments neglect at their peril. Simultaneously it helps to induce change and to enable people and societies to adapt to change with the minimum of disorder. They identify it closely with community development and the concept of self-help, especially in the French-speaking countries. Each of them is concerned about the sheer magnitude of the problem of providing an adequate educational service, for while deploying severely limited human and material resources and lacking good communications all their countries have to deal with large and scattered adult populations that are largely uneducated; India, above all, is confronted by appalling problems. The very weight of the resulting burden is hard for adult educators in more developed countries to appreciate.

Most countries must also decide to what extent they should retain the colonial legacy that they inherited willy nilly. It is often supposed that developing countries entered upon independence with nothing to build on. This is no more true of adult education than it is of any other social institution as Professor Bown demonstrates in her fascinating account of adult education before independence in Zambia. All colonial governments made some provision for adult education though it was usually very little. Countries such as Ghana and Nigeria, for instance, were strongly influenced by the practices of university extra-mural departments in England. More importantly, traditional societies have almost invariably had their own ways and means of educating adults, particularly through the process of socialization within the tribal group. The dilemma for the adult educator is whether to build on or to reject existing structures and customs. In some places institutions and practices ushered in by the old colonial regimes may be inflicting damage and yet be difficult to root out; in others, the borrowings may be beneficial but seem obnoxious simply because of their alien provenance. In deciding what to do about traditional behaviour patterns, the problem is not so much whether to accept or reject them as to ensure that they are identified and exploited, especially in the more remote rural areas. Nothing could be more dangerous than to introduce schemes that duplicate or run counter to well-established customs.

A second major dilemma is to decide just how many people to educate and for what purpose. The doctrine of universal primary education has been widely taken over from the Western world so that by extension it could be argued that adult education should also be universal. Yet how many developing countries have painfully come to realise that primary education for all can have disastrous consequences, that, indeed, both secondary and higher education can often be a curse when neither jobs nor an adequate standard of living are available for those who have experienced them; nearly all the countries under review, at a time when they are desperately striving to foster rural development, are embarrassed by the presence of large numbers of unemployed products of the formal school system and by a flight from the land by young people lured by the apparent attractions of the towns. It would be compounding past errors to raise among the adult population as well as the young expectations that cannot be fulfilled. Who, then, is to be educated out of the available resources? Should it be the potential community leaders, or the inhabitants of particular regions, or should an attempt be made to give everyone at least something? There is no stock answer. Professor Jones-Quartey graphically describes the dilemma in his account of the way in which in Ghana 'the philosophy of "excellence in little"…was broken by the ideology of the second historical period', that is, belief in a mass education movement. Mr Nettleford discusses the concept of 'centres of emphasis' enunciated by Professor Houle of the University of Chicago. What can be said is that to spread resources thinly in pursuit of the ideal of social justice may be to throw away the chance to create enduring institutions. Far better to concentrate resources upon particular sections of the community, a particular need, or a particular region. The danger here is that adult educators will simply respond to market demands by providing facilities where least effort is called for; thus urban centres are sometimes quite generously treated whereas rural areas are neglected. The most equitable and, as is now being recognized, the most profitable policy would seem to be to draw up a list of priorities, to apply resources where they will have the maximum impact, and to concentrate upon 'community development' in the rural areas, as the Philippines and Senegal are doing.

As might be expected there is continuing concern about the low levels of literacy; in Kenya, for instance, approximately 80 per cent of the population are illiterate. But literacy is plainly no longer an obsession, presumably because too many high hopes have foundered with the relative failure of mass literacy campaigns. Today the stress is fairly and squarely laid upon functional literacy, that is, upon ensuring that the newly literate should be able to consolidate what he learns by having abundant opportunities to apply his knowledge through regular reading and writing about topics and problems directly connected with his daily life.

In nearly all the countries under review the literacy problem is inevitably aggravated by a serious linguistic problem. When there may
be as many as nine or ten fundamental linguistic groups it may well
be impossible to organize national programmes, and even regional
programmes may run into cruel difficulties. In the Philippines, for
instance, the planners are confronted with the gigantic problem of
providing reading materials in eight major and eighty minor dialects.

Except in Zambia there is an acute shortage of finance. The trouble
is that too large a percentage of educational budgets is committed for
political reasons to full-time education – very often to prestige institutions that yield a small return on the invested capital – and that such
money as is set aside for adult education is administered by government officials, for whom education usually means schoolroom learning. Adult education will always remain a poor cousin so long as
governments fail to award it a fixed and equitable percentage of the
educational budget. Charging students economic fees as so many
western countries do will not provide a solution since those most in
need of education are those with least money – indeed, many of them
are subsistence farmers who have never owned any money to speak of.

The lack of qualified adult educators is frequently referred to, and
indeed for adult education planners the provision of appropriate professional training facilities may well be the most pressing of all their
problems. Educated manpower is scarce. Furthermore, outside India
at any rate, those graduating from the universities find themselves in a
sellers' market, and ignore the field of social service at large because it
is neither lucrative nor prestigious. The result is that only a sprinkling
of Asian, African or Latin American graduates enter the profession
of adult education. Without higher standards at the summit of the
career pyramid it is hard to see how the quality of middle-grade and
field officers can be raised to the required level of proficiency. Somehow more university graduates must be attracted into the field and
somehow they must be given a professional academic training so
that they can command competitive salaries and status. Associated
with the shortage of trained adult educators there is also, as Professor
Bown observes, a desperate shortage of trained adult teachers. Too
much teaching is done '...by amateurs, or by men and women who
have been trained as school-teachers and have not faced up to the
difference between children and adults'.

Not surprisingly in the absence of highly qualified staff little research
is being carried out. Busy people can scarcely be expected to devote
their own time to or to encourage others to engage in pure research.
Nevertheless the need for fact-finding inquiries, surveys of Community

wants and evaluation studies is imperative. This entails establishing a claim for adult education as a recognized field of academic study.

The contributors are interested in using methods of communication outside the traditional conventions of classroom teaching. The mass media are regarded as crucially important because they can reach a vast audience at relatively low cost and influence people to change their attitudes without their realising that they are being educated. Hence the resort to Radio Literacy Schools in Latin America, 'listening-discussion' groups in The Philippines and the important educational role of Radio Ethiopia. The value of instruction by post (correspondence education) as a teaching medium is also receiving recognition. For example, a Correspondence Course Unit has been established at the Institute of Adult Studies in the University College of Kenya.

As almost everywhere in the world there is a shortage of suitable teaching aids and of accommodation appropriate to adult expectations. Four other areas of particular concern are : rural development which calls for agricultural extension methods and the formation of co-operatives; the education of workers; the unemployed youth problem; health education.

On turning to differences we find that they exist not so much in relation to ends as in relation to means or methods. The Philippines have adopted the community school approach, the idea that schools should not only provide children with formal instruction but also serve as centres of practical guidance and inspiration for a neighbourhood. Even the curriculum is so designed that children can go home and influence their parents to change some of their habits and attitudes. Another innovation in The Philippines is the Folk-School, which is clearly modelled on the famous Danish Folk High Schools. Yet again The Philippines also tries to stimulate development through the 'purok', the small self-help community.

In English-speaking countries the independent states that were formerly French colonies have the reputation of going their own idiosyncratic way in adult education just as France is alleged to do. Such a judgement is too simple and arbitrary. The truth is that though there is precious little mutual understanding between Francophone and English-speaking countries, each has much to teach the other. It was particularly fortunate, therefore, that two distinguished French-speaking adult educators should have given such a clear indication of what 'rural animation' implies and what is the role in adult education of 'les animateurs', thus clarifying two terms that needlessly mystify outside observers.

The essential principle in French practice is that *animateurs*, the agents of social change, cannot be produced by the formal educational system but must be chosen from among the natural leaders in local communities. M. B. M. Cisse describes in detail the selection procedure used in Senegal and how extension workers are trained at 'Centres d'Animation Rurales'. As an expatriate working in the Ivory Coast M. Pauvert writes with exemplary detachment about the difficulties involved in making adult education a truly popular movement.

Of all the institutions referred to the most significant may well turn out to be the Kenyan Adult Education Board, for it represents an attempt to integrate all the adult educational facilities in one country and to ensure a truly comprehensive system of provision. Not the least important of its plans is one to set up a single multi-purpose training centre where all those destined to work in the social development field will be housed together and attend a certain number of common core courses. The Philippines already has a close-knit system thanks to the dominant role of the Adult and Community Education Division of the Ministry of Education. India is now planning to set up a 'Central Board for Social Education'.

Also noteworthy is the Military Civic Action programme in Bolivia. One or two other countries such as Persia use their armed forces in a social action role but Bolivia is unique in the intensity with which it has carried out its programme. It is also noteworthy that in Bolivia as in Zambia the army has its own well-conceived system of education.

In Peru Dr Wenrich describes the Vicos Community Development Project undertaken by a team from Cornell University. In Latin America, in general, agricultural extension programmes have been widely developed. Kenya has instituted a system of Farmers' Training Centres. In Kenya and the South Pacific prominence is given to co-operative education. On-the-job training is a feature of the provision in the South Pacific. The Department of Extra-Mural Studies in the West Indies regards one of its main functions as providing in-service training courses for professional groups, especially for social workers

Ghana is distinguished for having introduced as long ago as 1949 a national consumer movement, the PEA, The People's Education Association. Two voluntary associations bear the brunt of the literacy campaign in Ethiopia. In countries where a centralized system of government is often unavoidable the value of popular voluntary associations is particularly great.

Ghana, along with the West Indies and Kenya, has also taken over from Britain the practice of appointing resident tutors to university extra-mural departments. Some of the borrowings from Britain have proved to be inappropriate and even an encumbrance, but there seems little question that the resident tutor has been invaluable as a source of stimulation and creative ideas. Very often, indeed, he has been the sole torchbearer of adult education throughout a large region.

Other special features attracting attention are the Youth Centres, the experimental village polytechnics and the Harambee scheme in Kenya, the setting up of Cultural and Youth Clubs in The Ivory Coast and the Janta (People's Colleges), 'Educational Caravans', and mobile libraries in India. It is also important to note how invigorating is the dissemination of a concept such as Zambian Humanism or African Socialism, to which Dr Thomas refers when speaking about President Nyerere in Tanzania.

Priority needs

The pre-requisites for growth in adult education obviously vary in detail from one country to another. At the same time, certain major needs are shared in common. It will now be useful to consider what these are. To begin with, it is obviously essential to arouse in the common people a desire for change and a recognition of the part to be played by adult education in inducing change. Here the teacher-statesman, or 'teacher-preachers' as Professor Bown designates some of the Zambian politicians, and the mass media when imaginatively used, can wield great influence.

Pride of place should then perhaps be given to the need to preserve at least some liberal values. When education aims are narrowly conceived and there is an importunate demand for manpower, it is fatally easy to overlook long-term goals by omitting the liberal content from education and relying upon authoritarian or purely didactic methods of communication. This is all the more easy to do since it is virtually impossible to measure the effectiveness of liberal adult education and much simpler to adopt the utilitarian policy that if a programme fails to yield immediate economic or in some way measurable results it should be abandoned; adult students themselves in developing countries encourage the utilitarian approach by demanding a formal certificate or diploma as their reward for attending classes. As Mr Nettleford puts it: 'The old philosophy of preparing people not for examinations and certificates but for their own personal fulfilment and enrichment was a borrowing from British adult education traditions which, though still praiseworthy and even useful, does not meet fully the needs of today's West Indian ambitions.' An undue emphasis upon industrial, technical and technological programmes may well produce a higher economic output but in the meantime great damage may have been done to the quality of life in a society. Mr Prosser, whose outlook is that of an economist and an administrator purposefully seeking measurable gains, nevertheless draws attention to the neglect of civic education in Kenya. Mr Nettleford describes the use of public lectures to awaken a civic conscience among the people of the West Indies. In his penetrating article Professor Jones-Quartey discusses what happened when 'the state ideology of a oneparty regime given to propaganda was made to take the place of an educational philosophy which should have been teaching people both how to think independently and how to work constructively and democratically for the advancement of their country'. And here, too, it is vital that governmental institutions should not smother individual initiative, a point insistently made by M. Pauvert and M. Cisse.

Related to the preservation of liberal values is the need to encourage and respect the work of voluntary agencies. In seeking efficiency and a comprehensive coverage government officials may be tempted to destroy or at least to make life difficult for non-statutory bodies. Suspicion of the work of the churches in particular is understandable but today largely unjustified. Consider their valuable work in Zambia and Ethiopia. To reject the voluntary principle is a mistake for two reasons : first, the more educational provision is privately endowed, the more widely central funds can be distributed; secondly, government agencies may become arrogant and inefficient if not exposed to competition and open to advice.

A high priority must be the education of women, since they often exert a potent influence not only within the family nexus but also in the larger community. Among educators and politicians who have to talk about education much lip-service is paid to this subject but the evidence gleaned from such statistical inquiries as have been carried out proves conclusively that the education of women almost invariably lags far behind that of men. Yet it is not too much to claim that in a traditional community the key to improved living standards usually rests with the womenfolk. The South Pacific Commission recognizes this fact and has taken special care to serve women's needs. Not the least interesting of its methods are the courses in homecraft for both men and women, especially for married couples.

Fourthly, it is vital to make provision for joint planning and consultation among all those concerned with the education of adults. The loss of a sense of purpose that ensues when co-ordination is wanting is revealed by M. Pauvert, writing about the number of different ministries in the Ivory Coast claiming responsibility for providing adult education. How co-ordination can be achieved is recorded carefully by Mr Prosser and M. Pauvert. It is probable that in most developing countries adult education facilities will always remain paltry in the absence of a government-backed and centralized scheme. At the same time, centralism for purely political reasons may well do more harm than good.

Fifthly, methods of communication should clearly be extended and improved. The wider use of teaching by correspondence is necessary. All countries must aim at making extensive use of radio and television as the Ivory Coast and American Samoa.

Sixth, those who serve adult education, as administrators, organizers or teachers require to be properly trained. At all levels, there must be training courses; for the full-time and part-time worker; initial training and advanced training courses; short courses and long courses.

In general, experienced adult educators in the developing countries try to obtain financial and technical assistance from other countries. But by and large adult education receives far less support from external aid than any other branch of education. Though this is not perhaps surprising in view of its lowly status, it is still a great pity, for international aid spent on adult education would probably yield exceptionally advantageous returns. Maybe one of the functions of adult educators should be to urge their governments to attract more foreign aid for their area of work.

One remarkable feature of adult education in developing countries is the frequent disregard of practitioners for one another's innovations. It seems that they much prefer to turn to Scandinavia, or North America or Russia. Yet very often the most interesting and relevant experiments are taking place in an adjacent country. Chauvinism is often a costly luxury. More effective machinery is clearly required for facilitating the exchange of ideas and information.

In order that there can be an effective exchange of ideas and information it is, of course, essential that publishing resources should be readily available; a point made by Mr Prosser when highlighting the valuable part played by the East African Literature Bureau and the East African Publishing House, and by Mr Nettleford when referring to the publications of his own extra-mural department. Though there is undoubtedly a market for books and pamphlets about adult education, publishers do not as yet show much interest. One reason for their indifference may be that little good material is offered them. The moral is clear : adult educators should find time to write, even if it means neglecting other aspects of their work.

Finally and above all what is needed is purposeful planning. Because it is such an amorphous field adult education will always be parsimoniously subsidized unless its social, economic and political relevance is made crystal clear. In every national plan there should be not only the usual ritualistic reference to the singular importance of adult education in fostering development but an attempt to relate its expansion to forecasts of manpower and other requirements. This implies, of course, that the onus is upon adult educators to make their voices heard and to have something clear and purposeful to say.

Prospects

By singling them out for special study the present work may seem to imply that the developing countries face specially daunting problems. In quantitative terms so they do, but this does not mean that the efforts of adult educators in developing countries suffer by comparison with those of the developed countries. On the contrary, if critical comparisons are to be made the boot is on the other foot, for as a rule adult education in the developed countries is less dynamic and experimental, mainly because administrators tend to be inhibited by conservative practices and their relative lack of public influence. It is as though the developing countries are galvanized by the stark urgency of their problems and greatly helped by the fact that they are unburdened by old attitudes and priorities. They are also extraordinarily willing to experiment and innovate and to go far afield in search of ideas. Thus, you will find an African adult educator may look for ideas to North America, to Scandinavia, to Russia...whereas, until very recently at any rate, in the developed countries the adult educators have tended to be inward looking, to assume that they have little or nothing to learn from other countries. There is little doubt that the average university extra-mural department in Africa is more likely to use up-to-date methods than the British counterpart. Adult educators in developing countries are also helped by the national commitment to educate the adult population. Though they may well be constrained to fulfil requirements dictated by their governments, they can normally count upon at least some public support and they know that they are playing a central rather than a peripheral part in the evolution of their countries.

In short, some of the most exciting work and the biggest challenges in the field of adult education are to be found in the developing countries. If they, in their wisdom, look for help to UNESCO and to specialists in other countries, adult educators in the developed countries would be well advised to take keen note of what they are doing and how, faced with unprecedented problems, they are turning to unprecedented solutions.

NOTES AND REFERENCES

The chapters on the Ivory Coast and Senegal were translated by the editor.

1. UNESCO, *Literacy and Education for Adults*, Geneva 1964.
2. A. A. Liveright and N. Haygood, *The Exeter Papers*, Boston 1969, p 8.
3. R. Prosser, *Adult Education for Developing Countries*, Nairobi 1967, p 5.
4. 'Problems of Priorities in the Planning of Adult Education' in *Development and Adult Education in Africa*, Uppsala 1965, p 26.
5. Liveright and Haygood, op. cit. p 9.
6. But compare Mr Prosser's classification. See below, pp 79–81.
7. *Education, Manpower and Economic Growth*, London 1964.
8. Ibid. p 27. Seven criteria are formulated as statistical indicators of human resource development.

1. English-Speaking West Africa

K. A. B. JONES-QUARTEY

Historical Background

Society anywhere, as we know, is a cloth of closely interwoven fabrics, or, to change the figure, a skein of relationships : political, economic, cultural and any other form in which the processes of human life may be cast or conceived. In traditional society this truism is even more relevant than in technological society. In the latter the degree of co-hesion is usually eroded by those imperatives of economic develop-ment, industrialization and urbanization, and one of their inescapable results, progressive individualism. Such erosion means, for good or bad, the weakening of personal ties, especially as organized within the socio-religious mix.

In most of black Africa, on the other hand, the condition of social cohesion still pervades the life of the community. It is the matrix in which men and women are educated to the demands of our kind of society, and this process is no more and no less than the universal one of educating the individuals for life. But since life in traditional society is essentially communal, education is not for individualism but for group existence. This points to a profound difference between the socialization that goes on within developed countries and that which goes on within developing societies. In the former the stages of in-tense intra-group cohesion have passed and been replaced by less personal but more utilitarian relationships; in the latter the bewilder-ing, painful processes of change are only now being slowly experi-enced. The adult members of still largely traditional communities are both the chief vectors of the inexorable conditions of change and the worst sufferers from its pains. For it is an obvious and accepted fact of change in the developing countries that the adult population is poten-tially the readiest means of transition between the old and the new, between the ancient and the modern.

The desirability of change implied here is not an equation which reads *Old* (Ancient) = *Bad*, or *New* (Modern) = *Good*; it is, rather, the admission as a fact of people's lives that though 'pure' culture is essential and should be preserved, it cannot supply the economic needs of man and must therefore be backed by the acceptance and use of modern means to material welfare. Slowly and painfully the realities of this situation are being accepted, learned and put to practical tests as well as converted into direct experience among the adult populations of the under-developed communities of the world today. A modern means to material progress which is being thus put to use in what is now known as The Third World is adult education. In one of its most recognizable, most distinctive forms, that is, the university-based type, adult education came to West Africa after the end of the Second World War.

Among the revolutions created directly and indirectly by that war was what happened to the minds, the perceptions and the reactions of adult communities all over Africa. Particularly in West Africa the fires of enlightenment through enlarged experience began to burn in great, sweeping arcs. Soldiers returning home from East Africa, Burma and above all India carried the torch; their experience of life and standards elsewhere, though not necessarily always higher standards, supplied the fuel. Back in Ghana, Nigeria, Sierra Leone or Gambia, and even, some said, in Liberia and certain of the French territories of West and Equatorial Africa (notably Senegal and Chad[1]), the returning African veterans of the war not only narrated their hair-raising or enlightening experiences abroad but also began to demand a general upward change in the standards of life and work in their respective countries. In this they were in fact only joining the train of their civilian countrymen, among whom there was already a ferment for improvement, for greater participation in their own governance, and for much more besides, long before the end of the war.

Since education in under-developed areas, in particular, is the principal path to upward economic mobility and social status for most people, it was one of the immediate objects pursued by civilians and returning ex-soldiers alike. The experience of American veterans assisted by the G.I. Bill of Rights supplied a far-away but real inspiration and incentive. Activity and thinking along similar but less spectacular lines in Britain brought the inspiration of a struggle for rights nearer home. The reputation won by the West African countries as wartime dollar earners for the Allies – such as Ghana and Nigeria with oils, cocoa and other food products – sharpened even more the demand for reciprocal rights and benefits. With political agitation growing daily and the writing beginning to show on the wall, the British Colonial Office in 1945 appointed the (Elliott) commission to examine the apparently intensified appetite for advanced education in West Africa; and in early 1947 the Oxford University authorities made the first move towards meeting the needs of those of the adult populations in the West African colonies who were also calling for their own share in the new deal for education. The first results of this initiative were thus recorded by Dr David Kimble in his first report[2] as pioneer Resident Tutor in the then Gold Coast:

'Oxford has a special tradition of pioneer and experimental work in adult education. Nevertheless, it was an imaginative step when the Secretary of Oxford University Delegacy for Extra-Mural Studies – Mr T. L. Hodgkin – paid a brief visit to the Gold Coast in February 1947. His aim was to discover if there was any potential demand for the kind of adult education such as is met in Britain through courses provided by University Extra-Mural Departments in co-operation with voluntary organizations. He discussed the idea with a large number of people in all walks of life, and as a result of his report the Delegacy arranged for Mr J. A. McLean – their Resident Tutor in Kent – to give a 12-week series of lectures in Cape Coast, Sekondi, Kumasi and Accra from May to July 1947. The subject of these lectures was "Economic History and Problems". In the words of this Tutor : "The fear entertained that the initial enthusiasm everywhere displayed for the classes would be ephemeral, fortunately proved unfounded. Everywhere sizeable groups of students emerged who soon showed that they would stay the course, and would indeed certainly have undertaken longer and more ambitious courses of study if such had been available. In stability of membership and in regularity of attendance, classes in the Gold Coast compared very favourably with their English opposite numbers." At a postmortem conference held at Achimota with Mr M. Dowuona[3] in the chair – attended by representatives of the four classes – it was unanimously decided to ask Oxford for a further tutor for a longer period. This time it was suggested the subject should be politics rather than economics and the title provisionally proposed was "Problems of Government".

Purpose

As a direct result of this promising response the Oxford Delegacy in April 1948 seconded Mr David Kimble – their Staff Tutor in Berkshire – to a long range appointment as Resident Tutor in the Gold Coast for a period of up to two years...'

A more recent research work goes into even greater detail as to the genesis of this establishment, bringing neatly together all the principal elements already mentioned : the personalities, the role of Oxford University, and the involvement of ex-servicemen during and after the Second World War. Kwa O. Hagan, one of the original staff members of the then (Gold Coast) Department of Extra-Mural Studies, in his thesis for an Oxford B. LITT., *The Growth of Adult Literacy and Adult*

Education in Ghana – 1901–1957 (Trinity Term 1968, unpublished, pp 176–8), supplies the missing links, as follows:

'...The invitation to the Oxford Delegacy to engage in an experimental scheme of Extra-Mural Courses in West Africa, prior to the development of higher education in the area seems, therefore, to have fitted well into Oxford's own past role in this field.

The initiative taken by Oxford to experiment in adult education in West Africa was considerably influenced by Col. George (now Lord) Wigg, MP (then an advisory member of the Oxford Tutorial Classes Committee) who visited West Africa in 1945, "to survey and report on the position in regard to Army education in the area". [Quoted from OUELC, Agendum 5, 9 March 1946.] On the possibilities of university adult education in West Africa, Col. Wigg commented unofficially in 1946 to the Oxford University Extension Lectures Committee:

"During my tour of West Africa last year I think I saw most of the developments which resemble adult education as we know it in this country. In Kumasi, Gold Coast, the Labour Officer, Mr Oswald Kitching, who possesses considerable knowledge of the WEA both as a student and as a member of the Yorkshire North District, had gathered a group of ex-Achimota students and courses had been planned covering a period of a year...The experiences I record, added to general impressions gained there by countless talks with Africans and Europeans, convinced me that an enormous and vigorous field for work on extension courses lines is ready to be developed in larger centres of population in West Africa...The prestige of an established and respected university as the Sponsor of such a scheme is essential...some day it must be started if self-government is not to remain a meaningless slogan...I believe the time is ripe to experiment on the lines I suggest and I am convinced that such an experiment would be a success." [OUELC, loc. cit.]

Thus Wigg's comment [concludes Hagan on this point] provided a means whereby the Oxford University Delegacy was called upon to launch an experiment in West Africa...'[4]

It is at this point that we can resume the narrative, where David Kimble had then been appointed as Resident Tutor in the Gold Coast for at least two years.

Similar arrangements were soon under way in Nigeria. By the end of 1948, when the recommendations of the Elliott Commission had borne fruit in the establishment of a University College in each of the two countries, a university-based adult education movement was also in operation in each of them. In Sierra Leone this vital new line of development came a little later[5] and has made much slower progress, although for more than a century that country had led the rest of English-speaking West Africa in western-type education. The main reason for this lag was the incidence of intractable economic difficulties, although some traditional conservatism was also a restraining factor. Nevertheless, in principle the three countries have together provided the same basic experience of an evolving pattern of modern adult education.[6]

They have not progressed without difficulty, however. It was the British Government and people, so to speak, who had advised themselves of the nature of the political situation overseas and had taken action. This was both to meet legitimate, justifiable claims to rights and also to anticipate trouble. But the post-war movement against the colonial regimes had already started and was gaining momentum daily. Thus the colonial governments were under heavy fire and individual Englishmen under equally heavy suspicion. It was therefore thorny going for years for the pioneers of the new adult education movement as David Kimble indicated in his Report:[7]

'Meanwhile the mental climate of the country had changed. It is hard to exaggerate the distrust and suspicion of anything and everybody to do, or *thought* to do, with Government that was rife in the Gold Coast after the disturbances in February and March 1948. What was really behind a European coming to give public lectures at such a time – especially in politics? Was it an elaborate manoeuvre by the Colonial Office and the Gold Coast Government? There was little understanding that even although a University may be subsidized by State funds (how else?) it is nonetheless absolutely independent of Government as regards teaching content and approach.[8] A recent letter from the Secretary of the Togoland Union requesting the inauguration of an adult study group in Hohoe typically illustrates this sad outlook : "Even although we have been reading of your activities in the Gold Coast Press from time to time, we viewed them as another camouflage of...old officialdom." '

Exposure to the suspicions of Africans was only one-half of the burden of the pioneers. The other half was what they suffered at the hands of the self-conscious and equally suspicious colonial government officials themselves. Since these first Resident Tutors had to be essentially liberal and even radical in outlook to take the new jobs on at all, and since their initial classes dealt with the explosive subjects of politics and economics, they encountered the resentment and antagonism of certain colonial officials. In Ghana, especially, which eventually became the first African colony to gain independence in the modern era, the anti-colonial fires were soon in a blaze. The years 1947–51 saw the agitation at its most heated, and these were also the years in which Dr Kimble and his first team from Britain – including Miss Lalage Bown, William Tordoff and Dennis Austin – were struggling to organize the new system. It requires no more than a superficial acquaintance with colonial history to imagine how their efforts were viewed by their own countrymen, officials and businessmen alike. Ghanaians involved or even merely interested in the movement heard stories daily of warnings and threats from these quarters against the new teachers, although the latter themselves, for obvious reasons, had to report on their situation with caution and restraint. To quote again from *Adult Education in the Gold Coast*:

'One or two Europeans have criticized these popular meetings basic-ally on the ground that certain matters are far too controversial and dangerous to be handled safely by anyone at the present time – let alone by, or in conjunction with, a university.'[9]

But the team persevered, supported and strengthened by a growing number of participating citizens both notable and ordinary. And in the end they triumphed. An editorial in the then *Gold Coast Express*, cited in *Adult Education* (no date supplied), spoke for many when it said, *inter alia*:

'This happy linking-up of the Gold Coast with Oxford University in a permanent way – in the sense that wherever and whenever the PEA[10] is mentioned, Oxford University will be remembered as its source – was brought about by the co-operation of the University itself, the Gold Coast Government and the enthusiasm of our people, including the students.'

Aims and objectives

Since some of the contributors to this symposium already offer defini-tions and propound theories of adult education, it would be a wasteful and boring duplication to pronounce in general theoretical terms. Far better, perhaps, to state the principles upon which a local pro-gramme has been developed and to note to what extent variations or modifications, if any, have been introduced into it as a result of changing views, attitudes or circumstances. Here we shall first con-centrate on the Ghanaian (former Gold Coast) experience as our parti-cular case study, before offering any comments on similar activities and programmes both to the east and west of Ghana, that is, in Nigeria and Sierra Leone.

The history of the Institute of Adult Education of the University of Ghana falls into three distinct periods: first, the David Kimble era, running from the beginnings in 1948 until Kimble's retirement in

February 1962; then the 'ideological' era, from July 1962 until February 1966; and, thirdly, the current period since 1966. Each of the first two periods had its particular aims; the present period is in the process of acting out its own.

The aims and objectives of the pioneer period were summarized in Kimble's first report in which he stated that 'a tutor is normally satisfied with the class from which a few students emerge, maybe after two or three years, with a real power of independent judgement and the capacity to play an effective part in public life'.[11] Throughout the first fourteen years of the Ghana development, this then was the aim: throwing back into the community a body of citizens who would be more effective functioning units of society by reason of their trained independence of mind and objective approach to problems. Their number would be necessarily small, for as Kimble observed in the same passage 'this is not mass education'.

Although it was mainly with this élitist philosophy that the Institute was conceived and developed, it would be unfair to leave the description there, for the Institute sought to demonstrate at the same time that 'playing an effective part in public life' meant for those so trained an active leadership of and participation in community development projects of a practical, utilitarian nature. So it was that from the very beginning there were village projects involving well-digging, dam-construction, area surveying, road building, improved-latrine construction, and the like, which the Institute initiated, promoted, encouraged or joined in. But this was always done on the leadership principle: these were the men and women trained and inspired *to help the rest*.

This philosophy of 'excellence in little', as it may be described, was broken by the ideology of the second historical period. With the close of the Kimble era came the rapid take-over of most public affairs and processes by the Convention People's Party of the Nkrumah regime. From its highest level at the University of Ghana to village primary schools, education became not just the legitimate concern of government but one of the media of party-ideological propaganda. Adult education under the Institute had been for some time since the beginning of the Nkrumah era a target of ideological attack regarding its function and role in society; it now became a tool of the Party. The name of the Institution, which had under various changing circumstances been altered several times in the past, now became 'Institute of Public Education' so as to accord with the idea of the CPP Government doing everything for and in the name of the people alone. It was meant to and did break the old, admittedly debatable, élitist principle of narrow leadership *from* among the people, substituting for it the new one of leadership of the whole people – a mass education movement, in short, based on a university. This could have been a perfectly legitimate, proper and even upward trend in education for 'the masses'. Unfortunately it was nothing of the kind, and could not be so. As a consequence, the whole establishment was simply converted into another part of the CPP-Nkrumalist ideological propaganda machine, with adult education classes and conferences swollen into huge assemblies of people, for many of whom no honest claims to benefit could be made.

All this was most regrettable and not only for the reasons for which the Nkrumah regime has suffered so much discredit at home and abroad. What happened ideologically to the Institute during its second historical period was unfortunate because the IPE could at the same time take credit for many positive innovations achieved during its lifetime. To quote from a report published after the *coup d'état* in 1966:

'There is no doubt at all in our minds that the many new ideas and programmes introduced into university adult education by the IPE were a step in the right direction; indeed some of these were in principle exactly what the old Extra-Mural Studies Institute had envisaged as part of its then emerging developing plan. Under the IPE, an expansion of services to the younger aspirants to self-improvement did take place, notably in the GCE undertaking (see below); a new residential school, "Bu Bere" [Harvest] was added to the calendar of popular adult education events in the country; and many new courses were also introduced. In addition, more people were led into the widening embrace of the movement.

But all this was achieved in the context of a total process of politicization, in which academic principles and standards were treated with cavalier indifference, and in many ways with utter contempt. The increased participation of the people was only quantitative, and was a direct function of the forced-march strategy and tactics of the Party...'[12]

Thus the state ideology of a one-party political regime given to propaganda was made to take the place of an educational philosophy which should have been teaching people both how to think independently and how to work constructively and democratically for the advancement of their community.

In the third and current phase of development a synthesis of ideas and an amalgamation of objectives are being worked out. The aim is to provide an integrated system of university-based adult education in which several results would be achieved at once. The first of these aims is the traditional one of generally developing at least a part of our adult populations into a reservoir of independent-minded, thoughtful and well-informed men and women; secondly, from among these to continue to produce individuals who will be led on by their extra-mural learning experience to seek to resume their formal education by entering college to train for higher service to the country; and thirdly, the present philosophy aims to produce, to the best of the ability and competence of the Institute, manpower supplies able to contribute their quota to economic productivity in such an inadequately-developed country as Ghana – or in Nigeria or Sierra Leone.

In Nigeria and Sierra Leone the initial philosophy was the same as that introduced into Ghana under Oxford's experience. Indeed in Sierra Leone it was the Ghana team that had started the movement. First Kimble, followed by Austin and Tordoff, went to Freetown and delivered a series of talks or lectures, beginning from April 1949 and continuing through 1950 (Austin) to 1952 (Austin and Tordoff). The purpose of these visits was to explore possibilities in Sierra Leone, test responses, and lay the groundwork for immediate future development of the system then being established in the Gold Coast. In the subsequent sections dealing with organization, administration and programmes it will be seen how similar have been the lines of development among the three countries. The main differences have been due to such factors as the size of the operation, economic standing and variations in temperament, needs and supplies of many kinds : men, materials, physical facilities, and the rest.

These observations apply equally to the development in Nigeria. There Mr R. K. A. Gardiner, who has since risen through many posts to his present eminence as Secretary-General of the Economic Commission for Africa, Addis Ababa, was the first holder of the Ibadan-based Directorship of Extra-Mural Studies. An economist then given to few words about theory and philosophy and concerned only with the concrete situation, Gardiner supplied few direct statements on the purposes of his operations in Nigeria. An examination of his programmes over the early period of 1950–3 shows, however, that the aims underlying a combination of liberal studies with practical, utilitarian, and sometimes specialist or professional projects, were analogous to those of all the other pioneers. Indeed in his 1950/1 Report the Director mentioned being asked in Benin Province 'to explain the aims and policy of the University College in connection with Extra-Mural work'; he also reported giving an address on 'The Purpose of Extra-Mural Studies' at another place, and a public lecture on 'Extra-Mural Studies and Education for Citizenship' at Enugu.

To end this section on a 'Philosophy for Adult Education in Africa' I cannot do better than offer a summary quotation from the Introduction to his 1964/5 Annual Report by the present Director of Adult

Education and Extra-Mural Studies, University of Ibadan, Nigeria (Professor Ayo Ogunsheye):

'While the Department's traditional activities continue with un-abated vigour, this session has been one of innovation. Its work as a Department of Adult Education has been emphasized by two new developments, the start of a full-scale research programme in the African Adult Education Unit, and the completion of preparations for a two-year certificate course in Adult Education and Community Development. Both developments promise to add considerably to the Department's contributions to this country's development.'

To sum up : the philosophy explained and analysed in the above section can be summed up in three phrases : improvement of the individual citizen; service to the community; and development for the country.

Organization and policy

In this section we shall describe extensively only the organization of the Ghana establishment, since in broad outline it is very similar to that of Nigeria and would fairly represent the structure developed there. Where they exist, differences are in detail rather than in principle or in structure, and will be specified in due course for comparison and interest. The next few paragraphs are in the main a summary description of the Ghana organization, as prepared by the present author for the Report referred to above.

The aim of the Ghana Institute of Adult Education was to provide a university-based system of adult education for thousands of young Ghanaian men and women whose need for continuing education had been recognized and established. The Institute has done its work most of the time through a programme of extra-mural classes, residential courses, one-day schools, week-end schools and conferences, lecture series and occasional lectures. These are all based on liberal studies in history, economics, geography, politics, English language and literature, French – almost the whole range of liberal academic subjects. But they were designed and delivered to suit the admittedly mixed levels of ability and educational attainment among the thousands of entrants to the courses and classes. Up to 1962 no degrees, diplomas, or academic certificates of any kind had been awarded or offered, since the Institute had neither the power nor the inclination to offer any. However, as a result of the positive assistance which this programme offered, many mature students were enabled to pass external examinations with reduced difficulty; others followed through their advantage and prepared themselves successfully for admission into full degree and diploma courses at the University of Ghana and the Kumasi College of Science and Technology.

Until the end of the academic year 1961/2 the then Institute of Extra-Mural Studies operated this programme through and in partnership with the People's Educational Association (PEA), a voluntary organization established in 1949 almost simultaneously with the Institute. Its members formed the classes for which the Institute organized the teaching and supplied the tutors. The tutors were of two groups: permanent senior members of the Institute, who were also on the academic staff of the University of Ghana; and part-time Tutors, who were university graduates or specialists in technical or artistic fields working at other jobs outside the University. The Institute of Extra-Mural Studies and the People's Educational Association became well-known at home and abroad as an intellectual partnership providing for thousands of Ghanaian adults old and young a unique experience for thirteen unbroken years. The PEA is the pioneer organization later copied in Nigeria as the Nigerian Extra-Mural Association (1952/3) and in Sierra Leone under the same name of People's Education Association.

For some time during the period preceding 1962, many of the younger and more ambitious extra-mural students had constantly pressed the Institute for more formal courses which would lead them to academic examinations, degrees, diplomas, and/or certificates, for in West Africa these pieces of paper are a passport to status and economic betterment. In the end, Kimble and his colleagues decided to assess the demand for such courses among their extra-mural students. They entered into negotiations for the service of a North American expert, who would come to Ghana for one academic year, do some lecturing and meanwhile test the potential of adult student demand for degree courses. Before this plan could be carried out, however, the Ghana Government appointed an International Committee to examine the whole of the higher education structure in the country and make recommendations. Among these, when submitted, were strong pleas in favour of the expansion of adult education. The Government would not entertain the views of the Institute on the recommendations of the Committee and did not even consider to any extent the recommendations themselves. They simply proceeded to change the nature and the programmes of the Institute in order to satisfy political interests rather than to meet educational needs. The results and some of the consequences of this change in orientation were profound as well as disastrous. It was also an ironic confirmation of the prophetic popular suspicions about governmental interference in education which the first Ghana Director had so innocently tried to dissipate at the outset of his mission.

Thus between July 1962 and February 1966 the role of the PEA suffered a temporary eclipse, for massive party-ideological operations were no substitute for systematic learning; they therefore failed utterly to sustain the movement. After the overthrow of the C P P regime in the coup of 24 February 1966, the P E A started back on the long road to resuscitation, and eventually revived itself at a resumed Annual Conference in July 1967, the fifteenth in a series sadly interrupted during the 'ideological inter-regnum'. Fortunately, however, the extra-mural movement itself, though severely threatened during this period, was not destroyed. Indeed credit has already been given above to the innovations introduced into the system in the same period, many of which were sound in principle and laid the foundations of future development along certain foolproof lines; for instance, the more formal courses already envisaged in the pre-1962 plans of the Institute and introduced during the period under discussion by the 1962–6 administration.

Now at last it is hopefully true to say that the position has been re-stabilized in relation to an educational philosophy, social realities, and programming. Before looking again at structure, organization and programmes, however, let us return for a moment to a consideration of what I have called above the 'social realities' in the context of adult education policy in black Africa. These realities have to do mostly with what the economists and social philosophers call the 'expectation-demand explosion'. During the colonial era there was for the 'educated' African an employment expectation scale which can be related to the education scale in a scheme such as this:

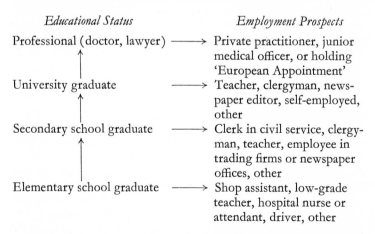

Educational Status	*Employment Prospects*
Professional (doctor, lawyer) ⟶	Private practitioner, junior medical officer, or holding 'European Appointment'
University graduate ⟶	Teacher, clergyman, newspaper editor, self-employed, other
Secondary school graduate ⟶	Clerk in civil service, clergyman, teacher, employee in trading firms or newspaper offices, other
Elementary school graduate ⟶	Shop assistant, low-grade teacher, hospital nurse or attendant, driver, other

These educated classes were the ones among whom social mobility in the modern context counted to a feverish degree. In traditional society there was stratification into chiefs and elders and commoners and slaves; into age groups carrying status and prestige in ascending – or descending – order; and so on. But there was also easy social mobility[13] both horizontally and vertically, in this arrangement, and economic welfare was guaranteed in what was a largely protective community. For better or for worse, industrialization and urbanization changes all this everywhere, and will do so in Africa, too. But meanwhile, in between the traditional and the technological, there is transitional society, and this is where there is in black Africa a ferment in the matter of status-seeking and social mobility.

The simple diagram above needs amplification to bring out the point. An African doctor or lawyer in the colonial era enjoyed as a private professional the highest social status outside of traditional organizations. But if he sought government employment in those professions he either would not get it or would be given it at a junior, depressed level; moreover, he would then become a little black island completely surrounded by a sea of free-flowing white contempt and discrimination. For professionals like engineers and accountants even contempt-surrounded islands did not exist. And when, once in 20 years or so, the 'European Appointment' status was conferred on one African, his professional elevation became the talk of the town for ages, except in the late 1800s when there were quite a few Africans holding 'European Appointments'.[14] One had to list here, too, job possibilities for such as African university graduates and secondary school products. But in truth the expectation of actual appointment to respectable jobs was small. The great Sir Gordon Guggisberg himself,[15] as late as the 1920s, had to argue and fight with his English contemporaries for the appointment of 'suitable' Africans to commensurately high office; and in the Gold Coast Civil List of 1928, for instance, the proportion of African to European senior staff in the Political Service, the largest of them, was $1 : 10.7$.[16]

The issue of more and higher jobs for native sons was of course one of the big ones in the anti-colonial agitations which culminated, in Ghana at any rate, around 1950. Economic expectation, status achievement and social mobility, all began to rise to unprecedented heights from this twilight period in colonial history and into the independence era. Then during the heyday of the Nkrumah regime social mobility became a riot, as the ranks of the middle class were filled to overflowing with the *nouveaux riches* – or, to give them their more expressive Sierra Leonean name, 'dem Jes' Cam'' (those *Just-Comes*). In the under-developed world at all times in general, but in colonial times in particular, education *is* the key to automatic social advance, in spite of the bleak employment outlook. In the first flush of independence, however, when general poverty so enticingly beckons to naked power for self-emancipation, it is political manipulation that becomes the key to status and social mobility for many who could not make it otherwise. There is, in the unsettled first stages of independence, not only an expectation-demand explosion but the means of attaining status, namely easy access to power through political manoeuvre and manipulation, and, secondly, the power to loot. This analysis does not, however, completely ignore the existence of normal means to status : ascriptive or acquisitive. There were always, for instance, the men and women of royal birth or with regal connections – the chiefly houses; and there have always been the gifted traders and 'Merchant Princes' of all these countries. It is for the rest that education becomes the legitimate means to sure status or politics the short cut.

The hope is that with the routing one by one of unprincipled ideologies, dictatorial regimes and loot-politics from these modernizing societies, the motivation drives and incentive patterns lying behind the response to adult education will return to their proper forms and levels, and that merit and achievement will come permanently to be the measure of and the principal means to success in these countries. Social mobility would then assume its natural characteristic, still full of stresses and strains, of good fortune and bad luck, of inequalities and roguery, of rewards and punishment, but also shorn of colonial mass frustration as well as of the independence-period psychosis of grab-and-carry.

Administration and programmes

The pattern of organization and administration in these institutions, as has already been indicated, is almost uniform. Each has nearly always carried a director, tutor-administrators, and a cadre of assistants and supporting staff at headquarters, together with a field staff of full-time tutors, organizers, and the usual office personnel consisting of a wide spectrum of functionaries and grades of workers. The whole of this framework is supported by a large body of part-time tutors and voluntary workers, the latter drawn from the various groups, classes and branches which carry the bulk of the adult student population for whom the system is operated. In each country the university establishment is partnered, to a greater or lesser extent, by a voluntary people's organization from which the extra-mural class is mostly drawn. The closest relationship in this arrangement seems to be in Ghana, and perhaps the least definite in Sierra Leone.

In proportion to size and coverage the Ghana establishment has always been the most fortunate of the three, though in terms of a universal ideal even this advantage – considered on the basis of *per capita* of population and per square mile of territory – falls far short of the desirable. Here it may be useful, for quick comparisons, to lay out for the reader a comparative table of sizes in territory and population among the three countries under consideration:

Country	Size of territory	Population[17]
Sierra Leone	27,925 sq. miles	2,180,355 *
Nigeria	356,669 sq. miles	$\begin{cases} 30,100,000 \,† \\ 55,653,820 \,‡ \end{cases}$
Ghana	92,100 sq. miles	7,500,000 §

* 1963 Census (S. L. Year Book 1968)
† 1953 Estimate (Government Department of Statistics)
‡ 1963 Census
§ 1967/68 Estimate (Government Department of Statistics)

Sierra Leone is thus the smallest of the three countries in respect of both territory and population. For mostly economic reasons, as has been previously indicated, its programme is also the least developed in terms of variety, scope, and coverage in area and numbers. Yet with increased funds and a good deal of boldness and radicalism it could mount a complete-saturation system with less difficulty even than Ghana, having regard to those same features of population and land area which in other ways seem to place her at such a disadvantage. For a comprehensive picture of the nature and extent of the operation in West Africa, a selected schedule of statistical and other factual data in the form of tables is presented at the end of this article.

The administration of the operations[18] follows an organizational pattern which cannot but be in line with general principles. It is made up of several bodies of people. First, there is the permanent departmental staff, employees of the respective universities, in their various categories (Director, Resident or Staff Tutor, Organizer, etc.). As elsewhere, their work is subject to the general academic and administrative control of the university, usually represented by a small committee or board. It is under the authority of this board that the Institute disburses its funds – however derived[18] – usually under the strict supervision of the university's finance officers. A third body participating in the policy and control of West African university-based adult education is the familiar larger council combining university and outside membership.[19] At the moment in Ghana this body does not exist but waits to be reorganized, following the changes brought about by the 1966 coup and the ending of ideological interference in education. When achieved, this reorganization is expected to feature the return of members of the People's Educational Association to their traditional partnership with the Institute in the work of adult education in Ghana.

Equally important is the idea of making the movement a joint effort with the two other institutions of higher learning in the country : the University of Science and Technology at Kumasi and the University College of Cape Coast. Since 1948 the Institute at Legon has operated alone, but with two other university institutions now part of the higher-education scene in the country it is felt that even pioneering, tradition, and history cannot justify the exclusive operation of university-based adult education by one out of three such institutions. The proposal is for a joint-universities board or committee to be the executive body carrying out the broad policies of a wider-based adult education council of fairly large membership and completely representative character.

In Sierra Leone and Nigeria, for their part, the positions are also interesting. There are two institutions joined into one 'federal' University in the former, while in the latter there are five separate universities (counting Nsukka in Biafra as one of these). It should be the easiest of procedures and arrangements to erect a single university-based adult education programme between the two institutions in Sierra Leone, Fourah Bay and N'jala, and no doubt only the shortage of funds prevents for the time being the establishment of an adequately-staffed regional centre at the latter place as merely one end of an axis of operation. In Nigeria, however, the position is profoundly different. This is so both from the nature of the original and permanent factors involved (size of territory, distances, number of people affected, the economics of operation, etc.) and from the political changes which have come over the country since Independence in 1960. Ibadan, like Legon, has carried the burden of the movement since 1948/9, and is the only centre of its kind in the country. But unlike Legon it seems limited, ironically enough, by the very 'limitlessness' of the factors enumerated above, from sharing its experience and its expertise on a partnership basis with the Universities at Nsukka, Zaria, Ife and Lagos. But perhaps in the future it can work out some basis of useful co-operation between itself and two or three of its sister institutions within delimited areas of interest or specialization.

I. GHANA

Table 1. Statistics of operations

	1950/1	1955/6	1960/1	1964/5	1966/7
No. of admin. centres	4	6	6	12	11
No. of permanent staff	19	29	32	69	105
No. of tutors (full time)	6	7	6	11	11
No. of tutors (part time)	41	120+	132	408	414
No. of organizers (full time)	4	5	6	15	20
No. of staff in overseas programmes	2	5	7	No record	8
Overseas visiting lecturers, speakers, etc.	7	8	3	No record	4
No. of permanent programmes	5	6	6	8	8
No. of class centres	55	132	121	125	121
No. of classes run	76	157	143	617	527
No. of major schools	1	2	2	3	5
Attendance at major residential schools	140	540	636	1038	580
Conferences and special courses	4	2	5	1	3
Total expenditure	N¢66,820.00 £G33,410.0.0 £27,192.1.0	N¢87,520.00 £G43,760.0.0 £35,714.7.0	N¢93,554.00 £G46,777.0.0 £38,022.1.0	N¢262,944.00 £G131,472.0.0 £107,242.0.0	N¢276,000.00 £G138,000.0.0 £112,653.1.6

Table 2. Statistics of programmes

	1950/1	1955/6	1960/1	1964/5	1966/7
Liberal (extra-mural) classes (10–19 weeks)	36	89	99	81	117
Liberal (extra-mural) classes (20 + weeks)	24	55	34	↓	↓
Short courses (5 – 9 weeks)	11	13	10	↓	↓
GCE classes	—	—	—	481	362
External degree classes	—	—	—	28	34
Major residential courses	1	4	3	3	5
Other residential courses	1	2	7	1	3
Trades union classes	4	—	—	12	12
Special courses (M PS, clergy, civil servants, etc.)	2	3	5	1	—

Note: In 1964/5 and 1966/7 there was no break-down of the number of Liberal Classes into those which met from 10 to 19 weeks and those which met more or fewer times during the year. The arrows in this Table should therefore read down to 'Short courses (5–9 weeks)'.

Table 3. Volta Region. Occupational distribution of students :
1966/7

Occupation	Number	Percentage
Teachers	286	31%
Clerks*	283	31%
Technical assistants*	108	11%
P. & T. officers/workers	59	6%
Nurses	40	4%
Draughtsmen	31	3%
Artisans*	28	3%
Policemen	20	2%
Unclassified	18	2%
Soldiers	17	2%
Store assistants	13	1%
Mass education assistants	12	1%
Traders	7	·07%
Unemployed	3	·32%
Local court magistrates	1	·10%
Total	926	

* Each of these groups is composed of three or four different sub-groups.

Note : The Volta Region is one of nine into which the country is divided politically and which form the Institute's administrative centres also. It has a population (1960) of approximately 777,000 (probably increased to approx. 800,000 in the 1966/7 estimate), and is one of seven of the Regions with populations of much under 1,000,000.

Table 4. Brong-Ahafo Region, 9 Liberal Studies Centres : 1966/7.
Occupation, sex and age distribution

A. *Occupation*
    (a) Teachers   81
    (b) Civil servants   69
    (c) Self-employed   44
    (d) Others   71

B. *Sex*
    (a) Females   8*
    (b) Males   257

C. *Age Group*
    (a) 16–20   Nil
    (b) 21–25   98
    (c) 26–35   103
    (d) 36+   64

*In all cases women students fall far short of men in numbers. But, as in Table 5, it can be shown that the incentive of 'paper qualifications' makes a significant difference to the ratio of men to women.
Brong-Ahafo is smaller still than Volta; its 1960 population, 587,920.

Table 5. Brong-Ahafo Region. Occupation, sex and age distribution of GCE students

A. *Occupation*		
	(a) Teachers	4
	(b) Civil servants	13
	(c) Self-employed	2
	(d) Others	52
B. *Sex*		
	(a) Females	10*
	(b) Males	61*
C. *Age Group*		
	(a) 16–20	4
	(b) 21–25	33
	(c) 26–35	29
	(d) 36+	5

* See Note to Table 4.

II. NIGERIA

Table 6. Statistics of operations*

Year	1952/3	1956/7	1960/1	1964/5	1966/7
Administrative centres	4		5	5	3
Permanent staff†	23		14	27	
Tutors (full time)	10		5	7	5
Tutors (part time)	84		53		
Organizers (full time)	1		2	5	
Voluntary organizing secretaries	116		50		
Class centres	84	89	51	37	37
No. of classes	212	89	99	86	71
Enrolled students	5,529	1,801	3,263	1,881	1,024 (53 classes)
Visual aids programmes (film shows)			115		
(TV programmes)				13	
Attendance at all courses		307	394	473	
Vacation courses, seminars and conferences	9		3	9	5
Industrial relations classes				9	10

* Some of the statistics for this Table were not immediately available to the writer, due to difficulties at his end of the line of investigation.
† The quantitative difference between this and the Ghana Staff expresses the differences in advantage mentioned in the text : page 26.

Table 7. Distribution of classes* by subject and region 1964/5 and 1965/6

Subject	Federal Territory		Mid-West		West		Total	
	1964/5	1965/6	1964/5	1965/6	1964/5	1965/6	1964/5	1965/6
Economics	4	4	9	—	3	6	16	10
Geography	2	2	3	—	1	2	6	4
History	—	—	1	3	2	—	3	—
Industrial Relations	2	1	—	3	3	1	9	8
Languages other than English	3	3	—	—	5	3	8	6
English Language and Literature	3	3	14	—	11	6	28	9
Political Science	3	2	2	—	4	3	9	5
Science and Mathematics	1	1	—	—	3	5	4	6
Other	2	2	—	—	1	2	3	4
Total	20	18	29	3	33	28	86	52

* The relatively small numbers involved in the whole Nigerian operation is in part due to inadequate funds, but in large part also to the political crises there of the last few years. All figures in Tables 7–11 are to be read with this qualification in mind.

Table 8. Class figures for federal territory, 1965/6
(including Industrial Relations and other special courses)

	1961/2	1962/3	1963/4	1964/5	1965/6
Total number of classes	19	24	21	20	18
Classes (20 + no. of meetings)	19	23	21	20	18
Classes (10–19 meetings)	—	1	—	—	—
No. of enrolled students	351	518	600	623	636
% of students qualifying by attendance	50%	69%	72%	73%	57%

Table 9. Record of attendance at residential courses, conferences and seminars

1954/5	230
1955/6	306
1956/7	307
1957/8	381
1958/9	452
1959/60	520
1960/1	471
1961/2	683
1962/3	510
1963/4	352
1964/5	473
1965/6	491

III. SIERRA LEONE

Table 10. Statistics of operations

	1958/9	1965/6	1966/7
Administrative centres	2	5	5
Permanent staff	5	7 (plus clerical)	8 +
Tutors (full time)	2	5	6
Tutors (part time)	42	51	31
Organizers	—	1*	1*
Administrative secretary	—	1*	1*
Class centres	15	21	19
No. of classes	57	64	51
No. of enrolled students	848	884	570
No. of effective students (60% attendance)	592	640	432
Residential courses, schools and conferences	1	1	1
Attendance (courses)	35	64	59
Non-residential courses and conferences	2	—	—
Attendance (conferences)	73	—	—
One-day schools/seminars	—	5	} 5†
Week-end schools/seminars	—	6	
Special courses/lectures etc.	—	14	12
Overseas lecturers, speakers, etc.	5	—	—
Revenue (class and other fees only)		LE 1,066 (£533.0.0)	

* Both being of Lecturer status, unlike the Ghanaian model.
† No separation shown in 1966/7.

Table 11. Statistics of programmes : 1966 / 7

A. *Tutorial* classes*

Area	No. of classes	No. of tutors	No. of meetings	Formal enrolment	Effective students
Western Area	18	15	315	181	129
Southern Province	12	6	135	161	131
Eastern Province	16	11	159	161	113
Northern Province	5	3	97	67	59
Total	51	35	706	570	432

B. *Courses, group discussions, etc.*

No. of events	No. of lectures	No. of meetings	No. of students
12	8	77	880

C. *Single public lectures (provinces)*

No. of lectures 13   Approximate attendance 1,120

D. *One-day schools, week-end seminars, etc.*

No. of events 5   Attendance 113

* There is no practical difference between 'Tutorial' classes in Sierra Leone and 'Extra-Mural' or 'Liberal' classes elsewhere, except in the nomenclature.

UNIVERSITY COLLEGE OF THE GOLD COAST
DEPARTMENT OF EXTRA-MURAL STUDIES
in conjunction with the PEA, announce an important series of
ONE-DAY SCHOOLS
on

'PRODUCTION FROM THE LAND'

Saturday, April 29th, 1949
COCOA FARMING
THE COCOA MARKETING BOARD

Saturday, May 6th
TIMBER
MINING

Saturday, May 13th
THE SOIL
WATER SUPPLIES

Saturday, May 20th
THE VOLTA PROJECT
MECHANIZATION

Saturday, May 27th
LIVESTOCK
THE TSETSE FLY

Saturday, June 3rd
FOOD CROP PRODUCTION
CO-OPERATION

Saturday, June 10th
SOME ECONOMIC QUESTIONS
PROBLEMS OF ADMINISTRATION

Saturday Afternoons at 3.00 p.m.

THE SUHUM BRANCH OF
THE PEOPLE'S EDUCATIONAL ASSOCIATION
announces
A ONE-DAY SCHOOL
Beginning at 2.00 p.m. on Saturday, April 14, 1951
on
'THE DEMOCRATIC CITIZEN AND
HIS LEGISLATURE'

---

1. THE VOTER AND HIS REPRESENTATIVE IN THE ASSEMBLY
   by the Editor, Department of Extra-Mural Studies
2. MINISTERIAL RESPONSIBILITY
   by a University College Lecturer in Government
3. POLITICAL IMPLICATIONS OF DEVELOPMENT PLANNING
   by the President of the PEA and Part-Time Tutor in Economics

---

arranged in conjunction with the
University College of the Gold Coast Department of
Extra-Mural Studies

UNIVERSITY OF GHANA
INSTITUTE OF ADULT EDUCATION

FOURTEENTH ANNUAL EASTER SCHOOL
on
'THE VOLTA RIVER PROJECT AND YOU'

AWUDOME RESIDENTIAL ADULT COLLEGE
TSITO, VOLTA REGION
Monday, 10th April–Saturday, 15th April, 1967

Seminars
1. The Economic and Financial Aspects of the Scheme
2. The Agricultural Potential of the Volta Scheme
3. Social and Resettlement Problems of the Scheme

Open lectures
1. 'International Co-operation in the use of Akosombo Power'
2. 'Some Economic Aspects of the Volta River Scheme'
3. 'Financing the Volta River Scheme'
4. 'The Possibilities of the Volta Lake'

UNIVERSITY OF GHANA
INSTITUTE OF ADULT EDUCATION

19TH ANNUAL NEW YEAR SCHOOL
on
'THE CONSTITUTION AND THE ECONOMY'

COMMONWEALTH HALL, LEGON
Wednesday, 27th December, 1967 to Friday, 5th January, 1968

Seminars

1. Ghana's External Relations
2. The State, the Citizen and the Law
3. Local Government and the Democratic State
4. The Church and the New Society
5. Co-operatives and Trade Unions
6. Secondary Industries and Private Investment
7. Agriculture and the Ghana Economy
8. Business Management and the Economy
9. History Workshop (conducted by the Historical Society of Ghana)

Morning lectures

1. 'The United States Constitution'
2. 'The Constitution of the USSR'
3. 'New Ideas for Ghana's Economy'
4. 'Economic Development in Ghana and Related UN Activities'
5. 'The New Constitution : Some Major Issues'
6. 'Problems of Business Management'
7. 'Political Disqualification : An Objective Analysis'

Evening lectures

1. 'Politics and Education'
2. 'Man's Historic Quest for Material Welfare'
3. 'The State and Economic Controls'
4. 'Foreign Participation in a Developing Economy : A Symposium'
5. 'Socialism : Eastern, Western and African'
6. 'Capitalism : Advantages and Disadvantages'
7. 'The Moral and Material Ends of Man' : A Platonic Tetralogue
8. 'In the Opinion of this House, Political Disqualification is Anti-Democratic' : A Debate

NOTES AND REFERENCES

1. Chad had produced Felix Eboué for the Franco-Allied cause and also sheltered Charles de Gaulle and provided him with a base for his notable *résistance* operations.

2. *Adult Education in the Gold Coast: a report for the year 1948–49 by a Resident Tutor* (University of Oxford Delegacy for Extra-Mural Studies) p 3. Dr Kimble went from this post to a Professorship in Political Science in Dar-es-Salam (Federal University of East Africa) and thence to a position with UNESCO in North Africa.

3. Mr Dowuona later became Registrar of the University of Ghana, then of the Ahmadu Bello University in Zaria, Northern Nigeria (as a voluntary exile from the Nkrumah regime); then, after the Ghana coup, Commissioner for Education under the National Liberation Council. His crucial role in the critical days even before the time of the political emergency is to be fully recorded by Kwa Hagan in a revised version of his study referred to below, pp 20–1

4. Hagan completes the picture by describing the roles of the other principal personalities who participated in the activities that culminated in the Oxford undertaking : Mr (later Sir) Christopher Cox and W. E. F. Ward (historian of the Gold Coast), both then education advisers to the Colonial office; the late Colonial Secretary Arthur Creech-Jones; Dame Margaret Read; and Thomas Hodgkin himself, greatly influenced and encouraged by a group of distinguished Oxford dons. (See Hagan, op. cit. pp.176–81.)

5. See below, p 26.

6. See below, p 212 for a similar conclusion.

7. Kimble, op. cit.

8. This is the ideal and the normal order in normal times and places. That the ideal can be subverted, and that popular suspicion of an alliance between government and education can be valid, were to be quite unexpectedly proved in Ghana itself a few years later. (See under the second section below, p 24f.)

9. Kimble, op. cit.

10. People's Educational Association. See below, pp 28–9.

11. p 5.

12. *Report of the Advisory Committee for the Review of the Institute of Public Education,* University of Ghana, Legon, Accra (June 1966), p 10. The present author was the Chairman of the Committee of Enquiry into the IPE and was responsible for phrasing the part of the Report from which the above passage is taken.

13. See Rattray on Ashanti social organization for the ultimate illustration, in, e.g. *Ashanti Law and Constitution* (2nd impression 1956), chapter v, p 38, 'The Family – Slaves' : 'A slave might marry; own property; himself own a slave; swear on "oath"; be a competent witness; and ultimately might become heir to his master.'

14. See various Colonial Office *Bluebooks* covering the fourth quarter of the 19th and the first quarter of the 20th centuries. Part of the reason for 'European Appointments' among a few Africans was climatic.

15. Governor of the Gold Coast from 1919 to 1927, and the best regarded colonial ruler in Ghanaian history. Through him Ghana got back 'Aggrey of Africa' from the United States and gained

Achimota School, Takoradi Harbour, Korle-Bu Hospital, and an extensive road and rail expansion system.

16. See Gold Coast Colony, Civil Service List, 1928, pp 3–80. The exact numbers were 97 Europeans and 9 Africans, the latter being placed at the tail-end of a long scale.

17. Total population figures here are not meant to suggest the same as indicating the relative numbers involved in this type of education. Literacy rates are only 15–20% in these countries, of whom only a smaller fraction still are served in university-based adult education.

18. The Ghana Institute derives its funds (see Table 2) from the Ghana Government, separately in the beginning, then as a part of the general University budget, and now again separately. In Nigeria the Department (of Adult Education and Extra-Mural Studies) receives its funds regionally. In 1951–2 for instance it got £5,000 (recurrent at the time) from Northern Nigeria, £4,000 from the East (now 'Biafra'), and £6,000 from the Western Region (see Report for 1951–2). Today it is financially supported by the Federal Government, the Western and Mid-Western Governments, the Ford and Rockefeller Foundations, etc.

19. In Ghana a Board of Extra-Mural Studies was first set up in 1949 by the Academic Board of the University College of the Gold Coast, as a committee of the latter. The membership of the BEMS was exclusively academic and was headed by the Principal of the College, with the Director as Secretary. In 1950 the Board was replaced by the first of the wider-based bodies of control, the Council for Adult Education. This body was made responsible directly to the College's Council of Convocation through the Principal – who was still Chairman – and the other academic members of the Council. These were : the Director of Extra-Mural Studies, the Director of the Institute of Education of the College, and six nominees of the Council of Convocation; nine members from the public made the Council for Adult Education a body of 18 members. In Sierra Leone today the equivalent is known as the Delegacy for Extra-Mural Studies and has 12 members : in Nigeria there was first an Extra-Mural Academic Advisory Committee, then later control passed into the hands of a Board of Extra-Mural Studies – now called Board of Adult Education and Extra-Mural Studies.

Ethiopia

SOLOMON INQUAI

Introduction

Ethiopia is a vast country with an area of 475,000 sq. miles and an estimated population of over 23,660,000 people. The Ethiopian people are divided in a number of ethnic groups and speak some 40 to 60 languages and dialects. Most of them are farmers and a substantial number are nomads. Amharic, the national language, is not widely understood in the rural areas, but is fast becoming a language of commerce and business in the urban centres. All instruction in the elementary schools is in Amharic. The country is divided into fourteen administrative units or provinces each with a governor-general appointed by the Emperor.

For centuries Ethiopian education has been in the hands of the Ethiopian Orthodox Church, which belongs to the Monophysite group of Churches of the Eastern Orthodox Church. Through the ages, churches, monasteries and individual members of the clergy conducted what was essentially religious education. Graduates were either ordained in the church or became private tutors in the monasteries and the houses of the nobility. It was not until the middle of the nineteenth century that the concept of secular education was introduced by the Protestant missionaries and only six decades ago in 1908 that the first public school was opened. Secular education then made some progress until 1935, the year of the Italian invasion. During this period some Ethiopians were sent abroad, especially to Alexandria, Egypt, and to France, in order to pursue their education beyond the elementary school level.

Educational progress was interrupted by the 'war of aggression' and not resumed until 1941–2 with the help of the British Military Mission to Ethiopia. Today, Ethiopia has many primary and secondary schools and various vocational and trade schools scattered throughout the country. In addition, it has a National University situated in Addis Ababa. Church, mission, and private schools exist side by side with government or public schools. Some of the Church schools are now following the curriculum prescribed by the Ministry of Education, thereby offering more secular education and less of the traditional religious teaching. Yet there is still not adequate provision for all those who are capable of benefiting from education and it will be many years before primary education becomes universal.

It is in the light of this lack of full-time facilities that one should view the state of adult education in Ethiopia. The spread of education, public or otherwise, has not been matched with an awareness of its value on the part of the general public and a demand for increased provision. Adult education seems to fare well wherever schools have been established.

In this survey the provision of adult education in Ethiopia will be treated under several headings : literacy, primary and secondary education, vocational and technical education, and higher education. This division is made purely for the sake of convenience, since the process is in most cases interwoven and interconnected; the existence of one type of adult education for the most part depends on the presence of another. In addition, the chief problems facing adult education in Ethiopia today will be discussed so as to give the reader a comprehensive picture of current conditions.

The problem of illiteracy

The question of what segment of the population is literate or what segment is not cannot be clearly established, mainly because it has not been properly studied. Until very recently such educated adults as were about had received their education in religious institutions. With the spread of public education, however, interest in learning has also grown among adults. Currently, the percentage of literacy in the country has been variously estimated at between 10 and 15 per cent. An incomplete study by the Central Statistics Office (cso) shows that perhaps the national average is not even as high as that. According to recent published findings of the cso for certain sectors of the country, the range is from as high as 30 per cent for the few urban centres and as low as 4 per cent for some rural areas. The study also showed that illiteracy among women is much higher than among men. Moreover, since schools are not evenly distributed throughout the country, the literate population is found concentrated around education centres, thus leaving some sections of the adult population almost 100 per cent illiterate.

Through the years adult literacy has found its champions among the people. Its most ardent supporters have been teachers and students who, on their own initiative, and often free of charge, have from time to time taught adults to read and write or to do arithmetic. However, in recent years a more systematic and organized approach has evolved. Two of the well-known organizations engaged in the war on illiteracy are the National Literacy Campaign Organization (NLCO) and the Yemisrach Dimtse Literacy Campaign.

The NLCO is a private organization largely supported by individual contributions from all sectors of the population. Some of its staff have been seconded from the Ministries of Education and National Defence. It mobilises volunteers to conduct classes in the schools, which are made available free of charge. Most of its work is conducted between July and September when schools are closed for the long vacation and teachers and students alike are available for extensive voluntary work. For the duration of the three months vacation the NLCO hires fifteen field organizers and supervisors, one for each of the fourteen provinces and one for the national capital. Their job is to travel from place to place interesting people in literacy classes, organizing classes, and recruiting volunteer teachers. This effort of the National Literacy Campaign has enabled thousands every year to acquire the status of literacy. During the academic year small classes are organized everywhere with books supplied by the organization. Its endeavour to create regional organizations has so far faltered through its failure to devise appropriate machinery. The organization suffers from lack of adequate staff, especially to carry out promotional and supervisory work. The executive committee is composed wholly of volunteers from among leading personalities in the Society. The need for full-time professional staff is urgent.

The Yemisrach Dimtse Literacy Campaign (YDLC) is the educational branch of the Mekane Jesus Churches (Lutheran) of Ethiopia. This organization has done a commendable job in the few years of its existence by coupling literacy work with community development and ensuring that some basic hygiene, nutrition, agriculture, and child care are taught to the adult students. It employs the services of a full-time staff, of whom there were 432 in the academic year 1965–6. They are, to a great extent, permanent employees of the organization and they enjoy the support of volunteers from the schools of the congregations. It is financed in large part by the Lutheran World Federation. Since its inception in 1962 about 100,000 people have benefited from its services. As one of its several services, it produces different forms of literature for adults, which are especially valuable as follow-up material.

The Ministry of Education has not so far directly involved itself in adult literacy. Although a few years ago it started what were called community schools, presumably to educate both the young and the old up to the fourth grade and to encourage some community development, today these schools are in no way separable from the regular elementary schools. All, or almost all, of them have been expanded to cover instruction up to the sixth grade and if they do any literacy work it is in conjunction with the NLCO rather than on their own initiative. Lately, however, there have been discussions as a result of which proposals have been submitted to UNESCO for an experiment upon an intensified literacy project. If this proposal materializes, the Ministry will be directly involved in adult literacy work. Meanwhile, the Ministry has raised the Department of Adult Education and Literacy to the Director-General level, and is preparing to undertake adult literacy work either on its own or in conjunction with existing organizations. To each province an official will be specifically designated for this work. The Ministry has allotted some funds. It is also experimenting with the uses of radio and television.

Prior to this intervention of the Ministry there has not been any organization to co-ordinate work in the adult education field. This was true in regard to establishing standards, producing teaching materials, and gathering information and statistics. Each organization has gone its own way and prepared different types of literature, almost all of which has been at the primer level; the standard has also varied from organization to organization. In most cases literacy teaching has implied rudimentary work; people have been taught the three Rs at a very elementary level and issued with certificates. Four recent reforms may help remedy the situation. First and foremost is the publication of a syllabus for use by organizations which are conducting literacy classes. This syllabus, issued under the auspices of the Ministry of Education and approved of by many agencies, defines the minimum education a student should reach before he can be certified literate, and includes instruction in the three Rs, civics, and some geography and history. Secondly, the Ministry is setting examinations for those who want a certificate to show that they have completed the prescribed syllabus for a literacy class. Thirdly, the Imperial Ethiopian Government has established a National Committee for Literacy and Adult Education which has a general mandate to co-ordinate activities and to advise the government. The Committee is under the chairmanship of the Prime Minister himself and has already held a few meetings. Fourthly, the Ministry of Education has just distributed the first issue of a monthly paper designed for the newly literate. In the past the most glaring shortcoming in the literacy programme has been the absence of follow-up literature to sustain the interest of adults who had attended literacy classes. Many people are known to have lapsed rapidly into illiteracy for this reason alone. The initiative of the Ministry of Education may help to improve matters.

Other bodies working in the field of adult literacy are the Ministry of National Community Development and Social Welfare, the Ministry of Agriculture through its extension agents, the YMCA, YWCA, the Ethiopian Women's Welfare Association, the University Student Union of Addis Ababa, various mission bodies, and the Ethiopian Orthodox Church. This combined effort will no doubt have an impact upon the state of adult literacy in Ethiopia.

Primary and secondary education

Once kindled, the desire for education seems to be insatiable. Many of the adults who acquire literate status want also to acquire elementary education. Those adults who left school for various reasons at one level or another wish to continue their studies. For many, education, especially secondary education, becomes the pathway to a better future.

Primary and secondary level adult education is characterized by the absence of any central organization. Schools, be they private or public, teachers, and students decide, on their own, whether or not to organize evening classes. If the use of public school premises is required, they must secure permission from the school director. Such permission is normally easily obtained provided they pay for the light, chalk, and such other teaching aids as they require. Some school directors, especially if they have a direct hand in organizing classes, make school text-books available for the use of night school students.

Night schools normally prepare students for the school-leaving examinations, given at the end of the sixth, eighth and twelfth grades. As a result they follow strictly the curriculum prescribed by the Ministry of Education. At times, in order to cover a year's syllabus, teachers rush through the course by dint of watering down the quality of the instruction. Normally, admission requirements are very lax, the student often being left to choose himself which grade he prefers to join. This is especially true of the evening schools run by private bodies, which are usually commercial rather than educational ventures. The subjects most commonly taught are Amharic, English, Mathematics, General Science, Geography, and History. At the elementary level one often finds students taking only English, but at the secondary level students normally register for five subjects at a time. Some well-meaning school directors who have control over evening classes have tried to limit the students' load during a prescribed period.

Most evening classes are taught either by teachers in the local school or by students in senior classes. The majority of teachers in evening classes view this work as a source of additional income. Fees for evening teachers vary from school to school. Private schools running evening adult classes seem to pay on an hourly basis ranging from 15s. to £1 10s.[1] However in some schools income-sharing is practised. This means that after the general expenses have been paid for, the remaining income is divided among the teaching staff on the basis of the number of contact hours per week. This mode of payment is widely used in night schools run by students or teachers in the various public schools.

Evening students are usually required to pay tuition fees and to bring their own text-books. In those cases where classes are organized by volunteer groups such as the Peace Corps or the Ethiopian University Service Participants, no fees are charged. A survey of the fee structure conducted by the author showed that great diversity exists. Progressive fees, that is, higher fees for higher grades, were commonly paid. Fees range from as low as 9d per month in Addis Semen to as high as £1 10s per month in Dessie. Some schools do not charge fees for grades 1 to 3 as this work is considered part of their effort to reduce illiteracy.

The work of the State schools in providing elementary and secondary education for the adult population in Ethiopia is supplemented by foreign correspondence schools, particularly at the secondary level. Many adults in Ethiopia are today pursuing their studies through correspondence, especially those preparing for the London GCE 'o' level or the Ethiopian School Leaving Certificate Examination (ESLC). The best-known correspondence schools enrolling Ethiopian students are the Bennettee College and Wolsey Hall in Great Britain, the British Tutorial College of Nairobi and the International Correspondence Institute from its branch offices in Nairobi or Cairo. Enrolment in these and other corresponding schools is variously estimated at a total well in excess of one thousand, money being the limiting factor. A licence to export money for educational purposes is seldom denied provided foreign exchange is available.

Since the war the provision of primary and secondary education for adults has depended purely upon the whims and wishes of teachers, students or school directors. The presence or absence of electric light has in places determined the existence or non-existence of an evening school despite the willingness of students and teachers to establish one. There has been no effort to speak of on the part of the Ministry of Education to standardize the practices of evening schools and to accredit them. A few schools have been accredited in the sense that they can present candidates to ESLC examinations. There is no financial or technical support or guidance available whatsoever, except the permission to use school premises. Teachers of adult classes have had no special training in methods and techniques, nor is there any provision for such training. As a result most evening schools are ill conceived and badly administered, at best offering an inferior education. Their only redeeming quality is that they have kept a torch burning in the absence of any alternative and at least some schools offer instruction comparable with day schools in its rigorousness and care for standards.

Vocational and technical education

Regular schools offering vocational education for young people are very few. Until recently most of the secondary schools were offering purely academic studies with the aim of preparing a select number for college and university entrance. Lately, many regular secondary schools have been converted into what are called comprehensive secondary schools offering a wide range of vocational instruction as well as academic education. According to their interests and aptitudes students are directed to one of the various streams, commercial, metalwork, woodwork, agriculture, electronics, drawing, home economics, and purely academic. Though these new comprehensive schools have yet to open their doors to evening-school students, some have started business classes, mainly centred around typing and book-keeping. The commercial school of Addis Ababa has been offering evening classes for a long time.

The major centres of part-time vocational education for adults are found in the private schools. Business skills and sewing for women are taught by private commercial institutions. Apprenticeship, especially in automechanics, woodwork, drivers' education, and all types of metalwork, is a widespread practice. The Confederation of Ethiopian Labour Unions is also training its members in various skills.

However, both private and public employers do run their own training schemes at various levels and for varying lengths of time depending on the type of competence desired. Such organizations as the Ethiopian Electric Light and Power Authority, the Telecommunications Board, Civil Aviation, and Ethiopian Airlines arrange training schemes designed to meet their specific manpower needs. Candidates for these classes are required to have reached a certain level of education in order to qualify for training.

Both the Ministry of Agriculture and the Ministry of National Community Development and Social Welfare, through their field staff, the agricultural extension agents and the village development workers, try to pass on to farmers some basic technical knowledge related to agriculture and rural life.

Mission bodies have recently opened residential farmers' schools and technical and vocational schools, aimed primarily at the rural people and the improvement of rural life. The farmers' schools at Selekleka and Wutchale, run by the American Lutheran Mission in conjunction with the Mekane Yesus Churches of Ethiopia (Lutheran), give a one-year training in modern farming methods and contemporary living. The farmer and his family move to the school and are given a house and five hectares of land, which are also supposed to serve as a model farm. The wife learns about modern housekeeping and the husband about modern farming methods. At the end of the year they return to their own land where the school continues to supervise their labours. The vocational and agricultural schools run by the German, Norwegian, and Swedish missions offer training in woodwork, masonry, metalwork, and agriculture, courses ranging in length from six months to two years. They also try to develop cottage industries based on local resources.

Higher education

Haile Sellassie I University was inaugurated in 1962, incorporating all existing colleges in the country. These colleges were the University College of Addis Ababa, an Arts and Science college, the Agricultural College at Alemaya, and the Public Health College at Gondar. Since then the Faculties of Business and Education have been inaugurated as faculties separate from the Faculty of Arts. Schools of Law, Social Work, and Medicine have also been added to make up Haile Sellassie I University.

The colleges, especially University College of Addis Ababa and the Engineering College, started evening classes for adults as early as the academic year 1952–3. Students were enrolled in Liberal Arts classes and were given an intermediate certificate after completion of the equivalent of two years at college. Part-time legal education was introduced by the University College Extension Department and a number of people obtained diplomas in law. The arts curriculum was more or less a replica of the day programme. Except for the law programme, no effort was made to identify adult needs in higher education and to develop programmes to meet those needs. Some students were also enrolled in the last year of secondary level courses which were offered by the University College of Extension. These efforts were supplemented by a series of lectures on specific issues. Often the topics for public talks were determined by the availability of qualified speakers, especially those visiting Ethiopia for a short period.

Engineering extension on the other hand had a more practical orientation. Students were enrolled for a period of one or two years and took classes in surveying and drawing and, at times, pre-engineering courses, which would qualify them for admission on advanced standing to the day-time programme. Many were taught drafting and surveying in those extension classes. Nevertheless the offerings, which to a great extent depended on the desire of a teacher to offer classes, were irregular, From the meagre reports it is evident that there were some years when no classes were offered.

When Halie Sellassie I University was inaugurated in 1962, it created a centrally-administered and co-ordinated programme of University Extension. That extension programme is run by a Dean, who is directly responsible to the Academic Vice-president and the President, like all other Deans of the faculties and colleges. However, since the extension does not have its own teaching faculty, all teachers hired on a part-time basis have to be approved by the departmental heads and the dean of the faculty under whom the courses are normally given. All courses and curricula are developed in co-operation with the faculties, which have the ultimate say in academic affairs.

The Dean of Extension is assisted by an Associate Dean and Centre Directors. To date, there are six centres in which extension classes are conducted, two in Addis Ababa and four in the provinces. Lack of qualified lecturers in the provincial centres and inadequate library facilities are the limiting factors. Students in these centres are restricted to some introductory courses and secondary level courses. However, diploma programmes have already been introduced in two of the four centres.

Students enrolled in the extension programme work towards a degree, diploma, or certificate in one of the various courses offered. Students also enrol in the last year of secondary education or as a special or auditing student in various degree and diploma classes. University extension also offers a number of non-credit and non-graded courses for interested groups.

The degree programmes for which extension students can enrol are the BA and BBA (Bachelor of Business Administration degree). Students in the Arts Curriculum can choose an area of concentration from among Amharic–English, Geography–History, and Economics–Political Science. This is in addition to the general education requirement that all candidates for the BA degree must take. BBA candidates can choose between Management and Accounting for their area of emphasis in addition to the general educational requirements. Candidates for degree programmes must finish their studies within a period of seven years.

Diploma courses are offered in the following areas (a) Accounting,

(b) Economics, (c) Political Science, (d) Advanced Secretarial Course, (e) Junior Secondary Teacher's Diploma, (f) Advanced Diploma in Elementary Education, (g) Librarianship, (h) Drafting, (i) Surveying, (j) Pre-engineering, (k) Highway Technology, (l) Computer courses, and (m) Law (taught either in Amharic or English). Certificate courses in Law (taught in Amharic and English) and some secretarial courses are also offered. These courses are reviewed from time to time so as to ensure that they meet student needs. Plans are under way to introduce correspondence education, especially at the secondary level. The duration of diploma programmes varies with each course, with the shortest course being three semesters and the longest six semesters.

Finance

The University extension programme is financed from two sources : the income from tuition fees paid by students and a supplementary appropriation from the university's general funds. The trend is for the operation to become as self-supporting as possible. This object will be difficult to achieve for some while yet, especially in outlying areas where the level of enrolment is low.

Students attending extension classes are required to pay for their education. The fee is normally assessed on the basis of hours of contact per week during a semester. For most of the courses the fee is £1 10s. [2] per hour per semester, foreign students paying double. Thus an Ethiopian National carrying a six hour per week load pays £9 [3] and a foreigner £18. [4] Tuition fees in some of the provincial centres are lower than those in Addis Ababa. Revenue from tuition is not adequate to cover the cost of the programme, which the University is thus obliged to subsidise to a great extent.

Enrolment in the various programmes has grown from year to year, the current enrolment rising above the 2,000 mark. The admission requirement to University Extension degree programmes is the same as that for the day students. The various diploma programmes have their specific requirements, completion of secondary education being the basic one.

University Extension is meeting a demand from the adult population for post-secondary education. The need to expand the programme is only too evident. It is envisioned that in the future there will be at least one extension centre in each of the fourteen provinces of the Empire of Ethiopia.

Informal education

This paper will not be complete without some reference to the type of informal adult education that is going on in Ethiopia. The most important agent of informal education is the mass media – radio and television. Radio reaches every corner of the country whereas television is limited to Addis Ababa. Various ministries and government agencies arrange programmes of an educational nature. Most of the programmes are of ten to fifteen minutes duration and are on the air once or twice a week. Some of the regular radio features include programmes on agriculture, health, civics, child care, and the informal study of science. Radio Ethiopia also features a programme called English by Radio, which was developed by the BBC. A similar programme is also broadcast by the Radio Voice to the Gospel, a Lutheran radio station operating in the country.

The method of presentation is the straight talk occasionally punctuated by a spell of question and answer. There is very little dramatization or adaptation to the needs of the different segments of the population. The problem about providing good radio programmes is a lack of knowledge of the characteristics of the audience. How many people in the areas to which specific programmes are directed actually own radios? Do they understand the Amharic language? The absence of feedback and the lack of qualified educators to plan meaningful programmes seem to hamper the efficiency of broadcasting. There has been no attempt to create or stimulate the creation of radio listening and discussion groups. Radio and television are also the main means of entertainment for the general public. For the time being television programmes are available to the residents of Addis Ababa only.

Another important source of informal education is the various cultural missions stationed in the capital city and some of the major towns. They offer valuable educational facilities, especially in the field of languages. Evening schools run by the English, French, Italian, German, Russian and, recently, Spanish speaking countries have taught hundreds of Ethiopians to read and write and to speak a foreign language. Some organizations like the United Nations Economic Commission for Africa have installed modern electronic language-teaching equipment.

Various government departments have cultural centres where talks and discussions are conducted and films are shown to the adult public with a view to helping people acquire an insight into the affairs of the wide world.

Conclusion

Adult education in Ethiopia is still in its infancy. The base is too small to meet the staggering demand for education at all levels.

Adult literacy, although now off to a good start, has to expand very fast if it is to make any impression upon the vast illiterate population. Furthermore, adequate follow-up and reading material of interest to the newly literate must be produced in quantity. At the elementary and secondary level co-ordination and supervision of the programmes are of paramount importance in order to ensure an acceptable level of education for adults. Government participation, both administratively and financially, and in all aspects of adult education, is imperative. Voluntary effort can only go so far and is bound to falter unless strengthened by government intervention. One can foresee the day when it may be necessary to mobilise the youth of the nation, especially during the long vacation, to help combat illiteracy. Thousands of schoolchildren are idle every year for some three months. Can they not teach the adults in their villages ? Finally, the mass media must be thoroughly exploited.

One very important aspect of the field of adult education that is not given adequate attention is the training of adult educators. Many organizations, including the Ministry of Education, give a brief orientation course to would-be teachers, especially on the use of books. This 'briefing' ranges in duration from as short a period of two days to as long as two weeks. The only educators who are given satisfactory training are the village level community development workers. The special problems involved in teaching adults should be given due attention and could perhaps be dealt with by the Faculty of Education of the University.[5]

NOTES

1. $5·00 — 10·00 Ethiopian
2. $10·00 Ethiopian
3. $60·00 Ethiopian
4. $120·000 Ethiopian
5. *See* Select Bibliography pp. 242–3. Unpublished statistical information from various organizations and a survey of part literacy adult education (elementary and secondary) conducted by the author were used in the preparation of this passage survey.

Adult Education in Ethiopia

Adult literacy	Primary and secondary	Vocational and technical	Higher education	Informal education
Ministry of Education	Private efforts schools state	Ministry of Agriculture	Haile Sellassie I University programme of University Extension	Government Agencies
Other Ministries	Foreign correspondence schools	Ministry of National Community Development and Social Affairs		Government Cultural Centres
National Literacy Campaign Organization (NLCO)		A few State schools		Radio Ethiopia
Yemisrach Dimtse Literacy Campaign (YDLC)		Private schools		Some television programmes in Addis Ababa only
YMCA		Confederation of Ethiopian Labour Unions		Radio Voice of the Gospel
YWCA		Private and public employers		Cultural museums
Ethiopian Women's Welfare Association		Mission bodies (mainly farmers' schools)		
University Students' Union				
Religious bodies				

3. The Ivory Coast

JEAN-CLAUDE PAUVERT

Introduction

In most of the French-speaking countries in Africa, and also in Madagascar, adult education occupies a marginal place in such few eductional plans as exist and more often than not it is not mentioned at all when the aims of a country's educational system are being formulated. Whether it be a question of literacy or remedial teaching, of professional retraining or social and cultural progress, public planning in this sector of education still remains limited, whereas overall educational planning, articulated with social and economic development, is becoming increasingly fashionable.

This neglect is all the more surprising since, in countries whose educational systems are based on the French model, tendencies towards centralization and state control might have been supposed to constitute an incentive to overall planning. But the simple explanation is that in many French-speaking countries in Africa the very concept of adult education has yet to be considered in any depth.

The Ivory Coast is no exception. It has been selected here for study, however, because it illustrates a new departure which may eventually lead to a more rational system of national education in which adult education will have its due place. The situation in the Ivory Coast poses what is surely a fundamental question : is it possible or indeed desirable to draw up official plans for the education of adults ? In this article an answer will be sought to that question. Beforehand, however, it will be helpful to describe some of the agencies of adult education to be found in this West African country, their principal aims, and the problems that they face in relation to methods, personnel and organization.

Aims and definitions

The key document in the national plan, *Perspectives Décennales de développement économique social et culturel 1960 – 1970*, expounds the aims in out-of-school education of several ministerial departments, and enables us to describe adult education as it exists at present in this country.

(a) The *Ministry of National Education* is responsible for cultural programmes, under which head it deals with public libraries and art education, not only at the school but also at the adult level, and encourages research into and dissemination of the traditional culture. In addition, this Ministry controls centres providing professional training for adults.

(b) The *Ministry of Agriculture* arranges a rural scheme designed:
'First to train the farmer during a prescribed number of years by means of a quasi-permanent programme, and then, more sporadically, to tender advice and keep him informed about technical changes...While waiting against the day when everyone in the rural areas will have received an adequate general and professional training, thanks to the spread of primary school education and vocational schools, it is important to do something for illiterate adults and young people. The important thing is to convince them of the value and interest of rural improvement, to stimulate them to modernize their villages, and to teach them the techniques of modernization.'

(c) The *Social Service* pursues the following objective: 'Family and Social Education,...contributing to community development and the formation of co-operatives', especially through a campaign directed at women and the socially handicapped. The 1960–70 plan noted that 'on all the evidence some of these aims overlapped with the tasks assigned to the public health agencies in the area of preventive medicine, and with the goals of the youth movement and the movement for popular education,...or even with agricultural training', since this latter, within the framework of rural development, is similarly striving to ensure some degree of education for women in the rural areas.

(d) The *Ministry of Youth, Popular Education and Sports*, as its name implies, is responsible for a further large section of adult education. The Ministry is charged with:
'the general organization of the literacy programme, and with the study of every possible measure calculated to ensure the success of this programme in conjunction with the external services; to promote the formation of agencies of popular education, to assist in their development, and to ensure regular supervision; to organize and control remedial education centres,[1] training centres for women and for popular education; to introduce and arrange every possible method of ensuring the appropriate smooth development of popular education; to form groups for cultural development and popular education.'

Leaving aside the programmes designed for young people, it may be useful to specify the aims of what we call 'popular education'. These are:
'Literacy and the education of adults considered as indispensable for

the realisation of how societies evolve and the role which each individual can play therein; training and instructing the common people with the aim of increasing production and enabling them to contribute more effectively to the cultural, economic and social education of the community; co-ordinating those habits and customs of the people which are judged to be valuable, with a view to enriching the traditional culture; giving special attention to the general role of women in fostering family education; encouraging the most fruitful possible use of leisure.'

In short, to quote the official text:

'Popular education must bring to bear new insights and original methods on all those areas of interest to the common people such as civics, co-operatives, hygiene, agriculture and stock-rearing, not to speak of craft groups and artistic groups. In addition, it must help men and women to adapt to changing conditions and to contribute fully to the well-being of the community.' [2]

At first, centres for Popular Education are formed under the guidance of an organizer who operates in the rural environment and strives to arouse in the villagers an awareness of new needs such as the desire to know more about things and to have at their disposal premises which can house a centre. Women's clubs and youth clubs will also eventually be accommodated in these Popular Education Centres.

Some degree of a hierarchical structure is envisaged. Thus at a higher level the Cultural and Youth Clubs will be set up under the supervision of a statutory association which will guarantee managerial control and administrative support and development. These 'clubs' will be designed for urban centres of population where there are upwards of 10,000 inhabitants. Finally, there are now in operation eight Cultural Centres which constitute the highest institutional form of continuing education administered by the State and welcome participants from every walk of life, providing them with all essential means of acquiring information at an advanced level.

The dissemination of educative and cultural information is also one of the specific aims of the Ministry of Information, which controls the mass media : the press, radio and, not least, television. The Ivory Coast is one of the few African countries to have the benefit of an effective broadcasting network since its transmitters cover an area inhabited by more than two-thirds of the country's four million population. Apart from educational programmes prepared for television and radio by the several ministries referred to above, other programmes, no less educational in content, are prepared by the Ministry of Information, which has its own conception of popular education, ill-defined though it yet remains.

AENB F

Complexity of adult education provision

As we have seen, the objectives pursued by these various ministerial departments are by no means clearly differentiated. Above all, it appears that Popular Education, as conceived by the Ministry specially responsible for it, includes a variety of educational activities also sponsored by other ministries : women's education; the training of skilled workers; health education; the bringing of farming and co-operative techniques to the people; cultural activities; and the provision of general information. It is not easy to discern behind all this the application of a comprehensive philosophy of adult education related either to an ideology or to principles underlying social and economic development.

However, one general characteristic of the education of adults does emerge, namely, that it is administered and controlled by the State. It is always conceived within the context of a centralized and hierarchical administration of a ministry and leaves little room for private efforts by individuals or local groups, be they professional, cultural or whatever. Thus it follows the French tradition in education where the tendency is to concentrate maximum responsibility in the State. In this respect it is essentially different from the practice in the Anglo-Saxon and Scandinavian countries, to name but two examples. It was already noted some years ago that when the French-speaking African countries gained their independence[3] this characteristic of their educational systems persisted, leaving little room for local enterprise. As with development, education is based upon a framework more or less hierarchical, more or less integrated, always bureaucratic, affording little scope for traditional or spontaneous institutions or for self-help. Schools, universities, adult education in all its forms – public lectures, theatre, cinema, workers' education, family life education, literacy, every part of the educational system – apart from the denominational religious schools – are organized from the centre by the State.

Paradoxically, as we have already noted, such centralization is not accompanied by a co-ordinating and unifying conception of adult education. Upon close inspection the paradox emerges as only apparent. The various educational activities are envisaged as part of the framework of national development which each ministry (Agriculture, Health and so on) must carry out on its own account rather than in response to felt needs expressed by individuals and groups working for community development. Moreover, the broad outlines of a philosophy of national education are in fact beginning to take shape in the Ivory Coast with the promulgation of a 'loi-cadre d'éducation et de formation' for the years 1968–70, integrated with the economic, social and cultural plan already adopted for the same three-year period. These broad outlines may appear to be determined less by a philosophy of education than by economic and financial considerations. There is a strong wish to ensure that the existing educational machinery is used to the full either at school or at the higher level and that such extra-budgetary resources as are available shall indeed be applied to education. The system of continuing education which is emerging will therefore be one designed not only for the personal improvement of the individual but also for the organization of groups in the field who will engage in educational projects at the same time as community development.

Further, but still within the same framework of reference, a desire for greater efficiency in education has led to investigations of the extent to which education can be based upon the national culture. If there is any philosophy of adult education in the Ivory Coast, therefore, it is that educational planning must be explicitly associated with a cultural policy.

It is in the light of these general considerations that this study of problems posed by the organization of adult education has been conducted. Relating to programmes, personnel, material and monetary resources, and administration, these problems will now be briefly considered, alongside the solutions that it is hoped to apply in those cases where they can already be discerned.

Content and programming

The general educational programmes envisaged for the Ivory Coast naturally cannot fail to include certain factors previously mentioned : the spread of more up-to-date and efficient agricultural techniques and of more rational commercial practices; the improvement of technical skills either through work-release or on-the-job training for workers in the secondary and tertiary sectors, and through preparation for promotion; family life education, especially women's education; general civic education (politics, economics and social affairs) – all these must continue to be the object of yet more intensified effort.

But it is now also emerging that planning educational programmes for adults requires a better understanding of real cultural needs. Even the method of approach is not yet quite clear. There can be no question of an approach conceived merely as a study of the cultural market. Our desire must be to escape from the notion of a uniform consumer culture which might well constitute a more or less totalitarian programme. The content of adult education must encourage individual enterprise and personal development along creative and imaginative lines. In other words, it must develop individuals who are capable of

escaping from that area which in advanced societies is known as 're-
pressive satisfaction'.[4]

Thus, it is at the precise stage when programmes are in the making
that the participation of all those interested appears necessary, particularly the participation of all the intermediary agencies and of the various
local and professional groups. At this stage, moreover, and under the
same heading, it looks as though where programme design is concerned, as in the case of method, it is involvement itself which must be
stimulated and encouraged, in such a way that the evolution of a
national culture is fostered, not the diffusion of a prefabricated culture.
For, allowing for the fact that there are countries with a well-formed
unified culture,[5] the ultimate goal of adult education in the Ivory
Coast, as in many of the developing countries, is precisely the construction of such a national culture.[6] The role played by the University
of Abidjan and by The Institute of National Arts will be the determining factor in the search for the emerging culture which must form the
very essence of the adult education programme.

So much for methods. Without going into detail it is especially
worth noting that in this context of programming and determining
the final form adult education shall take, the uses of such extremely
powerful media as television must be studied with the greatest care
precisely because they can promote either the active involvement of
all the people or, on the contrary, total apathy.

Staffing

A recent report of the Ministry of Popular Education indicated that:
'the selection, training, improvement and supervision of adult educators presents an array of truly formidable problems as one attempts to deal with large numbers in a country where the shortage
of qualified personnel is one of the factors limiting action...One
solution must be to use existing trained groups connected with projects being undertaken. The "animateurs" must be agents of the
Ministries directly concerned, service agents for agriculture, societies for promoting agricultural improvement through the television
clubs in rural areas, employees of movements for workers' literacy,
and so on.'

These training problems have yet to be solved. Although several
ministries have set up training centres, the training they give does not
adequately cater for the requirements of a body of adult educators
who shall be truly aware of the real needs and aspirations of the social
environment concerned.

A more fundamental question has arisen : to what extent does the
education of adults necessarily entail the intervention, on the ladder of

contact with the educated, of intermediaries who are more or less formally trained. Without doubt these agents often appear as indispensable activists in a given human environment. As Radlinska has said with reference to the goals of social training:

'the job of education consists in arousing the energies (both actual and potential) of individuals and groups so as to create more favourable conditions for their self-fulfilment. What is decisive is the degree to which the educator knows how to contribute to the activation of the milieu so that each person can become a conscious participant in the nation's life.'

All the same, two factors must be borne in mind. The first is that certain forms of adult education have less need of activists than have some others. This may well be true of television, although we must admit that more study of its uses is called for. Certainly, where the content and form of the message correspond closely to the very nature of the spectacle that is televised, a face-to-face relationship can be created in which an intermediary might seem superfluous and even an interference.

The second factor is that, where the use of the mass media is concerned, the 'activist-intermediary-educator' often starts with a great advantage if he has been designated one of the natural leaders of the group he is dealing with. A study of the relationships between community development and public administration in some African countries has already led the present writer to stress the importance of using existing local groupings if efforts towards self-help and collective improvement are to succeed.[7] The old system of district chiefs can be reorientated along more modern lines, as was observed in 1950 among the Fang du Woleu-Ntem in Gabon. It is true that the mass media were not used in those cases. But certain sociological studies of mass culture in the United States tend to show, for example, that decisions taken by vote can be explained only by the actions of the leaders of public opinion, better informed and absorbing more from the mass media, who disseminate verbally among their fellow-citizens the information they have gleaned from reading the press or listening to the radio, a process described as the *two-step flow of information*.[8]

It does not seem possible therefore to arrive at any clear conclusion but it is useful simply to raise the problem. Let us add only that in the Ivory Coast some indications have been provided by an inquiry into the uses of sound broadcasting. Completed in 1966, the inquiry concluded by emphasizing that:

'the literate bushmen, above all the young ones, have reserves of enthusiasm which it would be possible to exploit in the cause of popular education in the context of a broadcasting exercise. There is, however, no point, as is often the tendency, in expecting them to manifest their energies in individual enterprise; they show willingness to act only within an organised scheme and with the support of all the official apparatus.'[9]

Therein is to be found one of the consequences of the centralized and state-centred administrative form which every educational undertaking in the Ivory Coast has so far assumed, any spontaneous initiative and organization no longer seeming conceivable to a population waiting upon official directives. The same report added:

'The preoccupations of and the need for information expressed by the villagers, their consciousness of the changing nature of the world around them, leave them profoundly disoriented : they know they can no longer be what they were, they recognize that changes are necessary, but they remain afraid, they are distrustful. As a consequence, they need constant reassurance concerning all that they hear, concerning all the advice that is lavished upon them, together with repeated explanations of everything that has to do with them.'

What seems to emerge from these various comments on the general problems faced by adult educators, on the nature of their role in expanding interest in education, on the kind of intermediary who is most effective, and on the question of whether intervention is necessary or not, is that more searching studies than any we have had so far are essential. Such studies must naturally take heed of the auxiliary adjuncts of teaching, of the use of radio and television, and of other methods not involving the problem of intermediary agents.

Methods

This term can give rise to confusion. Two particular sets of problems may stem from its use : the first have to do with material means, techniques, the tools placed at the disposal of the educational activity; the second is more generally concerned with methods of finance. Both have attracted the attention of those responsible for the national plan.

In the case of tools and techniques it is essential to refer to the use in the Ivory Coast of radio and television. The national radio covers the whole of the country. An inquiry undertaken in 1964 estimated that 11 per cent of the population listened in once a week and 13 per cent listened in several times. Listeners were more numerous in the Centre and South-East (34 per cent) than in the North (4 per cent). Naturally the proportion of listeners was by far the highest in the towns (75 per cent in Abidjan and 66 per cent in the other urban centres). Since there is some correlation between listening figures and the standard of living, the educational level and the rate of urbanization, it seems reasonable to infer that radio is not an ideal means of teaching the large rural population that is in greatest need of benefiting from basic education. This warning note having been sounded, it is noteworthy that a good deal of general education had been carried out by radio, arranged by the Ministry of Information as a rule on its own account but sometimes in conjunction with the technical ministries, conveying to the public a substantial body of information about hygiene, child rearing, schooling, fish production, agriculture, home economics, administrative planning, human and economic geography, and civil law. But it is a measure of the limited scope of education by radio that the number of receivers does not exceed 150,000.

As for television, by August 1968 it covered half the country, that is, two-thirds of the population or 2,700,000 inhabitants. By 1971 coverage of the whole country will be complete. This means that the Ivory Coast has at its command a very powerful instrument of education. Its use for educational purposes is, even so, as yet quite limited; of the three hours of daily transmission only a restricted period of time is set aside for educative programmes. At the same time, it is worth taking note of recent experiments with television clubs, thirteen of which are now in existence.

From January to June 1967 a series of ten experimental programmes was presented dealing with the following themes : rural depopulation, pregnancy and confinement, registration of births, marriage, divorce, the rural environment, weaning, death and inheritance, stock-rearing. These broadcasts were directed in particular at the rural public, assembled in the village television clubs and assisted by specially trained local organizers. The programmes were also viewed in 47 existing literacy centres and in a few government service reception centres. Using a similar format another series on rice production has been broadcast with specialist instructors from the agricultural service making explanatory comments at village meetings. All these television programmes were followed with great interest and stimulated animated exchanges. They afford a formula which provokes the active involvement of the population concerned and which it is intended to apply more widely and more frequently.

It is no less important to mention the teaching of literacy by television. In November 1962 the Association of Business and Industry requested that courses should be arranged in spoken French and in reading, writing and arithmetic so that qualified workers would be able to attend professional training courses and thereafter take up posts of responsibility. After two experimental sessions a third programme (1965–6) was shown on open circuit television and viewed by 1,500 people. In June 1967, 75 per cent of the viewing audience which took the final examination reached the threshold of fluent reading and corresponding writing skills. If those students who dropped out are also taken into account, the percentage of the enrolled students who succeeded was 35 per cent.

Radio and television can thus be regarded as two vital methods for educating adults in the Ivory Coast, though their use has continued to be restricted as much by the nature of the programmes transmitted as by the size of the public sector reached. Numerous inquiries into the potential uses of these media are still needed. A few are already under way. As a rule they are concerned with what may be called – albeit a very broad term – cultural equipment and aim precisely at defining the total potential of the Ivory Coast available for putting a cultural policy into practice. This particular notion will be reconsidered later on, but in respect of cultural equipment it is useful to round out what has just been said about radio and television by a rapid survey of the other methods of adult education : the public library system, the museums, the theatres and the rest.

To take them in that order, there is in the Ivory Coast a National Library, together with three public libraries in Abidjan. Though there are libraries in most of the secondary schools, they are never used for extra-curricular or post-school purposes. In Abidjan there is a museum. Of all the cultural institutions, however, the most important is the National Arts Institute in Abidjan since it provides a unique and indispensable means of training personnel necessary for the success of a decentralized and popular cultural policy. It consists of national schools of music, dance and drama, and includes a department of folk arts and traditions. As can be seen, all these cultural facilities are concentrated in Abidjan, thus making any penetration of the whole population on a national scale impossible.

Sources of finance

The amount of money allocated in the national budget to adult education, interpreted in the very wide sense described so far, does not exceed 400 francs per head. Moreover, if we were to take into account only expenditure on adult education in the strict sense of the term, the amount would be much smaller. Aside from the money it spends on young people and sporting activities, the Ministry of Popular Education, Youth and Sports had in 1968 a budget of 125 million francs (CFA)[10] approximately for adult education – that is, 30 francs CFA per inhabitant or 60 francs CFA per adult. As for the Ministry of Education, it had an allocation of 96 million francs, i.e. 25 francs *per capita*, for all its cultural activities, including museums, libraries and the fine arts. And even if it be reckoned that the aggregate activities of the Ministry of Information constitute a kind of adult education, its expenditure of 354 million francs for 1967 would represent only 90 francs *per capita* or 180 francs for each adult.

These several figures serve to quantify the amount of money set aside for non-full-time education. To see them in perspective it is sufficient to point out that the budget for the whole country in 1967 was 39·8 billion francs and the gross national product touched 250·5 billions.

It is therefore apparent that the financial resources at the disposal of adult education are restricted in relation to the scale of the national resources. Apart from State subsidies it must be added that this form of education benefits from severely limited private support. The various voluntary associations, groups and local collectives have little responsibility and few genuine activities.

At the present time, however, there is, as already mentioned, a disposition to define a more positive, more precise and more comprehensive cultural policy, with increased resources. The education plan for 1968–70 calls for larger sums to be allocated to adult education and to the cultural policy. It also prescribes the conditions in which existing facilities may be provided more efficiently through their full and systematic use. Their full use would imply, of course, the solution of administrative and coordinating problems.

Organization

The present diffusion of effort in the provision of adult education has already been noted. The authorities in the Ivory Coast are now trying to remedy the situation.

A first attempt to co-ordinate efforts is now beginning with particular reference to the use of the mass media, the press, radio, cinema and television. Thus, the Ministry of Planning has carried out a thorough inventory of all the existing facilities and an assessment of the way they are used by the various ministries. Based on this study, consideration is being given, on the one hand, to working out more coherent educational programmes, to the fulfilment of which the various ministries will contribute according to their competence, and, on the other hand, to the introduction of a more centralized and therefore less costly system of production such as a National Cinema Office or an Educational Television Department. At present, each ministry wants to use the resources of sound and television to transmit educative information, but each one wishes to control production and hence its own facilities. It is therefore profitable to study the conditions under which the concentration of production might best meet economic criteria in a way satisfactory both to the economist and to the educator, might cost less than the traditional means of education, while increasing its efficiency thanks to the use of services ensuring better integration and retention.

Another tendency is for the education of adults – or part-time continuing education – to be supported by organizations progressively introduced for stimulating local development. In fact, the Ministry of Planning controls a *Direction de l'Animation* which is seeking to lay down the conditions for a coherent educational programme, decentralized to the level of local communities and integrated with developmental planning. Investigations are in progress to specify what exactly should be the participation in such an educational programme of the various competent ministries. There would still be diversity but there would also be more co-ordination, since direction would be at the level of sub-prefectures. Co-ordination of this kind should enable the agents of the social services, of information, agriculture, health and national education to use as far as possible the same accommodation and the same educational facilities, for example, libraries, radio and television sets.

Furthermore, co-ordination of educational and local development operations would tend to involve the members of local communities in the actual organizing and financing of the educational programme. It must be stated that in practice there exist up to the present time in the Ivory Coast no institutions of a communal or institutional nature (with the exception of eight urban Cultural Centres formed in the big cities) and that consequently local communities do not have at their disposal funds which can be devoted to educational programmes or for that matter to economic development projects. The Ministry of Planning is proposing to remedy this deficiency.

This brief survey of the forms of adult education operating in the Ivory Coast, of its declared aims, of the many problems posed and the solutions which it is hoped to bring to them leads one to note in conclusion that numerous factors combine to make planning imperative: the centralized character of the administration, the State's dominant role in education, the need to remedy the diffusion of effort among the services, to bring about full use of existing means and resources, to define a cultural policy likely to guarantee national unification, and, finally, the task of integrating the educational process with the process of economic and social development.

So we are brought back to the question which seems impossible to avoid : is such planning either feasible or desirable ? Is there not a contradiction between the idea of culture and the idea of planning ?

Culture and planning

An international round table convened by UNESCO at Monaco in December 1967 took as its theme the study of 'cultural policies'. This study was occasioned by the fact that in many countries the growth of formal schooling, the extension of leisure, and the rise in the standard of living were causing manifest changes in the cultural needs of various societies. The participants were led to consider the eventual possibility of introducing a policy of cultural planning to be based upon an assessment of these needs and consisting of a realistic anticipation of future cultural requirements and the means to be adopted for satisfying them. But to proceed along these lines brings one up against the problem of defining the culture that is being planned for and of specifically raising the problem whenever adult education is under discussion. Must a cultural policy underlie every policy and every programme of action in the area of adult education? Can and should cultural policies and adult education policies be planned from above in the way that we plan economic development?

Without doubt the advantages, the very necessity even, of such planning are clear in the light of the experience of the Ivory Coast and of such imperatives as administrative co-ordination, the full use of resources, the harmonization of programmes and methods, the adaptation of adult education to the needs and possibilities defined within the framework of development plans and national cultural characteristics. Anticipation, co-ordination and choice plainly imply a planned approach.

Furthermore, as recent events in France have shown, it seems essential to impart significance and a sense of direction to development. A national development policy must presuppose human and social involvement as well as an economic policy – in other words, it presupposes a cultural policy. And if the essence of government is foresight (to govern is to have foresight) it seems wholly desirable to integrate cultural and general planning.

In such a context a cultural policy is far from being focussed upon the fine arts. It is education for a social and human situation of which the fine arts form part. It is a generalized, continuous educational process. It is in this sense that the Ivory Coast plan for education assigns to the cultural policy associated with it the function not only of organizing the spread of Ivory Coast and universal culture but above all of:

'giving to every individual, throughout his full-time and post-school education, the tools with which to play his part in the continual enrichment of that national culture, receptive also to outside influences, and directly involved in the development of mankind and of Ivory Coast society. Such a cultural policy seeks to give to every form of education and training a humanist dimension.'[11]

The popular culture diffused by adult education is not, according to this conception, a form of consumer goods. It is the permanent continuing production of a society engaged in the process of economic and social development. Perhaps, indeed, the term 'popular' should not be used since it leads to confusion and seems to be differentiated from an exclusive culture reserved for an élite, whereas what we are referring to is the culture of a whole people.

Are culture and planning then reconcilable, reconciled? It seems that we can claim so. Planning must also be regarded as a first step towards establishing channels of communication between the various sections of society both horizontally and vertically, that is to say, not only articulating economic organizations but social, religious and other organizations as well. In this light a planned adult education system may be seen as pursuing a cultural strategy aiming above all at facilitating social intercommunication while not stifling the growth of voluntary movements. On the contrary, by furnishing the conditions under which individuals and communities may attain self-expression, adult education will foster spontaneous growth, thus ensuring for each citizen a creative role in his own community by supplying what G. Gurvitch has called the appropriate social conditions for the germination and dissemination of the seeds of knowledge.

Thus, within a planned scheme the mass media would not be allowed to smother individual and community initiatives. Rather their function would be to encourage a sense of personal commitment to society as a whole, by bringing into contact one with another all the various levels and sections of a developing society at a speed which would have been impossible through the traditional channels for spreading knowledge. Psychological tests on the reactions of the individual to radio and television should tell us more about the real or supposed danger of passivity which they are alleged to inculcate and also reveal ways in which this danger, if it really does exist, could be reduced.

Provided, then, that the means used to promote mass education neglect none of the social agencies which can ensure the personal involvement of all citizens, it seems reasonable to envisage an adult education policy that is at the same time centrally planned and yet capable of stimulating organic growth from below.

The foregoing analysis of the present situation in the Ivory Coast and its plans for the future leads to the conclusion that only good can come from persevering with the regulated policy of cultural development already initiated. There is one reservation : planners must not bypass the existing social order but retain an anthropological approach to the culture of the people for whom their planning is designed.

NOTES AND REFERENCES

1. Centres for young people who left the primary school before obtaining a certificate of primary education.
2. *Ministère de la Jeunesse, de l'Education Populaire et des Sports : rapport sur les institutions de jeunesse et d'éducation populaire*, 1967.
3. Pauvert, J.C., 'Les tendances actuelles de l'éducation des adultes dans les états africains d'expression française' in *Cahiers de l'Institut d'Etude du développement économique et social de l'Université de Paris*, Paris 1967.
4. Here, of course, the theories of H. Marcuse are very pertinent.
5. Though we should remember that in these countries, too, culture is in a state of flux, due to social and technical changes, etc.
6. Without this national culture being necessarily confined to the country in question. Culture, as J. Berque has written, 'emerges from a dialogue between the manifold and the individual, between the world-wide and the limited'.
7. cf. Pauvert, J.C., 'La lecture publique et la culture populaire', in *Unesco : les bibliothèques publiques en Afrique*, Paris 1953; 'La formation des leaders locaux', in *International Review of Community Development*. Rome 1959.
8. Cf. Lazarsfield, Berelson and Gaudet, *The People's Choice*, 1944.
9. Marcomer, S.A., *La Radio éducative en Afrique noir : la Côte d'Ivoire*, Paris 1966.
10. 245 francs CFA are worth one US dollar.
11. Plan for the Education and Training Act, 1968–70.

4. Kenya

R.C. PROSSER

Introduction

Lying astride the equator though hardly to be described as equatorial, Kenya boasts in her tourist brochures of being a land of contrasts. This claim is not without foundation. The tropical coastline contrasts with the temperate highlands, the dry northern deserts with the humid plains of Victoria Nyanza; the spectacular Great Rift Valley with soaring Mount Kenya. But it is not simply in topography that contrasts prevail : while the true Kenyan emerges, peoples contrast with peoples. Races maintain their separate identity through customs, conventions and culture while graduating to a common likeness; Kenya is predominantly African, yet Asian, Arab and European communities preserve their distinctiveness. Even among the African peoples themselves contrasts are deep and clear. Ethnically, the Hamitic north-east is distinct from the Nilotic lake belt and the Nilo-Hamitic Rift from the Bantu centre. Socially, the progressive westernized Kikuyu differ sharply from the simple Turkana tribesmen untouched by modernity. All these lie within the boundaries of a country the size of Spain with a total population of some nine million and a *per capita* annual income of around sixty shillings.

Independent of Britain in 1963, the new nationalist government inherited a host of complex problems all requiring urgent solution but with no simple apparent answers. A lack of known raw materials has necessitated a heavy reliance on agriculture, though the quality of two-thirds of the land area makes farming difficult if not impossible. A very high rate of population growth, nearly three per cent per annum, implies a doubling of the population every twenty years or so. A steady migration to the towns from the countryside raises enormous urban living problems while cash employment becomes increasingly difficult to find.

Some eighty per cent of the population of Kenya is illiterate. Over half of the population is under fifteen years. Only half the number of children between seven and thirteen years eligible for school are actually attending school. Of those at primary school and completing their seven years just ten per cent are able to continue to secondary schools, and of the 150,000 who leave each year, 100,000 are destined to be unemployed. The finance or resources for rapid expansion of formal child education do not exist. The country is poor and already over twenty per cent of the national recurrent budget is being spent on formal education alone. By international standards this proportion is high to the point of overstraining and leaves little room for expansion beyond keeping pace with the population increase. It is small wonder that Kenya's Chief Education Officer was able to say : 'Access to education is perhaps the biggest issue in Kenya's domestic politics. Kenyans are avid for education, both for themselves and for their children.'

Pattern of adult educational provision

It is within the national constraints described above that the present adult education provision must be analysed and evaluated. It is only in very recent years that any clear picture has begun to emerge of the nature, role and scope of adult education in the Kenyan context. Inheriting attitudes and structures drawn from the British experience, Kenya has been slow to appreciate the need for a philosophical framework which links adult education to immediate national needs or which allows a body of professional adult educators to emerge able to take a wide view of the field. This is not to say that no adult education has been carried on, but it is a major contributory reason why the approach to adult education provision has been sporadic, often disorganized and generally unrelated to any predetermined order of priority or to overall national development.

However, the situation is now changing. The need to plan seriously for national development and to fulfil promises which were made by a democratically elected government, along with the urgent need to isolate the key factors governing the speed at which national development can take place, have necessitated a closer examination of the nature and role of adult education. More and more it is being realized that only through education, and through the education of adults in particular, will the essential breakthrough occur. A change in attitudes and practices is the necessary prerequisite to development, more important even than injection of physical capttal.

Such is the novelty of the concept of adult education as all-embracing that no comprehensive study of the existing provision as yet exists. Kenya is not alone in this omission; few developing countries, or developed countries for that matter, have been able to gather together for descriptive purposes all the strands which constitute the pattern of adult education.

For descriptive purposes it is useful to divide adult education into its functional component parts : formal, fundamental, liberal and vocational. Formal adult education can be thought of as the kind of adult education which provides opportunities for taking courses of study leading to examinations recognized within the State's formal education programme, normally from primary school to university. It embraces remedial opportunities for those who failed as children or who have not been to school at all or who had to leave school before completion; it also embraces that kind of adult education which in Britain is termed further education.

Fundamental adult education represents the most basic features of educational programmes for adults. It is that kind of adult education which attempts to teach the basic ways of modern living : simple new agricultural techniques, health education, forms of social and economic organization, literacy, child care. For Kenya, fundamental adult education poses the most searching challenge since it is of immediate value to the vast mass of the people in their efforts to help themselves to overcome their inheritance of ignorance, disease and poverty.

Liberal adult education is most easily understood by Western adult educators. Education for its own sake, for self-fulfilment, for leisure, for nothing more than a simple improvement of the mind, has for long been an important element in the Western adult education tradition. In Britain, this is for many the sole activity to be described as adult education, all other activities being seen as something different. There can be no doubt of the major importance of this kind of adult education and certainly it has its place in adult education provision in Kenya.

Vocational adult education covers the fields of in-service training, technical courses, professional training and, equally important, re-training. Essential to the life of a modern community, it must be included as an integral part of the total education provision of any national state.

This division into four categories is, of course, to a certain extent artificial. The categories are not mutually exclusive; there are close inter-relationships and much overlapping. The simplest kind of liberal education merges with fundamental adult education as does vocational education. Likewise, some courses which might be labelled formal adult education may well include students who themselves have a completely liberal motivation. Nevertheless, the categories are useful since they serve to identify the different emphases which otherwise may be overlooked completely.

As a rough guide the table on page 81 shows the various predominant types of adult education provided by major institutions.

Age group	Formal adult education	Fundamental adult education	Liberal adult education	Vocational adult education
Pre-literate	Nil	Agriculture, Health, Co-ops, Literacy, A.E. Div., Community Dev. } Govt. depts.; Churches; Mandeleo ya Wanawake	Nil	Nil
To 8 years of schooling (primary)	Municipal classes Institute of Adult Studies (IAS), University of Nairobi	As above	University (IAS) Churches (but generally very little)	Some industries and government (but generally very little)
To 12 years of schooling ('O' level)	University (IAS) Correspondence colleges	Not generally required	University (IAS) (but very little)	Good coverage by industry and government
To pre-university ('A' level)	University (IAS) Correspondence colleges	Not generally required	University (IAS) (but very little)	As above
University and above	Not generally required	Not generally required	Almost none outside Nairobi	As above

AENB G

Fundamental adult education

There can be no doubt that the kind of adult education which is given highest priority in Kenya is that which relates most closely to the total national development, namely, fundamental adult education. The provision of fundamental education is largely a government responsibility though voluntary bodies also make a significant contribution. The government ministries most important in this field are : the Ministry of Agriculture, the Ministry of Health, the Ministry of Commerce and Industry, and the Ministry of Co-operatives and Social Services.

One of the most notable features of Kenya's agricultural education is the pattern of residential Farmers' Training Centres scattered throughout the Districts. There are at present 28 FTCs, 22 of which are managed by the Ministry of Agriculture and 6 by the National Christian Council of Kenya, though the latter are aided by the Ministry of Agriculture. The Centres provide simple food and accommodation, range in capacity from 20 to 100 beds, and offer short courses in basic agricultural methods and techniques to peasant farmers who pay a highly subsidized fee. Courses generally last one to two weeks and are considered to be an essential part of the District extension service under the District Agricultural Officer, who is also responsible for running a small demonstration farm. An important subject in the syllabus of all FTCs is rural home economics and the Ministry of Agriculture has a specially trained cadre of women Home Economics instructors to teach this subject. Of the total intake to the FTCs some 30 per cent are women, often accompanied by children. The courses are heavily practical, and though no thorough evaluation of the impact of the FTCs has yet been carried out there is no doubt that they have made a great contribution to the development of peasant agriculture throughout the country. The Centres themselves, while supported by the Ministry of Agriculture, are available for use by other rural 'educational' staff so that short courses organized by co-operative staff and community development or health staff take place in them as space is available. There are plans for the building of six more centres in the near future.

In recent years the main difficulty associated with the FTCs has been concerned with staff recruitment and training. The basic educational level has not been very high and there has been no strong career structure, so that the best staff have tended to move quickly out of the agricultural educational field and into other technical fields. Moreover, while the staff are usually competent in the general field of agriculture, their training in adult education techniques and methods of communication and the running of residential institutions has been given little priority. The result has been a recent falling off in attendance, which is now being corrected by a reorientation of staff in-service training and the recruitment of better calibre staff, more frequently now of university graduate level.

Alongside the Farmers' Training Centres, the officers of the Ministry of Agriculture mount a continuous programme of Farmers' Field Days, agricultural shows and demonstrations to complete the picture of agricultural education in the country.

One of the rapidly expanding fields of fundamental education closely associated with the agricultural education programme is that organized by the *Department of Co-operative Development*. While co-operative activity has been a feature of Kenya's development since the late 1940s, it is only since the achievement of independence that it has been accorded any real prominence. Co-operative societies are formed mainly as peasant agricultural producer societies concerned with the marketing of agricultural produce. As yet, the development of co-operative societies in Kenya cannot be thought of as a 'movement' such as characterizes co-operative development in Britain or the Scandinavian countries. However, a movement certainly exists in embryo. Undoubtedly, the development of such a movement requires public recognition of the social as well as of the purely economic benefits of co-operation. Education can play a part in both these areas.

The growth of the Division of Co-operative Education within the Department marks the attention which the government is prepared to give to the educational aspects of a co-operative movement. The Division of Co-operative Education consists of two main sections : the first is concerned with the development of the Kenya Co-operative College and extension staff; the second is concerned with the in-service training of staff.

The Kenya Co-operative College is an important new institution in the field of adult education in Kenya. It began in 1967 and has as one of its main objectives the development of a co-operative movement. It seeks primarily to serve the officers and members of the co-operative societies and their unions. The College receives substantial aid both in staff and finance from the Scandinavian countries, whose expertise in this field is second to none. It operates in three different ways : the first is residential training within the college itself; the second is in extension and field activities; the third is in providing advisers to co-operative societies in such technical matters as credit and finance accounting. The College, at present temporarily housed, has room for around 45 adult students. In the new premises which are to be built soon there will be room for 120 students at any one time. In spite of the shortage of accommodation some 1,100 society committee members and over 3,000 society officials have passed through on short courses ranging from two to eight weeks.

Working in close collaboration with the Co-operative College are seven Co-operative Field Teams. Each team consists of two members of the Departmental staff who are responsible for arranging field courses for co-operative members and officials. They are deployed one in each major Province and one in a major settlement scheme. As yet, the field teams have no permanent premises of their own, though there are plans for Co-operative wings as extensions to Farmers' Training Centres. In the meantime, the teams make use of the Farmers' Training Centres and the Rural Training Centres run by the local authorities.

The Co-operative movement is in its infancy but the firm intention is that, as it becomes established, it will become an important vehicle for many different kinds of adult education activities.

Health education is a most important aspect of fundamental adult education embracing as it does such vital objectives as improvements in prevention of disease, hygiene, nutrition, child care, family planning and sanitation. It is here that voluntary agencies in Kenya play an important role. The Red Cross Organization has educational teams; the Churches have both residential activities and rural extension classes; the Family Planning Association has local branches; and, not least, the activities of an important women's movement founded in the early 1950s, the Mandeleo ya Wanawake or Progress of Women, have been significant in all aspects of women's education, including health education. The Mandeleo ya Wanawake organization deserves a special mention in any description of Kenya's adult educational provision since it is one of the few examples of a completely indigenous voluntary movement which has been highly successful. Its organization is spread widely throughout the country, reaching deep into the rural countryside and leaving few family lives unaffected by the work which it has set itself to perform.

To emphasize the work of the voluntary agencies in the field of health education is not to ignore the government authorities, for the Ministry of Health and the local authorities both work closely together. The main brunt of the work at District level is carried out by the cadre of Health Assistants, Health Inspectors and Health Visitors employed either directly by local authorities or as seconded staff from the Ministry of Health. There are too few of these workers and much of their time is spent on curative medicine or the enforcement of sanitation regulations. The amount of health education that is undertaken depends a great deal on the inclinations of the local authorities employing them and the inclinations of the officers themselves. All these staff are trained centrally by the Ministry of Health, and methods and objectives of health education are included as part of their training course.

Supporting the field officers there is in the Ministry of Health a Division of Health Education with a fully fledged Health Education Unit which incorporates an Audio-Visual Aids Centre. The Health Education Unit has a small staff of three Health Education Officers one of whom is posted to West Kenya while the other two remain at Headquarters preparing materials and teaching in-service courses. The Audio-Visual Centre is fully equipped and produces teaching materials not only for the Ministry of Health and the local authorities but also, on request, for other government 'educational' ministries such as Agriculture and Co-operatives and Social Services. Though the whole Unit has a very small budget and a very small staff, it has nevertheless built up a reputation for effective work out of all proportion to its size. It is expected that in the near future it will be possible to have at least one Health Education Officer in each Province in a supporting role to the Local Authority.

Traditionally, *the Department of Community Development and Social Services* has long been associated with adult education. Now, as part of the Ministry of Co-operatives and Social Services, it holds the government 'portfolio' and is administratively responsible for adult education. The Department incorporates, and is administratively responsible for, the Board of Adult Education. It has three main Divisions relating to Community Development, Social Welfare and Adult Education. It also has responsibility for Youth and Sports. The Division of Adult Education, although the youngest of the three Divisions, being now only two years old, has been expanding very fast. There are already four Education Officers (Adult Education) and thirty-one Assistant Education Officers (Adult Education). The intention is to increase the staff until there is one Assistant Education Officer (Adult Education) in each of the forty-two districts of Kenya.

The adult education officers in the districts are responsible for organizing and teaching in the National Literacy Campaign and for arranging classes in basic formal education. The first two operational years of the Division have been experimental and, of course, concerned with setting up the necessary administrative structure. In the main, recruitment to the new cadre of adult education officers has been from among trained school teachers, which has perhaps led to an overemphasis on formality of approach. As they gain in experience, however, the AEOs become more confident in their new work and a change in approach is already taking place. The programmes for literacy and

basic formal education are being completely separated and the development programmes of other ministries and agencies are being used
to integrate the literacy element. There is thus emerging a functional,
job-oriented literacy programme which is proving very successful.

For conducting literacy classes organized directly under the auspices of the Division part-time teachers are paid around 50 shillings
per month direct from government funds. There are, however, a large
number of classes which are organized on a self-help basis and which,
in the past, have been organized by Community Development Officers
and voluntary agencies. These are mainly self-financing with the
adult illiterates contributing small fees which are used as a small
honorarium for the teachers.

The National Literacy Campaign was launched by President Ken-
yatta in 1966 and is planned in four-year periods covering three main
geographical areas : the urban areas where classes are organized
through commercial and industrial firms; the plantation and large-
scale farming areas; and the peasant rural areas. After 1973 the programme aims to turn out around a million new literates every year.
The mounting of such an ambitious programme cannot be done without encountering many initial difficulties, not least amongst which are
the training of part-time teaching staff, the production of teaching
materials and follow-up literacy reading matter, and of course the
search for supporting finance to maintain the programme. Training
of staff is taking place while the programme is under way and short
courses are organized periodically as part of their in-service training.
For preparing materials the Division has a small production unit
equipped with printing machinery and the services of three UNESCO
experts who assist with both the training of literacy staff and the production of the materials. The question of finance is not so easily
solved; there is no doubt from experience that completely self-financing literacy classes are seldom very satisfactory and yet, increasingly,
the self-help principle is having to be invoked in order to expand the
programme.

While the Division of Adult Education in the Department of Community Development and Social Services concentrates primarily on
literacy and basic formal education, the staff of the Division of Community Development organize other adult education activities
through Rural Training Centres. These include courses for self-help
group leaders in community development techniques, health and
nutrition courses, youth and women's courses.

The Rural Training Centres number over twenty and are financed
through the municipalities or rural local authorities; a few are managed
by voluntary agencies. They have help from the Department and

from such bodies as UNICEF and vary a great deal both in size and quality, depending on the importance given them by the local authorities which they serve. Like the Farmers' Training Centres they have problems of staff recruitment, staff training and finance. They are residential, beds ranging in number from twenty to eighty, and unlike the Farmers' Training Centres they seldom receive any subsidy in the fees charged for board and lodging.

While not strictly concerned with adult education, mention must be made of the Youth Centres which are scattered throughout the more densely populated districts of Kenya. At first non-residential, these Youth Centres were set up during the days of the Mau Mau emergency as a means of giving unemployed youth a simple trade training in such fields as carpentry, leatherwork and masonry together with some basic formal education. While they cater for youths, the average age of the participants is often high, sometimes over twenty years. There are around 170 such centres, again run through local authorities with support from the Community Development Officers; they also vary a great deal both in size and effectiveness.

A pilot project in youth work started two years ago through the National Christian Council of Kenya. This is the provision of village polytechnics. There are now six experimental village polytechnics, which take primary school leavers who are unemployed and who often have been away from school for one or more years to give them craft training for self-employment in their own rural environment. It is too early to give any indication of the success of this experiment, but it is possible that the polytechnics are in the vanguard of a major development in the field of rural education for young adults. Most of the village polytechnics are predominantly residential, providing courses lasting from a few months to two years in agriculture, building, leatherwork, metalwork and some further education. The courses are based on the local manpower needs of the areas in which they are sited.

Opportunities for the peasant farmer and his family in the rural areas of Kenya to learn and improve their way of life are varied and scattered. Help and advice are available from the Agricultural Extension Workers, the Health Assistants, the Trades Officers, the Co-operative Officers, the Community Development Officers and the Adult Education Officers. For his wife and daughters there are the activities of the Mandeleo ya Wanawake and other voluntary agencies such as the Red Cross. The family may attend courses at the local Farmers' Training Centre or at a local Rural Training Centre. There will be club meetings and Farmers' field days, agricultural shows and demonstrations. Having left school, his sons and daughters may attend a local Youth Centre.

All these facilities exist. Yet it is difficult to estimate the value of their total impact. There is no doubt that the educational facilities provided for adults are exceedingly thinly spread so that large sections of the population may be untouched by them. Most of the more closely constructed classes and courses cost money and many of the rural folk are hard pressed to find the required funds. Where there are facilities it may be that only a small fraction of the adults wish to make use of them, most people having yet to find the basic urge to break away from their traditional way of life. Again, there is a short supply of highly motivated, adequately educated and sufficiently trained staff to maintain the educational services. There are insufficient materials and funds to maintain activities at the level at which they need to be maintained. Not least, the lack of co-ordination of serviced and integrated planning serves to accentuate the loss of a total impact. But nevertheless, day by day the provision increases and improves in quality, and more and more adults willingly and eagerly participate in the learning process, which in itself will form the basis of an economic and social revolution in the rural areas of Kenya.

One important new development which will undoubtedly help in solving many of these problems is the intended adaptation of existing training centres into multi-purpose centres. It is planned, and already some amalgamations are underway, that these new centres should retain their existing provision while adding new activities to provide a more rational and concerted general pattern of fundamental education. These centres will be the heart of the District extension work and will combine under one roof as far as possible agriculture, health, co-operatives, trading, literacy, women's courses and youth training. The future development of such multi-purpose centres could provide an interesting blue-print for rural development. If it achieves nothing else, it will certainly tidy up the present multiplicity of training centres and give some overall general guidance on the methods and direction of effective rural development.

Formal adult education

If the benefits of fundamental education are not always appreciated by the adults for whom it is provided, the benefits of formal education need no explaining to its clientele. The demand for formal education is most vocal. There are three main organizational groups working in this field: municipal councils, commercial organizations and the University College's Institute of Adult Studies. The municipal councils organize evening continuation classes generally taking adults from illiteracy through primary examinations to school certificates. As a rule the municipalities are poor so that the funds they are able to allocate to such activities are small. They do, however, provide the rudiments of an evening continuation centre organization for the urban areas. They employ school teachers, who are paid a small sum according to the level of class which they teach, and in some cases they supply text-books and writing materials. Apart from funds raised from their own sources, the municipalities also get small grants from the central Government ranging from £1,500 in Nairobi down to £150 according to their size. However, the scale of provision remains insignificant in relation to the demand.

Little is known of the private *commercial sector* engaged in adult education. But, as in most countries and especially in other developing countries, the usual mushroom variety of further education colleges and correspondence colleges proliferates. Some are bad and some are not so bad. They are able to feed on the insatiable public demand for formal paper qualifications and are scattered throughout the urban areas of the country. The better organized correspondence colleges can make a comfortable and steady income and clearly fill a vacuum in formal education provision. More often than not a correspondence course is the only way an ambitious messenger boy or clerk can get the necessary paper documents which employers require before they are willing to consider him for a particular job, and young adults are willing to make considerable financial sacrifices to attain their ends. However, inadequate provision, poor teaching, lack of learning materials, poor living and study conditions, relatively high fees and the constant mobility of young people, tend to make the drop-out rate from such courses very high and only a few of the very persistent are able to achieve their ambitions.

Students in the towns are more fortunate than aspirants in the rural areas for, apart from a few rural centres where the University College may organize classes, there are available only the very basic classes organized by the Adult Education Officers of the Division of Adult Education, and these are so thinly spread as to be almost negligible. The largest institution serving in the field of formal adult education is the *Institute of Adult Studies* of the University College, Nairobi. Some five years ago the emphasis of the adult education staff of the University College was mainly in the field of liberal and informal adult education. There has now been, however, a gradual shift of approach toward the formal field as the kind of classes in problem-oriented subjects like political science, economics and sociology, so eagerly sought just before and just after independence, became less urgent and therefore less popular. The pressure for paper qualifications caused an almost imperceptible transition to take place; for example, as discussion classes on the economy of Kenya became formal classes in advanced level economics.

The Institute of Adult Studies consists of three basic units : the Extra-Mural Division, the Adult Studies Centre and the Correspondence Course Unit. The Extra-Mural Division has a staff of four Resident Tutors based on the four main towns, Nairobi, Mombasa, Kisumu and Makuru. From, as well as in, these centres they organize classes, seminars and conferences. The bulk of the classes are run in the early evenings and are generally oriented towards formal or professional examinations relating to school certificate or professional examinations. While the main body of the programmes are centred in the Resident Tutor's base town, classes and activities are also organized in other more rural centres of the area which they cover. At present all classes are conducted in English and therefore attract the more highly educated, the average student being just below the school certificate level. Run almost throughout the year, extra-mural classes are heavily subsidized, though adult students pay a small fee. On average fees range between 1 /- and 3 /- per class and go up to 36 /- per course. As well as formal classes Resident Tutors arrange public lectures and weekend schools of a more liberal kind ranging from topics of current and local interest to cultural topics.

The Adult Studies Centre, which came into being as an independent adult college in 1960, is situated at Kikuyu some thirteen miles outside Nairobi. It has a staff of six tutors and runs two kinds of courses. The core of the teaching at the Centre is centred on the Certificate of Adult Studies, a University award roughly equivalent to Advanced Level standard. The syllabi for the certificate has been drawn up to relate to African needs and the course lasts one academic year. Students who attend are predominantly school teachers since the certificate is recognized for purposes of up-grading teachers.

The atmosphere of the Adult Studies Centre is an intimate one, helped by the small staff-student ratio of about one to six and the fact that teaching is done mainly through tutorials and discussion with an emphasis on informality. Students are recruited through the Ministry of Education or through business firms.

One of the attractions of the 'long course' leading to the Certificate is that it can be used as a preparation for mature-aged entry to undergraduate degree courses in the University. There is provision in the University of East Africa for a small number of adult students who lack the normal minimum entry requirements to sit a special entry examination which, if passed successfully, may allow direct entry to the University.

The other kind of courses which are organized at the Adult Studies Centre are 'short courses'. These normally last for between one and three weeks and are of a general nature, covering the economic, social and political problems of East African development. Short courses are used to help in the selection of students for the long course.

A recent development at the Adult Studies Centre is the introduction of short courses in the techniques and methods of adult education designed for adult educators working in the whole field. This interest in the wider field of adult education may be the beginning of a novel role for the Institute of relating its work more closely to rural development and fundamental adult education where it can give support in research and training – a university activity which is perhaps long overdue in such a national situation.

The Correspondence Course Unit is the youngest of the three Divisions, having been set up in 1966. The objectives of the Unit are to prepare courses for the Certificate of Adult Studies and to provide courses for the teachers employed by the Ministry of Education so as to help them complete the academic part of teacher up-grading covering the first and second year syllabi of secondary schools. These courses are also available to private students studying the secondary school syllabus. So far, only the secondary school courses have been written and there is some doubt about the advisability of teaching Certificate of Adult Studies subjects by correspondence methods.

The correspondence courses used so far have been planned as an integrated instructional system with radio. There can be no doubt from this development that correspondence methods have a bright future in the educational system of Kenya.

Through its three divisions the Institute of Adult Studies makes a sizeable contribution to the total educational provision in Kenya. There are, however, some who feel that the Institute has not yet found its correct place in the total national programme. Many questions are being asked – not least by the staff of the Institute itself. Is the strong trend toward courses in formal secondary school subjects appropriate for a university in a country like Kenya ? Is the expense of the long course at the Adult Studies Centre justifiable ? Why has the Institute not involved itself more closely in the supporting activities related to adult education training and research in rural development which is the most important problem area facing the country ? Why are the staff and programme of the three divisions not more closely related ? What can be done to reintroduce a stronger liberal and cultural element into the total programme ? The Institute is in the position of having to rethink its objectives and its priorities, and this is timely since it is in the position to make a real impact throughout the field of adult education.

Vocational and technical adult education

Vocational and technical adult education is well covered in Kenya in both the public and private sectors. In the public sector, the most important training institutions are the Kenya Institute of Administration and its sister, the Maseno Institute of Administration. The former is situated just outside Nairobi, the latter in West Kenya. The Institutes of Administration are responsible for the greater part of government In-service Training in public administration, local government, social development, co-operative development and senior management. A fine tradition has been built up since the Institutes were established under the Office of the President in the early 1960s. Special attention is being paid to teaching methods and there is a strong audio-visual section supporting the Institutes. Many of the courses are open to sponsored candidates from the private sector.

Other important training facilities are provided by the Ministry of Labour, of which one of the most interesting, the Nakuru Industrial Training Centre, provides courses for private small-scale businesses and tradesmen, giving them basic instruction in the running of small businesses and trades.

In the private sector all the large scale industrial and commercial concerns offer in-service training courses at all levels. The largest of these is the Railway Training School organized by the East African Railways and Harbours Corporation. Many of the training schemes include programmes of general education ranging from literacy upwards. At present the Institute of Adult Studies offers a day-release course to private industry and commerce for the middle-grade officer cadre in basic management organizational techniques.

Service organizations

Apart from the main providers of adult education programmes there are some very important supporting organizations. These include the Voice of Kenya radio and television services, the publishing houses, and the Kenya Government's Board of Adult Education.

The Voice of Kenya is part of the *Ministry of Information and Broadcasting* and over a period of many years it has built up a tradition of schools broadcasting. The policy of VOK is to co-operate as closely as possible with adult education bodies for the transmission of adult education programmes. Thus, in the past they have experimented in collaboration with the Nairobi Literacy Centre, a private body, in teaching literacy through television. They have also collaborated with the Institute of Adult Studies in its pioneering experiment in integrated correspondence – television instruction, which led to the establishment of the Correspondence Unit in the Institute. At present vo k collaborates with the Correspondence Unit in the production of radio programmes which are an integral part of the secondary school level correspondence courses run by the Institute.

The vo k has also experimented with listening and viewing groups of its own and the main constraint has been lack of funds to extend their activities. There is no doubt that for the population as a whole radio is very effective as a teaching medium since there are few families not within reach of a radio set. This is not true of television for, although there is almost country-wide coverage, the distribution of television receivers is very thin and it is only among the more affluent sections of the Nairobi community that television sets are to be found in any number. While there are efforts to increase the number of receivers through schools and community centres in the rural areas, problems of maintenance and organization still impede the large scale use of television as an important adult education medium of instruction.

Two important *publishing houses* which have built up an interest in adult education are the East African Literature Bureau and the East African Publishing House. The East African Literature Bureau is financed by the East African governments and is part of the East African Common Services Organization. Over the past fifteen years it has played a particularly important role in the preparation and the publication of literacy primers and follow-up books which it is enabled to do at a financially subsidized rate. There are now full sets of literacy primers published through the Bureau prepared both in Kiswahili and most of the major vernacular languages. Besides its work in the literacy field the Bureau has been instrumental in sponsoring small booklets covering various other aspects of adult education.

The East African Publishing House is a private non-profit making organization which has a special relationship with the Kenya government. It has been operating now for some four years and has concentrated upon encouraging local authors and specializing in writings on local problems thus making publications possible where the limited market has made foreign publishers less willing to collaborate. It has been able to produce published reports of conferences and books related to adult education which, while primarily of local interest, are enabling the publishing house to establish an international reputation.

The Board of Adult Education

There can be no doubt that the most recent adult education development of major importance in Kenya has been the establishment of the *Board of Adult Education*. It may well be that the Board of Adult Education will be Kenya's special contribution to the international field of adult education with special significance to all developing countries. Two of the most difficult problems in developing the broad field of adult education and in making its operations more effective are, firstly, how to establish a high degree of professionalism, and secondly, how to develop the pre-requisite corporate spirit amongst adult educators in whichever sphere they operate to allow for maximum integration and co-ordination, sharing of experience and development of a common approach. Adult education is carried out by a multitude of different organizations: different ministries, different departments, different public bodies, different voluntary bodies – so often unaware of each other's existence. This results in duplication, overlapping, failure to learn from the experience of others and a general lack of planning, confusion and waste. Certainly the developing countries cannot afford avoidable waste, least of all in an activity which is so central to their national development.

The Act enables the Board to advise on the coordination of the field of adult education; to prepare overall plans for its development; to advise on training and research; and to structure a national network of panels and committees to carry out these functions. The membership of the Board includes ten government 'co-ordinatory' and 'educational' ministries which cover the Office of the President, the Treasury, the Ministry of Economic Planning and Development, and ministries like Agriculture, Health, and Co-operatives and Social Services. It includes twelve non-official or voluntary bodies like the Kenya National Union of Teachers, the Kenya African National Union, the Central Organization of Trades Unions, the University College and the National Council for Social Service. It also provides for five co-opted members. There is thus a majority of non-officials to represent the voluntary contribution to adult education. The Board is administered through the Department of Community Development and Social Services and has a small secretariat consisting of a full-time secretary and supporting clerical staff.

The Board meets about four times a year and deals only with major decisions on policy and programming. To facilitate its day-to-day work it has a number of panels and committees. The panels consist of specialists from the Board and co-opted members from the major functional divisions of adult education. Thus there are panels representing Formal and Vocational Adult Education, Literacy and Fundamental Education, and Liberal and Cultural Education. The committees, which, unlike the panels, are non-statutory, cover interdisciplinary aspects of adult education, including Research and Training, Finance and Development, and Publications and Teaching Materials. There is finally an Executive Committee consisting of the Board's Chairman persons nominated by the Board and all Panel and Committee Chairmen.

At Provincial and District level there is provision for committees of the Board to ensure that the Board is kept informed of developments throughout the country and to provide administrative machinery so that organizations working in the field can make their needs officially known. These committees consist of the same kind of membership as the Board itself and cover the same areas of adult education activity. Normally the Adult Education Officers of the Ministry of Co-operatives and Social Services act as secretaries to the committees.

It has taken some time for the Board to organize itself and it is only in the past year that it has begun operating in the manner intended. Hence it is too early to evaluate its full impact.

The Board as such runs no adult education programmes of its own but supports the activities of its member organizations. It therefore requires few funds of its own. It does, however, receive a subvention from the central government to cover its incidental expenses and most importantly to carry out research projects in adult education.

Since little of a co-ordinated nature was known of the general adult education provision throughout the country, its first task has been to carry out basic research projects in order to identify the nature, cost and content of the adult education programmes being carried out. It has also been the initiator of the present proposals under discussion to amalgamate the existing various kinds of district training centres and to establish multi-purpose centres. It is reviewing the field of literacy teaching and formulating proposals for an adult-oriented examination structure which could lead to a vocationally based National Certificate at primary level to avoid the present necessity for adults to follow the child primary syllabus. It is centrally concerned with the development of training for adult educators in methods and techniques. It is also setting up an information centre for the adult education field which will be of international and national value.

Needs and prospects

Kenya is fortunate in possessing the rudiments of a comprehensive structure of adult education now strengthened by the Board of Adult Education. The organizational framework exists for expansion in a planned co-ordinated way geared to national development. There are many growth points, but a great deal of growth is required. All the services are very thinly spread. Only gradually is the relationship between economic and social development and adult education being appreciated. As this appreciation grows so resources are made available for its expansion. Kenya inherited no tradition or blue-print for a total adult education programme. She has, therefore, had to move forward slowly, experimenting here and trying out there. But there is still a great need for more co-ordination and planning and it is at this level that the Board of Adult Education has its most important role to play.

As yet, there is no sign of an adult education 'movement' coming into being. The trades unions and the political parties have yet to make a contribution. The Co-operative Societies have begun to move in this direction but have still to demonstrate their ability and willingness to provide programmes for their members.

There is still an urgent need to develop professionalism within the adult educational field. This will not come about until there is provision for an element of co-ordinated and common training for all adult education and extension workers as the cornerstone of a growing adult education tradition.

If one had to pick out an area which is being particularly neglected from among all the subject areas covered by adult education, that of civic education would come first to mind. In only a few places, thanks to individual efforts, is there any real attempt to teach citizens the necessary knowledge required by the good citizen. This is an area awaiting development and which embraces local government, simple economics, and the framework for the solutions to social problems.

There is no doubt that effective use of the mass media has yet to be achieved. If a nationwide impact is to be made on the people of Kenya through adult education, then the mass media must be used to their full extent. Experiments in the use of mass media have only just begun, but their future is assured if only by the fact that in no other way can a quick and sure impact be effected on the scale that is required.

Kenya is a young country. Her achievements in the field of adult education are considerable notwithstanding her lack of resources. Indeed, in many ways, the priority it is given by the Kenya government and the pattern which has already developed offer lessons for many of the developed countries. If there is much more to do, fortunately there is the will to do it.

REFERENCE

1. *Kyale Mwendar Report of the Kericho Conference on Education, Employment and Rural Development, Oct. 1966*, Nairobi 1967.

5. Senegal

BEN MADY CISSE

Introduction

With the coming of independence, freedom of thought was restored
and the people of Senegal faced the task of remoulding the nation and
determining their aims. Independence offered us no more, however,
than an opportunity to become totally free from colonial subservience.
The nation had still to choose its goals and to find ways of achieving
them.

The immediate priority was economic development. We did not
wish this to take place in unplanned conditions and when every factor
had been considered we felt obliged to adopt a socialist approach
which at the same time preserved the fundamental values of the
African people.

Our guiding principle may be formulated as follows : development
would be accomplished only if undertaken by the population as a
whole. Social consciousness, stimulated by the appropriate means of
communication, must release the will to work and the energies of both
individuals and communities so that they might themselves evolve
their own lines of development. This implies a change of attitude at all
levels of society, a dialogue between the professional élites and the
masses.

Thus Senegal opted for African socialism, but in its own distinctive
way. Its aim to transform social attitudes was addressed in particular
to farmers, who constituted the majority of the population. It attempted to create the right conditions for and to foster the spirit of participation. For this purpose Senegal chose the following administrative
structure : at *département* level the Directorate of Extension and Development, which is attached to the Ministry of Planning and Development and which operates through the directors of the Men's and
the Women's Rural Extension Centres and the directors and deputy
directors of the Rural Development Centres; at regional level, the
officials and regional assistants co-ordinate their work. A central
office provides essential subject matter together with material, equipment and guidance on teaching methods. Through its education
programme the Directorate guarantees a cadre of community leaders

who are expected to organize facilities in their own villages. Every opportunity is seized to promote and co-ordinate all forms of adult education, whether literacy projects, cultural activities or instruction in health and hygiene. By this means a sense of social awareness is created through which the people can themselves arrive at a point when they accept responsibility for their own development.

Various other countries have similarly devised original and adaptable educational programmes of this nature. Senegal's approach to the problem is outlined below.

The Extension Centres and their organization

Senegal is divided into seven regions each administered by a governor. These regions are subdivided into twenty-seven *départements* under the control of Prefects, to whom district chiefs are subordinate. As a first practical step the Directorate establishes at *département* level a centre under its own control. This Extension Centre becomes a focal point both for activities and for training purposes. At its head, a director, nominated by central office, having devised an extension plan with his regional superior, puts it into operation. The fact that centres are at *département* level facilitates effective liaison between our Extension services and the administrative and technical agencies of the State.

The prime concern of each centre is that farmers should feel that they are at home in their own familiar environment and should thus have confidence to express their ideas as freely as in ordinary social intercourse. A centre must avoid stimulating wants it cannot satisfy. Thus while enabling close contact to be made between the rural population and government officials, it is also the function of Centres to try to discourage rural depopulation. Rural extension centres must be situated either inside or at least within close reach of the main towns in each *département* so that the director may call upon public officials to act as lecturers during training sessions.

In addition to performing his administrative duties, a director must gain understanding of the local situation by going out among the people and meeting them. His basic task is to work out a plan, choosing the zones or groups of villages where he will begin so as to ascertain the present condition of the people in his area. Training will have provided him with the right techniques and methods. Once his choice of a zone has been completed, a seasonal training schedule is prepared in collaboration with the Regional Development Committee.

At the regional level the regional officer, co-ordinating the work of the directors of the extension centres, is expected to provide them with any technical advice they may require. His is a vital role for on the one hand he keeps the Regional Development Committee informed about the practical work and projects being carried out in the villages, and on the other hand passes back to the extension centres the views and policies of the Committee.

The recruitment of Extension workers

Once the idea of Extension has been presented to the local people interested villages are invited democratically to elect those who will become their Extension workers. The qualities sought are that the future extension worker must be an adult, aged 25–45, and a man known to wield influence in his village; he will be a volunteer *who is and who will remain a farmer*; he will not become a civil servant or an appointed official of any kind. It is in the name of his village and with his village that the Extension worker becomes involved in a programme. It is not a case of choosing a leading farmer but a member of the community. The Extension worker himself is not the important factor but the community he represents. There is no fixed ceiling to the number of Extension workers, the essential idea being to form a cadre which, even though recruited as the opportunity arises in successive training courses, is conscious of its contribution to local development.

To select truly representative Extension workers is not easy : experience has shown that in the early stages suspicious villagers send unrepresentative individuals, who push themselves forward and who are often highly extrovert and disposed to be critical. It is only after the training scheme has been in existence for some time that villagers are in a position to judge the method, to perceive its advantages and to nominate their natural leaders for the advanced stages of training. To avoid conflict when extension workers return from training it is wise to ensure that they are first chosen with the approval of the village chief, since he can be very helpful in facilitating their subsequent activities.

The method of choosing potential women workers is the same as for men but it is not, in general, adopted except in those areas where men's Extension work has already been in operation and where the male population has become convinced of the utility of educating women. In other words, where they have realised that there are not, in fact, on the one hand, men with their problems and potentialities and, on the other hand, women with theirs, but rather a village society with common problems and jointly responsible members who must act together to solve them. It is for this reason that men's and women's Extension organizations are merged at all stages of the work.

The initiation stage (or first degree stage)

The Extension workers, recruited from among the inhabitants of the chosen villages, receive preliminary training at what is known as the initiation stage, timed to take place outside periods of agricultural activity. The training is of a particular kind – there must be no question of a master-pupil relationship but of a dialogue in which two equals exchange ideas freely and frankly. This is an active and progressive method of training which must never become rigid. The following general features can always be distinguished:

(a) *Civic information* – enabling the Extension worker to place himself and his community within the structure of the nation as a whole, to see it against its historical and geographical background, its political and administrative organization, and the main characteristics of the country's economy.

(b) Information will be given about the role of the different technical services, relating them to local problems and pointing to the possibility of technical action by Extension workers in liaison with the technical services. The information need not always be the main thread of the teaching. Its primary object is to create an open mind towards *all* problems, especially the local ones which are of immediate interest to the farmer, and specifically towards political problems. A good deal of time must be set aside for discussion when each participant can let off steam without restraint or suspicion. Whether farmer or townsman, the future Extension worker must appreciate the importance of choosing his words carefully and understand that he is regarded as an adult and listened to with the respect that his questioners also deserve from him.

In these meetings all the technical services participate in turn. The dialogue between the technical expert and the population is thus begun: after the training period it must be continued as part of the daily task. Practical work in the field (notably observing agricultural techniques and visiting equipment centres) are important elements in the course.

(c) Lastly, evening training sessions are best for establishing communication between teacher and taught. Here, the role-playing method becomes a spontaneous means of expression, putting the problems the farmer encounters into concrete form and explaining the conflicts which arise within him from the fact that he belongs to a traditional society whose structures are breaking down and giving way to a new society which he has difficulty in understanding. The sketches are generally presented at an end-of-course celebration. (It should be noted that this method has been known to present numerous difficulties to Centre directors who are unskilled in its use.)

(d) One of the concluding days of the training period is often given over to a *village court of inquiry*. This does not imply staging a stereotyped inquiry conducted by a disinterested investigator. The teachers choose one village, try to see it with new eyes and to analyse its distinctive problems. This village might well be the students' own village, its problems might well be the same as those they meet in their own village. How would they like to see them resolved? The final summing-up of the inquiry is eventually made in the village itself, in the presence of the village chief, the community leaders, the Extension workers, and the villagers. It is during this discussion that the teachers seize upon the problems and the possibilities of development in the village. A feast at the close of the course, organized by the teachers, brings this initiation period to an end.

(e) The training period concludes with a session on 'Accomplishing the Task' during which each Extension worker ascertains, in consultation with the Centre director and in the light of the training he has received, how he will put his belief in development into effect when he returns to his village and starts work with the inhabitants. Thus each participant leaves with a programme of action to present to his fellow villagers on his return.

The training programmes in women's Extension work are roughly the same. Every effort is made to deal with technical subjects which are more specifically concerned with the improvement of women's working conditions, her particular role in society, her specific cultural tasks, the management of her family budget, the improvement of the general welfare of her family life, hygiene, nutrition, child care. A supplementary course either for men or for women is offered by each centre.

The reintroduction of the Extension worker to his community

The reinstallation of the Extension worker in his community will take place in front of the assembled villagers and it will be the Centre director who will present him. If he is to be effective, the trained Extension worker must be completely acceptable to the village. It does happen that, though influenced by the training he has received, an Extension worker may no longer respect the existing hierarchy and may seek to make himself the village chief, thereby coming into conflict with traditional customs. It may also happen that, feeling inspired, he tries to impose techniques instead of using persuasion. A well-managed induction at which the obligations and potential services of the new Extension worker are made clear to the population will avoid such aberrations.

The Extension workers in a village group will collectively form a focus of activity which will collaborate to put the plans for development into effect.

Further training

This is provided through (a) a second stage of training, (b) refresher courses, and (c) the Centre director's tours.

The second stage of training aims at improving the Extension workers' technical efficiency whether with regard to agriculture (harnessing and yoking animals), stock rearing (techniques of castration, vaccination), co-operation (co-operative management), hygiene and child care (day nurseries for female Extension workers). During each short session of 2–5 days a single technique is taught to a restricted number of about twenty Extension workers, the approach being through practical demonstrations and not through theory. These sessions take place at the request of the Extension worker or at least with his agreement and in accordance with the objectives of the plans upon which he is working. The technical services themselves assume responsibility for the training, the Extension service doing no more than make the administrative arrangements and sometimes provide the accommodation.

Refresher sessions. Training at the first and second stages is effective only if the Extension worker is constantly supervised, drilled and directed by the technical agencies operating in his particular area. Through this permanent framework, essential problems for which the Extension workers need extra training are identified and valuable opportunities provided for contact between extension workers and technical experts.

The Centre directors back up the practical projects started by the Extension worker. He acts as a mediator in conflicts arising between villagers and Extension workers and recommends the technical service to which they should turn for help with particular projects.

These, then, are the methods of instruction employed by the Directorate of Extension. They are obviously not inflexible in character; in such a field constant self-questioning must be the rule. We shall now consider to what extent our methods have been successful.

Extension work and its effects

In Senegal, as in many countries, we are dealing with a traditional society in the throes of disintegration which nevertheless has its own distinctive values and thus rebels against the notion of development. The task of the Extension Service is to carry out its programme within the framework of communities that have evolved organically, by redirecting existing values along channels which will lead to African socialism. The Extension workers, trained, supported and upheld by the Extension agencies and united in a cell of activity, perform this task within the villages themselves. Geographically, the development cell must group together homogeneous villages, gathered round a central village which serves as headquarters. Thus there is set up the framework of a multiple co-operative from which certain services can be distributed to the villages. From it local development projects will spread out. The areas, legally established, will coincide with the territory of the development cell. In the final stage, the *commune* will lose its artificial administrative framework to regroup several development cells and thereby create a social and political reality, a local union of co-operatives, with a market-town centre as an economic focus. The decentralization of the State services will thus be achieved. (An interministerial committee, presided over by the Minister for Planning and Development, is engaged in studying how best this scheme may be put into operation.) One of the difficulties facing Extension work is that village chiefs are having to reconsider their role in the community so that the authority and decision-making power which they traditionally enjoyed may do no more than modify the Extension workers' activities instead of completely cramping it, as has sometimes occurred. Training sessions for village chiefs concentrate on describing the administrative and economic structure of the nation, and the role which they as chiefs are called upon to play.

Co-operative presidents, weighers, and extension workers also need extra training every year before the opening of the commercial season for staple products (ground nuts, millet, rice), when they may attend an intensive refresher course designed to brush up their knowledge of such essential skills in arithmetic as addition, subtraction, division and multiplication.

It would be an onerous task, indeed, to attempt to assess the effect of Extension work in economic terms since its aim is to transform the social structure and social attitudes. How does one estimate a qualitative change in social relationships or in mental habits? In any case, it is difficult to attribute such tangible results as are achieved to the Extension department alone since in practice Extension is not an isolated activity but a way of ensuring that the people make full use of other government services. To what extent can we ascribe an increase in productivity to the effects of a Centre director who has worked on people's attitudes for several years as opposed to the efforts of the government team which disseminated information about new techniques?

Nevertheless, since the Extension Department employs no fewer than one hundred officials and has at its disposal more than 150 million francs per annum plus general resources, we are right to be concerned about its efficiency and to attempt to measure it. To do this we shall refer to a few quantitative as well as qualitative indicators.

Quantitative results. 27 men's Centres and 28 women's Centres functioned in 1966. Many of these, moreover, were housed in purpose-built premises.

Since 1959, 9,253 rural Extension workers, coming from 2,600 out of the total of 13,366 villages in Senegal, have undergone training at the first degree stage (of which 6,731 were men and 2,522 were women). Relating these figures to the rural adult population we have a ratio of 10 male workers per 1,000 men and 3 female workers per 1,000 women.

5,241 or 64 per cent of these male and female workers have experienced technical training up to the second degree stage in several agricultural techniques (oxen-yoking, fertilizer-spreading, market-gardening, grafting etc.), stock-raising (castration of cattle, bee-keeping etc.), fishing (fish-curing), motor maintenance, co-operation, health and other subjects. 1,903 people or 12 per cent have been given further help through sessions in the villages lasting several days, and 667 have attended refresher courses at the Extension Centres. Some of these Extension workers have been organized into 300 cells, in which male and female workers are usually brought together.

As for the formation of village units : 2,000 village chiefs (15 per cent of the total) have attended 4–5 day training sessions each year, and an average of 3,500 co-operative presidents, weighers and extension workers, that is over 7 per cent of the total, receive technical training before the start of the commercial season. Thus, through its teaching Extension has reached altogether nearly 15,000 farmers, that is 11 per cent of the adult rural population.

Qualitative results. The technical agents of the government, and in general all the organizations charged with work in rural areas, agree that their work is more effective in regions that have been reached by Extension activities. Other indications also bear witness to the conversion of mental attitudes, to the fact that very often in our particular villages the cleavage between different socio-economic categories and the hostility between different ethnic groups have been overcome. In effect, after three weeks of receiving training, and in common with others placed in a situation which ignores divisions and tries to promote communal growth, students of different ethnic groups, castes and villages forget what divides them and acquire a fellow-feeling stronger than traditional antagonisms. On returning to the villages this cadre of extension workers are a unifying factor. This aspect of Extension may well have very important political consequences.

In other respects, the Extension workers' task has consisted very often of reorientating certain modes of communal life along new lines of development. Thus there used to exist in the majority of villages common land cultivated by the various associations or classes of different ages, whose products were consumed at feasts. As a result of Extension work, the amount of this land has been multiplied and its products are gradually being appropriated either as provisions (for instance garden products for the household) or else pooled for investment in the construction of wells, or in buying medicines for the village. Furthermore, in such a background, the farmer recognizes his duty in the process of development. He knows henceforward what the technical services have to offer and what he has a right to expect from them. Frequently Extension workers thus have the effect of combating irregularities in the technical services (misappropriation of the social share in co-operatives, partial distribution of seed) of filling gaps (certain technical services lacking in the villages) and forcing officials to be of real service to the farmers.

Lastly, if the rise of the co-operative movement cannot be attributed to Extension, it must at least be recognized that the presence of Extension workers has aroused increasing enthusiasm for it, for they have played an active role in the general meetings of the co-operatives, supervised the presidents' administration and the weighers' activities, and persuaded the apathetic to remain within the co-operatives. Following the introduction of women's Extension activities there was a pronounced movement by women towards joining the co-operatives, an unprecedented phenomenon in Senegalese society. More generally, a greater receptivity is noticed in our villages, a readier acceptance of the theories of development, a more active participation in proposed innovations such as improving methods of cultivation, diversifying crops, increasing production, and introducing sanitary campaigns.

Particular results of Extension work with organizations

The Senegalese administration, like that of all countries in a similar position, stems from a colonial administration which had neither the need nor the inclination to exchange views with the population. The task of Extension consists in giving people a feeling and a taste for such an exchange so that they may respond to their own forward steps in development.

The linking of the technical services to the Directorate of Extension and Expansion has now made possible a more efficient distribution of responsibilities and revealed to the technical organizations the real needs of the farmers. The agricultural programme (the annual installation and delivery of products and materials for agriculture) is at last becoming, after many vicissitudes, the result of co-operation between government technicians and the people. The technicians are on the way to acquiring the planning techniques needed in their work and to establishing a teacher-pupil relationship with the people.

The training periods for intermediary organizations (originally conceived for individual teachers working alone) now provide an annual opportunity for all the organizations which work in direct contact with the field to meet, to reflect and exchange information about development projects, and to take responsibility for them on their return. By these methods organizations formerly only slightly influenced are becoming sensitive to new needs – 1,535 of these organizations were influenced in 1965 including district chiefs, the heads of departmental technical sections, employees of the National Office of Co-operation and Assistance for Development, teachers, political organizations, and agents of Rural Expansion Centres.

The creation of regional and *département* committees for development has made it possible for projects initiated by the government to be concerted; regional officials and Centre directors can thus have a positive influence on their colleagues : one movement in progress seeks to give the committees at *département* level efficient working methods for directing the operations of government technicians by means of a realistic monthly programme, calculated in accordance with the needs of the people and with available resources in finance and in technical personnel.

At the level of the Central Government a National Committee re-unites all the services. The future National Development Committee will henceforth make it possible to co-ordinate all the development projects which are undertaken.

The recent inauguration of the National School of Applied Economy is also in keeping with the Extension spirit – that of providing organizers at headquarters with courses based upon experience acquired in the field : four colleagues are responsible for courses lasting several years, of which a large proportion takes place in the field. Four special fields of study are covered : Extension, Co-operation, Planning, Re-allocation of Land. The organizers thus trained have a vocation to return and work in the field, and the school functions in close collaboration with the Directorate of Extension and Expansion.

Thus, along a thousand channels, the spirit of Extension is beginning to percolate through into all levels of society, but in opposition to many social reforms the direction of progress in Extension is from base to summit. The principle of taking Extension workers from the heart of the population leads to their reunification in cells of activity. These lead to the creation of *département* committees. Finally, at the national level, an overall committee including all government agencies has to be created. The combination of these measures results in raising the morale of Extension throughout its whole structure, especially at the top where it enjoys the firm support of the President of the Republic.

Extension does not limit itself, then, to a pedagogic effort during training. It begins in fact outside formal training. To assess the degree of Extension work in terms of the number of Extension workers is doubtless convenient, but it is in fact misleading. The success of Extension is to be measured in terms of the initiative of the workers produced, the retraining they undergo and especially the projects proposed to them; these projects will become one of the most important means of implementing the nation's overall development, especially in agriculture.

The problems of Extension

Extension is not a service, nor an Administrative unit, it is a movement, an idea of development put into effect by a service. As such, it cannot become set in a mould, it is confronted each day with new problems; it must constantly be engaged in research and perpetually renewing its methods. The most important of the current problems of Extension are as follows:

1. *The relationship between the technical and political aspects of Extension.* Extension pursues two aims which would seem at first sight to have little connection. It has a political aim in that it changes relationships between people and the State by awakening a social conscience, a desire for change and progress. People realise that they have a choice and this effects a transformation in the behaviour and composition of the mobile teams.

But Extension, as we have seen, has also a technical dimension. The people are given practical encouragement to make a personal effort towards development, and thus, necessarily, to call upon technicians. The technicians recognize the value of the influence of Extension upon the population, which becomes more receptive to the adoption of techniques (whether in agriculture, hygiene, or housing). The two activities are complementary, for Extension is all-embracing. But out of an excessive insistence upon one or the other, the following perversions can be born:

(a) On the one hand, if the technical dimension is lost sight of, Extension risks becoming confused with sterile political agitation. Indeed, Extension can raise hopes in people's breasts, stirring up aspirations without being able to provide immediate means for their fulfilment.

Resort to demagogy is then a danger. The Extension worker cuts himself off from all collaboration with the technicians, who distrust him, and the flame of enthusiasm aroused in the breast of the people seeks in vain for something to attach itself to, and eventually gutters out. It is through the laborious but sure way of technical competence and achievement that the revolution of thought and of social and political structures will come to pass.

(b) On the other hand, instead of seeking to impart a social conscience, Extension risks being reduced to a system of agricultural instruction centred exclusively on immediate technical projects. In such a situation it avoids 'meddling in politics'. But the techniques that it introduces into the rural setting are not neutral : they must shape the change in society in the way chosen by the nation; an increase in production is not an end in itself; economic growth is without interest if it does not involve development.

The relationship between these two aspects of Extension is extremely delicate and there is an ever-present risk of disturbing it in one of the ways indicated and thus compromising the idea of Extension in everyone's mind.

2. *Extension and political parties.* Being all-embracing, Extension necessarily has a political dimension, since it accelerates and improves the political awareness of the masses. It can, however, become difficult to distinguish it from the purely political organizations, the parties. Its task, however, is quite distinct.

The parties have the task of *representation*, of ensuring general political understanding, of clarifying the important choices at issue and of putting policies into operation through the medium of the government and the administrative hierarchy, which includes the system of Extension workers.

It is important to respect the distinction, to avoid exposing either the government or Extension cells of activity to the risks of 'politicians' politics'. Party members must not be given direct management, for this would impair their functions as representatives and throw doubt upon their impartiality.

Nevertheless, their contacts and co-ordination of activities is necessary at all levels : thus it is convenient for political officials to sit on Extension committees and to associate their party with actual achievements, provided that at grass-roots party cells of activity remain separate from the Extension cells, although lending mutual support to each other's activities.

3. *Keeping alive a sense of commitment and free discussions.* Extension may be a spirit, a movement, but in order to be effective it needs the paraphernalia of administration : hence the existence of the Directorate of Extension and Rural Expansion with its personnel, its vehicles, its credits, its procedures, and its hierarchy. The risk can immediately be discerned : putting Extension into operation needs militancy as well

as organization in its personnel structure. As part of an administration still only slightly receptive to development, the agents of the Directorate of Extension and Rural Expansion face the danger that if this militant spirit is lost they will no longer have influence on the officials. And who would then spread the gospel of individual participation? 'If the salt has lost its savour, wherewith shall it be salted?'

Alongside this danger is that of losing the sense of holding free discussions with the people; government officials, inheriting colonial practices which they have often made worse, are rarely in the habit of conversing with the people and instead limit themselves to an authoritative relationship.

A dialogue, which consists of knowing how to listen, of letting the respondent explain himself, of trying to convince him, and eventually of accepting the possibility of being convinced instead, requires an exercise in self-control at all times which it is difficult to insist upon in the inner circles of government.

4. *Extension as applied to the whole of society.* As Extension works with people at the grass-roots level it is clear that there will be resistance as much from the environment of the group as from the group itself: thus, a village chief may set his face against the specific activity which the Extension worker wishes to promote, a political or government official will be jealous of the worker's action and seek to hinder it, or government-employed technicians will not consider it in their own interest to collaborate with the Extension cells. Responsibility for overcoming this kind of opposition and for creating an environment of communities aware of and desiring development falls to the Directorate of Extension. Thus it organizes regularly not only courses for village chiefs, each lasting several days, and others for co-operative presidents and weighers, when the people and the organizations which work among them meet together, but also sessions for intermediate organizations when officials of a region who are working in direct contact with the people come together. In this way, a combined effort may be launched in which all those who play a role in the development of the community will participate.

Much the same happens at higher administrative levels, especially since Extension work was one of the State agencies started with the support of the President of the Republic. It would, indeed, have been ironical if the administration whose duty it is to provide the stimulus for development should have become a restraint and remained on the side of the people's out-moded ideas. Everything depends upon creating appropriate conditions. Competence, professional conscience, and precision are what matter; nepotism and veniality must be eliminated from inside the Services by those concerned. Thus it must be recognized that in this field tangible achievements have as yet been limited, and that the Directorate of Extension, one of several government agencies, has only limited resources and is still trying to define its methods.

Finally, confronted with the rapid urbanization that is taking place, Extension cannot remain inactive. It has to design and experiment with urban extension so as to guide the urbanized peoples not merely to endure their conditions of living, but to take responsibility for their own development. But, in this field, it cannot be a question of imitating the achievements and methods of rural Extension since the problems in a town are totally different where specific intermediate groups exist without an ethnic or family basis (trade unions, large firms) where problems are often part of a scale of extended collectivity (urbanization, housing, municipality, transport) or dependent on external elements (conditions of work). In this very complex field few concrete results have as yet been achieved. (A training course for organizations of urban Extension was held at Rufisque in August 1964.) But an inquiry and experiments are currently in progress, notably the participation of urban Extension workers in educational television programmes, one of the future instruments for arousing social awareness.

By these efforts among all sections of the population, Extension strives its utmost to respond to its duty, which is to enable each individual to become conscious of his responsibility for development and to participate actively in achieving it.

5. *The aim of Extension as a service – self-effacement.* The technique of Extension, and the administrative machine that implements it, have been created only to counteract deficiencies. If one day, in the wake of their activities, the people take charge of their own future without having to receive external encouragement, if the government and the political organizations reveal a spirit of inquiry and start a natural dialogue to promote development, then the Service will have fulfilled its mission, each group and each agent will effectively have taken up its responsibilities. The spirit of Extension must enter into structure and behaviour, and find itself within them. If everyone was doing his duty as he should be, the Directorate of Extension would no longer need to exist.

6. *Zambia*

LALAGE BOWN

Resources and difficulties

Zambia's social and economic situation is different from that of other independent African countries. An unusual concatenation of resources and difficulties makes it a special case, and gives adult education a special and urgent role.

Bluntly, Zambia embarked on political independence facing every disadvantage except lack of resources. In relation to its population (slightly under four million), the country is wealthy. It has ample land of reasonable fertility, good water-supplies and hydro-electric potential. It is also the non-communist world's second largest producer of copper; and the Copperbelt supports 16 per cent of the country's employed labour, provides approximately 70 per cent of Government revenue and brings in 93 per cent of all foreign exchange.[1] Although there is an element of precariousness in any economy relying so heavily on one commodity, independent Zambia was in a position to envision economic and social development in bolder terms than had been possible for most other African countries. For example, the 1966–70 First National Development Plan anticipated Government investment of £282 million and total recurrent expenditure of £339 million; by contrast, Nigeria's 1966–71 plan provided for total Federal and Regional spending of £340 million – for 14 times the population.

But besides bringing wealth, copper has brought difficulty : a sophisticated industrial complex set in a traditional rural subsistence economy. There is a consequent gross disparity of reward available to rural and urban workers. The towns draw in young men from the villages, and because many of them have little education and less skill, they join the ever-increasing class of job-seekers. The 1963 census listed 72,000 African unemployed, a figure which represented approximately one-quarter of the employable work-force at that time.

Most African countries have to overcome the inertia of village society. Zambia is almost unique in having to grapple at the same time with the malaises of an industrial urban community on a substantial scale. On the one hand, in the rural areas there are about 400,000 farm families whose standard of living is low, since their production is static and their purchasing power limited. The Government's publication on the Development Plan remarked that to change their situation would require, as well as capital, social reorganization, psychological reorientation and the acquisition of technical knowledge.[2] On the other hand, 25 per cent of the population live in towns along the line of rail (a high degree of urbanization compared to Eastern Africa). The towns are artificial creations, in which the majority of the inhabitants live in drab suburbs, known as townships, of closely-ranged, uniformly-designed houses – conditions which give rise to frustration, delinquency and such social problems as alcoholism. Just as gin was the quickest way out of Manchester in the 19th century, so today the quickest escape from a Copperbelt township is 'chibuku', a traditional opaque beer, now made industrially and retailed at 3/-($0.42) a gallon.

A further complication is the problem of a plural society, in a rather more drastic form than in Eastern Africa. For instance, there are about 700 European farm families, who contribute 66 per cent of maize marketed, and almost all the Virginia tobacco. In other sectors, the proportion of middle- and high-level jobs filled by non-Africans is formidable. In transport and communications, the figure is 58 per cent; in manufacturing, commerce and finance it is 75–80 per cent; and in major metal mining 88 per cent.[3]

The Government has firmly nailed its flag to the mast of non-racialism, but the existence of a noticeably foreign privileged class cannot but breed friction and mutual distrust. Moreover, no long memory is required to recall the social and economic discrimination against Africans which obtained when Zambia, then Northern Rhodesia, was part of the Central African Federation. During most of the Federal period, from 1953 to 1964, Africans were barred from responsible jobs on the mines (they were even excluded from the provisions of the Apprenticeship Act until 1959), had to tolerate indignities in shops and hotels and also had to watch much of their country's wealth being drained away to Southern Rhodesia, for the benefit of an alien population – the Southern Rhodesian capital was given a nickname in those days which meant 'Eat-up-everything'.

All these social problems – urban unease, village stagnation, racial dis-harmony – are exacerbated by, and to some extent stem from, *educational* problems. Of all the English-speaking African nations, Zambia perhaps was the least prepared educationally for independence. Dr Kenneth Kaunda, the country's President, has commented: 'Skilled and educated manpower is Zambia's scarcest resource',[4] and he and his ministers constantly recur in their speeches to the stark figures. At the time of independence in 1964, there were about 100 Zambian university graduates and 1,200 Zambians with secondary school certificates (Cambridge, London, or similar). There was already a comparable number of persons who had successfully completed secondary school in Ghana in 1943, Uganda in 1955 and Kenya in 1957. In Zambia, the whole educational pyramid rose until recently from a very narrow base, and the 1963 census estimated that 76·6 per cent of all men were illiterate or sub-literate and 95·6 per cent of all women. (See Appendix III, Table 2.)

Since independence, the Government has embarked on a Herculean attempt to make up for lost time, and has already expanded the school system dramatically. Total primary enrolments increased from 358,357 in 1964 to 609, 490 in 1968, while secondary enrolment went up five-fold, from 8,177 in 1964 to 42, 191 in 1968.[5] In 1966 the first 312 students entered the newly-founded University of Zambia; and by the opening session of 1969 there were just over 750 full-time undergraduates.

Until the school system can, however, catch up with the country's needs for skilled industrial manpower and for more enlightened farmers, schemes for the education and training of adults are bound to assume a quite peculiar importance.

The post-independence demand for immediate Zambianization in many fields and the planners' insistence on the urgency of up-grading the rural economy mean that the country cannot wait for the generation now being put through the schools to become available for employment. Further, in 1968 the President launched a plan for economic reform which requires the very much increased participation of Zambians in business enterprise at all levels; and numbers of men and women are newly involved in forms of economic activity for which they have had little opportunity to acquire training. In such circumstances, adult education is a desperate necessity.

Social and economic pressures are reinforced by a moral and political factor. Zambian politicians, like those of many other African countries, feel a responsibility to their electorate to provide for them what they missed through growing up in the colonial era – and they have to fulfil the expectations of those who put them into power. Adult education has become also a moral obligation.

Fortunately for Zambia, money became abundantly available after the Federal leaching ceased, and there has grown up a whole network of institutions for the education and training of adults. Zambia has now the completest range of adult educational provision of any African country. So complex has it become in a few short years that the University of Zambia's Department of Extra-Mural Studies appointed a research fellow, Dr Colin McCaffrey, to make a two-year survey of adult education agencies in the country, and evaluate the effective-

AENB I

ness of their programmes, as well as their response to the needs of the community. I believe this to be a pioneer venture. One full-length descriptive survey of adult education in an African country has been published,[6] but no attempt has ever been made to appraise a national adult education system in Africa in relation to its social setting.

In a short article like this, it is not possible to prefigure the more detailed survey at present nearing completion; one hopes though that it may be useful at this stage to give an outline of Zambian adult education, setting it against the plans and provisions of other developing countries.

Adult education before independence[7]

Independence and sudden access to wealth brought in a whole train of new adult educational agencies, but there are still some important links with the past.

I. *Traditional adult education.* The colonial period in Zambia, although it had a traumatic impact, was relatively short, and we must look first at pre-colonial society. The peoples of Zambia had a wide variety of institutions designed to transmit knowledge, ideas and codes of behaviour, as well as systems of training for particular functions in society, both economic and non-economic, and residues of these institutions and systems still persist.

Among modes of passing on the lore and values of the community, initiation was widespread; young persons on the verge of manhood or womanhood went through complicated rites and procedures designed to impress on them the accepted patterns of behaviour and, at the same time, to entrust them with new knowledge not regarded as suitable for children.[8] In full adulthood they came in contact with other educational forces. There were various types of political council, whether of elders or of a larger community, and speeches in these were often formal expositions of history, oral literature and political and social ideas. There were evening sessions of story-telling, in which adults and children had their memory exercised and learnt something of the accepted techniques of communication, as well as absorbing the mythological or historical content of the stories. Court musicians, as among the Bemba, set cultural standards and in songs also conveyed genealogy and cosmology. Some tribes had organizations for recreation and discipline, which served as guardians of values and ensured that members understood them; for example, the Nyau society among the Chewa.

Yet other organizations had the purpose of providing training for specific crafts or professions. Throughout Zambia there were guilds of smiths, carvers and herbalists, who had regular apprenticeship systems, as well as hunting societies in which techniques were learnt in less formal ways. Among the Ngoni, military training was an important feature of the organization of the men into regiments, while among the Bisa, who were engaged in long-distance trading between Kazembe and the coast, there were commercial guilds.

Of all these modes of education or training, perhaps particular stress should be laid on the tradition of didactic speeches at councils and meetings. Other traditions were impaired or rendered obsolete during the colonial period which followed, but the technique of using a public meeting to introduce new ideas was utilised by missionaries and colonial administrators, since in a largely non-literate society 'the living word' is the most effective means of communication. Hence the continuance into independent Zambia of the tradition of teaching-cum-preaching by persons in authority.

2. *The colonial period.* In colonial times, as has already been explained, Western-type educational provision, even for children, was exceedingly meagre. In the early part of the century, the country was very poor (the first major copper mine went into production in 1931), and, far from supplying pressures for popular education, European immigrants themselves were often ill-educated (about 14 per cent of them were illiterate in the first decade of this century). The work of pioneering Western-type education belonged to the missions; by 1923 they had reduced 17 Zambian languages to writing, and by 1928 five missionary presses were at work in the country.[9] Some of their efforts were aimed at adults, but inevitably their main stress was on teaching children. It must, however, be mentioned that with the coming of the Copperbelt, the missions began to tackle the problems of urban welfare, spurred on initially by the report edited by Merle Davis, *Modern Industry and the African*;[10] and their work on the Copperbelt emphasized literacy and women's education, as well as community development generally.

The government first assumed some responsibility for African education in 1925, with the setting up of a Sub-Department of Native Education. It suffered after 1931 from lack of direction (there were 6 Directors of African Education in the five years between 1931 and 1936) and at all times from shortage of funds (see Appendix III, Table 1), more Government money being applied to the education of the relatively small number of non-African children than to that of the whole African population. There was a strong emphasis on primary education, and no proper secondary education until the end of the '30s.

In a system which set its sights so low, one could not look for much adult education activity. There was, however, an adult educational philosophy built into the school system. Northern Rhodesia was strongly influenced by the reports of the Phelps-Stokes Commissions.[11] Starting from the conservative assumption that Europeans would retain key positions in government and in urban life, they saw education primarily as a tool for the uplift of villages. Educated Africans were expected to remain in their rural homes to pass on what they had learnt, and teachers were expected to act as agents of community development. It was in pursuance of this philosophy that a 'Jeanes School' was founded at Mazabuka (later transferred to Chalimbana). It is very hard to assess what the effect of this was in practice. Certainly by the end of the colonial period, the Jeanes philosophy had withered away, and the government had begun to view adult education as a separate activity.

The government formalized adult education in two ways. In 1954 it appointed the first full-time Adult Education Officer. This was Mr George Hardcastle, who with vision and energy set about organizing evening classes for adults and a badge scheme for women (women's education has since largely been taken over by the municipalities and the mining companies). By 1964, there were 4,498 men and women in the Government's adult education classes, studying to make up for a primary education they had missed, or never completed.

Other features of the decade before independence were the establishment of Development Area Training Centres, designed to provide courses in skills as well as to train councillors and local government officials (this scheme has since been submerged) and the founding in Lusaka of the Evelyn Hone College of Further Education. The College was planned to provide vocational skills and at present has departments of Business Studies, Communication, Technology, Health Science, Basic Catering and Social and General Studies. In 1969 it had an enrolment of 293 full-time students, 50 students on day-release and 625 evening students. In addition, it played a considerable part in the expansion of the Government night-schools, and at the time of writing still administers the night-schools in the Lusaka area, 7,861 students in 233 classes in 1969.[12] It was in the pre-independence decade too that the mining companies entered seriously into the whole educational field; before, they had regarded education as the government's responsibility, but after 1955, and particularly after the setting up of the Mines Educational Trust in 1960, they have founded schools and adult education programmes, as well as their own training schemes. These will be discussed later. The new atmosphere on the Copperbelt led to the foundation of the Northern Technical College in Ndola, with branches in other mining towns, and a fairly varied evening class programme.

Finally, as in other African countries, colonialism evoked a response among the population in the form of self-help organizations of various kinds.[13] In Zambia, they were puny compared to those in, say, Ghana,[14] since there was such a dearth of educated leadership, but they cannot go unmentioned; since they combined 'welfare' functions with those of expressing political protest, one may trace in them too one of the roots of the Zambian view that a political party has an educative function. The first of these bodies was probably the Mwenzo Welfare Association of 1923, among whose founders was the father of K. Kaunda, President of Zambia. Later, one such association on the Copperbelt proved the germ of the African Mineworkers' Union, established in 1949 and among the powerful unions which have shown a genuine, if spasmodic, interest in workers' education.

The present picture

1. *Remedial education.* Both the need for Zambianization and the sense of moral and political obligation led the government of Dr Kenneth Kaunda (President of the Republic) and his United National Independence Party to attempt to remedy the many deficiencies in the formal education system.

There are three main aspects to the programme of 'remedial' adult education : literacy, night-schools and correspondence education.

Before independence, no money at all was allocated to *literacy* teaching, whereas under the Government's first National Development Plan it was envisaged that an initial annual expenditure of £25,000 a year on literacy would be increased to one of £544,000 by 1970. The main aims of the literacy section of the Department of Community Development are:

'(a) To help accelerate the rate of national socio-economic development through:
  i. The provision of opportunities for basic literacy,
  ii. The provision of reading and study materials designed to help improve vocational efficiency,
  iii. The developing use of radio and television to further vocation-oriented education;
(b) To provide opportunities for communities, private groups and voluntary associations to exercise their own initiative and abilities in helping their illiterate members to become literate.'[15]

The section's most important achievements so far have been with regard to (a)i. and to (b). There has been a valiant attempt to provide basic opportunities to acquire literacy in the mother tongue throughout the country. In 1966, 4,564 men and women enrolled in literacy classes, conducted by 577 certified instructors, assisted by a total of 74 regular staff. The volunteers were each given 30 hours training, and

the regular staff (or Local Literacy Officers) had three months' specialized training at the Kabwe Community Development Centre. Other
figures showing development since the launching of the scheme in
1965 are : the devising by the end of 1967 of seven series of literacy
primers, 42 post-literacy readers, 5 fortnightly news-sheets for use in
the Zambian-language press, and 5 fortnightly broadsheets for distribution to literacy classes.

The Department of Community Development is not unaware of
the problems of preparing for truly functional literacy and of the need
for evaluation. A UNESCO team of experts was requested, to advise on
functional literacy, and visited Zambia in August-September 1967.
Their report is still under consideration at the time of writing, but
suggests special approaches to farmers, miners, construction-workers
and housewives. Evaluation of the existing literacy classes was held up
by adventitious obstacles, such as the shortage of petrol after Rhodesia's illegal declaration of independence*; but a UNESCO adviser on
evaluation has now been appointed.

Government literacy work is the best documented, but there are of
course private bodies undertaking literacy teaching. Several churches
work in this field, and among religious groups the Jehovah's Wit-
nesses make perhaps the most concerted attack on illiteracy among
their members. Owing to beliefs which result in their remaining aloof
from the school system they have evolved their own educational provision.

The night-school and correspondence schemes have reached out to
larger numbers so far than the Government's literacy work. These
schemes, under the Ministry of Education, provide opportunities for
men and women to pursue the whole primary course and the first two
years of the secondary course anywhere in Zambia; and in some
centres GCE classes are provided too. There is a very strong demand
for the night-school classes, and even certain people in high positions
have been prepared to attend them – including at least one Minister of
State, a woman MP, and the mayor of a town. The night-school programme depends on a network of full-time Ministry staff and the recruitment of paid part-time teachers. Some 35,000 persons enrolled in
these classes in 1969, and the contribution of night-schools and the
Government Correspondence Unit to Zambianization appears to be of
real significance. Some research by Mr Hans Noak would indicate that
as many as 27 per cent of Form II entrants to Government training
courses may receive at least part of their education through night-

* Shortage of petrol affected the class programme too. One resourceful
Senior Literacy Officer took to doing his supervisory rounds on horse-
back.

schools and correspondence courses.[16]

This is not to deny that there are imperfections in the night-schools and correspondence courses, of which the responsible officials are well aware. For one thing, when school places are short, it is hard to keep juveniles out of classes supposed to be for adults. For a second, the content of the courses is designed for the schools and for school-children and may not be either relevant or appealing to adults (one English text-book used at upper primary level includes the poems : 'If all the sea were one sea', and 'The Rainbow Fairies'). There is, too, an unsolved problem of relationships; at present an illiterate may go either to a Community Development literacy class or to a Ministry of Education night-school.

Embarras de choix is obviously better than dearth of provision, and it should be mentioned that the strong Government lead in remedial education is followed by other agencies – municipalities, mining companies and voluntary bodies, which reinforce and complement the Government's programme. There has also been one successful voluntary night-school organization, the Bwacha Adult Education Association in Kabwe.

2. *Vocational training.* Both private enterprise and Government are involved in a form of education more strictly economic – training for specific jobs. Zambia is uniquely well provided, in Africa, with training schemes. Appendix 11 gives a list of 40 separate Government training institutions, though there may be some rationalization following a recent report on technical education and the appointment of a Minister of State for Technical Education in the President's Office. Quasi-Government bodies, such as Zambia Railways, also have comprehensive training arrangements (the Railways had a crisis of skill owing to a large post-UDI exodus of expatriate workers).

At this point, tribute is also due to the training efforts of private enterprise. Almost all employees of the mining companies go through induction courses, and the mines have large-scale provision for development training and for retraining that is combined with systematic selection processes.[17] An enumeration of types of operation for which training is required on the mines would include : research and development, and mining, metallurgical, engineering, management, administrative, medical, community and personnel services.[18]

(Incidentally, the mining companies also give serious attention to literacy classes and adult schools for the inhabitants of the mining townships, probably having a smaller drop-out rate than that in the country at large, owing to the stability of the labour force.* The mines

* The average length of service among Zambian miners on the Copperbelt is 6·8 years.

have been imaginative in experimenting with adult teaching methods and financed a pioneer experiment in television teaching.[19])

The Manpower Report comments : 'More surprising perhaps is the extent to which training is required, provided and obtained in the mass of private firms, large and small, throughout the rest of the private sector.'[20] A survey of 3,368 African workers with at least secondary education in the private sector other than the mines and railways showed that at least three-quarters had either received training or were undergoing it. Perhaps it is not invidious to single out the training dispositions of Barclays Bank[21] and the Booker Group. All programmes are likely to expand when an expected Industrial Training Act is passed; and since the appointment of Government committees on Zambianization, there is more interest in Management training (professional bodies, the Zambian Institutes of Management, Personnel Management and Supervisory Management are promoting this too).

The training so far mentioned relates to the urban economy. The rural economy is catered for by an extension service run by the Department of Agriculture on a pattern similar to that in other ex-British dependencies. There are extension workers all over Zambia, as well as farm schools to which farmers are brought for short courses. Outside the usual range, there are large ranching schemes on which people can learn husbandry, and a developed system of Farm Forum broadcasts beamed to organized listening groups in the villages.

3. *Informal adult education.* The heavy emphasis I have placed on formal education and training reflects Zambia's urgent and immediate preoccupations. It is here that most money is spent.* It would, however, be a caricature not to mention other less formal types of adult education. There are a number of projects designed in one way or another to improve the quality of life, among them women's programmes organized by Government, municipalities and missions, the National Nutrition Commission efforts, and at another level the Government Directorate of Cultural Services and the voluntary Zambia Arts Trust. Further, the national broadcasting service is officially viewed as a vehicle of education and time is allotted to many agencies to teach about such matters as health, road safety, soil conservation and the dangers of excessive drinking.

4. *Some special features of Zambian adult education.* This survey should not omit certain special features of Zambian adult education.

First, groups which by their nature are cohesive and also partially separated from the rest of society (e.g. prisoners, the police) need special provision, and in Zambia *the Army* has a flexible and well-

* See Appendix 1 for allocations under the Plan.

thought-out educational system. Apart from training at all levels (and officers are at present promoted by examination), there is a broad scheme of education geared to the secondary school examinations but more flexible in content and method than the civilian counterpart. Instructors are encouraged to remember that they are educating adults and soldiers learn under less arduous conditions than civilians, since they are released for extended periods to attend educational courses full-time.

Secondly, in most African countries, *missions* and religious bodies have made substantial contributions to adult education (e.g. Sir Albert Cook, the doctor, who worked in Uganda and kept detailed notes not only of his patients' medical histories, but also of whether or not he and his wife taught them to read).[22] The Christian missions' tradition on the Copperbelt flowered into a lay training centre with a very individual flavour, Mindolo Ecumenical Centre. It is run by a Board of Governors representing several Protestant bodies and including a Catholic observer, and its staff at any one time may represent up to 20 nationalities and almost as many different denominations. Its contribution to social and economic progress, on the relatively slender budget of £60,000 a year, includes the training of youth leaders and community development workers, courses for women in Christian homemaking (one was attended by the President's wife), three-year practical farming courses on its own farms, programmes for junior management and trade unionists, and a range of activities under the general heading of National Development : before independence, it provided a meeting-ground for Zambian politicians.

Mindolo has a very beautiful lake-side setting, and also provides a home for other organizations such as the Y W C A Training Centre and the All-Africa Conference of Churches' African Literature Centre. It has the important advantage too of containing the Dag Hammarskjold Memorial Library. All this makes it an unusually varied community and an unusual adult educational complex.

Thirdly, one of the most significant modern adult educational forces (and this is true of Tanzania too) goes back to the tradition of didactic speech. Zambian *politicians* take seriously their role of teachers-cum-preachers. They constantly stump the provinces, and speeches are used to convey a message. The Minister of State in Northern Province may exhort people to use a new fish market, the Minister in Southern Province may tackle race-relations, the Minister of Labour may make a point about industrial discipline, the President himself about the Churches and morality.

Archbishop Temple once said that the whole work of education was to raise the level of what a man is to what he has it in him to become.[23] The politicians are conscious of what their fellow-men could become and are feverishly anxious to help along the transformation. A result of this approach is the President's study-pamphlet on Zambian Humanism,[24] and, more recently, the establishment of a Ministry of National Guidance.

Exhortation to change is not all. The African tradition of discussion is also called into play. There are constant seminars of special groups (traders, information officers, permanent secretaries) in which an endeavour is made to thrash out difficult issues – although it has to be admitted that sometimes discussion takes second place to harangue. But when the National Development Plan was launched, a Convention of 800 people met and worked hard in discussion groups to study it; and this was followed up by mini-conventions in the provinces.

It may be seen that there is a certain ambiguity in Zambian adult education. The government responds to pressures for adult education by the provision of formal courses, which are necessary for *economic* betterment, and spends heavily on them. At the same time members of the Government devote their own time and energy to types of educational activity aimed at *social* and *political* betterment, showing in this way how important they rate this, but somehow very little money is applied to these objectives.

Some problems

There are two glaring problems arising from all this activity, one technical and one relating to objectives.

The *technical* problem is that while the country so obviously is committed to large-scale adult education and training, most of the teaching in these projects is done by amateurs, or by men and women who have been trained as school teachers and have not faced up to the difference between children and adults. All too many literacy classes and night-school classes are deadened by methods suitable to a rather old-fashioned institution for child education : question and chanted response, authoritarian discipline, the quelling of any original idea or query. This is exacerbated by students' expectations. The only form of education they have seen is a primary school, and they want to conform to that model since it is all they know; and this is what they demand of the politicians to provide. They can only be made to realise the excitement and relevance of learning if their teachers are trained to handle adult groups in an adult fashion.

Zambia therefore needs a scheme for training in the principles and methods of adult education if much of the money applied in the National Plan is not to be wasted – and 18 per cent of the annual recurrent expenditure in 1970 will be on adult education and training. Drop-outs mean waste and examination failures mean waste, and many of both can be avoided if the adult teachers are properly trained.

This is not to imply that no thinking has been done about the problem, and about the general professionalization of adult education in Zambia. A number of conferences on adult education has been promoted, notably by the Evelyn Hone College and the Friedrich Ebert Foundation, and Zambia has played an active part in the organization now known as the African Adult Education Association. But there is still need for a coherent system of training. The University called a conference on this[25] and has started acting on its recommendations. It has begun conducting short courses for specific groups, arranged for a visiting expert in adult education training,* and started work on a sociological manual for adult educators; and it has plans for a full-scale professional course. The Government too now has within the civil service several people well-versed in training methods, and they are having an impact.

The second problem is the consideration of *objectives*, and it is an acute one. Most of the difficulties mentioned at the beginning of this paper should be soluble by carefully-planned long-range adult education programmes. But at present they are not being solved because most effort goes into tackling the immediate short-term economic difficulties; and even these attempts have dangerous facets, since many of the products of the night-schools will swell the ranks of the unemployed or at best the discontented, because their hard-won piece of paper does not fit them for anything much.

It is easy to forget the long-range goals of education when the immediate manpower needs are pressing, and it is even easier when educational values themselves are narrow. Understandably, for most Zambians the advertisement of a Lusaka correspondence college is all too apt : 'To earn the *most* money – get the *best* education'. Education is seen as a means to individual emolument, and it is often not realised that emolument itself should be a means to a better life for the individual and to a better society, and is not an end in itself. An education with a value-content is an unfamiliar concept in a country where most school-teaching is dull and at secondary level is geared to foreign examinations taught by foreign teachers (of the 1,030 graduate teachers in 1966, only 21 were Zambians). But it is a necessary pre-requisite to achieving the ideal of Zambian Humanism, a society in which the haves help the have-nots.

There are three sides to this problem. One is the need to persuade public opinion that education can be different in character from that

* Dr Alan Thomas, Executive Director of the Canadian Association of Adult Education; his visit was financed by the Commonwealth Foundation.

bequeathed by a colonial government. The second is the need to decide the long-term goals to which adult education should then be applied. And the third is the need to transform the content of adult education to make it relevant to modern social, economic and political changes. Perhaps one can even start to tackle the third first, since one wonders particularly at the immense devotion and expenditure going into teaching adults school syllabuses instead of material more suitable to them. There are examples in Africa, the Makerere Adult Studies Certificate for one; and in Zambia itself the cry for separate teaching about the National Plan and Humanism is an implicit comment on the formal adult educational system.

There are some institutions, such as Mindolo, which have already been concerned with long-term objectives. There are now two new institutions in Zambia which may also help to provide adult education geared to the larger-range social problems – the President's Citizenship College and the University.

The Citizenship College is financed by Government and a foundation and its main purpose will be to provide a broadening for trade unionists, co-operators and party workers to fit them to be better members of society. It is not to be a propagandist institution, though it will inevitably be committed to the goals of the National Plan, Zambian Humanism and the Mulungushi economic reforms.

The University has been in operation for two years and the policy of its Extra-Mural Department is to help people to think straight about their own problems. Through classes, seminars and the radio it hopes to teach subjects which are relevant to this. It too cannot be partisan (and it tries to encourage objectivity), but its teaching is designed to enable people to understand the modern world, and to control changes that occur, rather than merely being buffeted by change.

In effect, the College and the University may help to convey to co-workers in the adult education field the significance of Professor Busia's comment : 'What is done in education must be seen within the concept of man and society in their totality and inter-relations, and within a vision of the foreseeable future of Africa and the world.'[26]

APPENDIX I

Abstract of expenditure on training and education of adults envisaged in Zambia's first National Development Plan
(1966, Lusaka, Government Printer)

The Plan has been subject to substantial modification since it was issued, but the tables indicate the order of priorities.
Note: These figures are taken from the Sector Tables. Annexure xxx on Training is incomplete and contains several discrepancies.

A. *Adult education programmes affecting the community at large*

Programme	Annexure reference in plan	Total capital expenditure 1966/70	Additional annual recurrent expenditure in 1970
Literacy campaign (Ministry of Youth, Co-operatives and Social Development)	XVII, Education, p 260	161	544
Youth work			
Zambia Youth Service	XXI, Off. of President, p 270	340	235
Rural Youth Work (Ministry of Youth, Co-operatives and Social Development)	XVI, Social Welfare, p 258	32 〕 372	18 〕 253
'*Adult education*' Provision of formal schooling for adults (Ministry of Education)	XVII, Education, p 260	427	501
President's College of Citizenship For trade unionists, co-operators, party workers, etc. (Ministry of Labour)	XXI, Off. of President, p 270	114	40
Zambia library services (Ministry of Education)	XVII, Education, p 260	503	74
Government information services Including Zambia Broadcasting Services, Audio-Visual Aids and Provincial	XX, Information, p 267	847	427

Co-operative Building Training Scheme (Ministry of Co-operatives, Youth and Social Development)	XIX, Co-operatives, p 266 (& XII, Transport and Works, p 248)	26	26	36	96
Agricultural extension					
Farmer training and extension on farm	II, Agriculture and Lands	740		696	
Specialist tobacco farming training	II, Agriculture and Lands	400		—	
Extension by broadcasting	II, Agriculture and Lands	393		120	
Farmers at Chipembi	XXX, Training, p 282	—	2,533	30	846
Fisheries extension (Ministry of Natural Resources and Tourism)	II, Agriculture and Lands, p 232		93		37
Training of Blind					
Mission Blind Schools and Clerical Training for Blind	XVII, Social Welfare, p 258	59		2	
Farm Training and Settlement of Blind (Ministry of Co-operatives, Youth and Social Development)	XVII, Social Welfare, p 258	65	124	20	22
Totals			5,200		2,840

Notes: President's College of Citizenship – Additional funds from outside sources are likely to be available (e.g. a contribution from the Friedrich Ebert Foundation).

Government Information Services – Included here since the broadcasting system is regarded as primarily for public service, and the Provincial Information Services disseminate a fair amount of semi-educational material.

B. Training schemes affecting government and non-government employees

Programme

Technical and further education
New Technical College
Expansion and development of Northern Technical College
College of Further Education
Provisional additional allocation
Carry-over from previous plan
(Ministry of Education)

Industrial and building training
(Ministry of Labour)

Training of local government staff
(Ministry of Local Government)

Urban community development training
(Ministry of Co-operatives, Youth and Social Development)
Totals

Notes: Technical and Further Education – part of the last two heads apply to technical and trade schools and not to the training of adults. Training of Local Government Staff – the Ministry of Local Government Training schemes embrace councillors as well.

Annexure reference in plan	Total capital expenditure 1966/70		Additional annual recurrent expenditure in 1970	
xvii, Education, p 260				
	300		56	
	510		73	
	920		220	349
	350			
	108	2,188		
xvi, Social Welfare, p 258		154		175
xv, Local Government, p 256		54		10
xvi, Social Welfare, p 258		25		23
		2,421		557

C. *Training schemes designed primarily for government employees*

Programme	Annexure reference in plan	Total Capital expenditure 1966/70	Additional annual recurrent expenditure in 1970
Administrative and clerical			
Staff Training College and Law School	xxii, Sec. to Cabinet, p 272	82	35
Clerical Training Schools	xxii, Sec. to Cabinet, p 272	98	45
Training schemes	xxii, Sec. to Cabinet, p 272	131	—
Training grade posts	xxii, Sec. to Cabinet, p 272	197	—
(Cabinet Office)		508	80
Police and armed forces			
Police Training School	xxi, Off. of President, p 270	340	39
School of Military Training	xxi, Off. of President, p 270	1,075	489
zaf Training Wing	xxi, Off. of President, p 270	787	415
(Office of the President)		2,202	943
Agricultural sector training			
Agricultural staff	II, Agriculture and Lands, p 228	525	279
Veterinary staff	II, Agriculture and Lands, p 228	30	1
Forestry staff	II, Agriculture and Lands, p 230	40	—
Game Dept staff	II, Agriculture and Lands, p 232	30	20
Marketing	xxx, Training, p 282	—	50
(Ministry of Agriculture and		625	370

Item	Reference				
Roads Training School	IX, Roads and Harbours, p 243	30		—	
Civil Aviation Training School and temporary facilities	X, Civil Aviation, p 244	120		24	
PWD Training School and dormitories	XII, Transport and Works, p 248	43		110	
Mobile Training Workshops (Ministries of Works and of Transport, Power and Communications)	XII, Transport and Works, p 248	48	241	18	152
Nursing and other health training					
School of Hygiene	XVIII, Health, p 262	60		10	
Medical Assistants' Training School	XVIII, Health, p 262	69		15	
Training schools at major hospitals (including accommodation for trainees)	XVIII, Health, p 262	475		63	
Other staff training (Ministry of Health)	XVIII, Health, p 264	26	630		88
Training of teachers (Ministry of Education)	XVII, Education, p 260	1,539		297	
Totals		4,206		1,633	

Notes: Forestry and Game Department Staff – a small amount of non-staff training is included. Works and Transport – the Ministry of Labour's building training scheme will be found under B. Nursing and Other Medical Training – the proposed Teaching Hospital is not included (capital expenditure of £400,000 on it is envisaged during the period of the Plan)

APPENDIX II

List of government training institutions, 1967 (compiled from various sources)

Administrative and clerical
1. Staff Training College and Law School, Lusaka (now National Institute of Public Administration)
2. Chalimbana Local Authority Staff Training College, Chalimbana, near Lusaka
3. Clerical Training School, Lusaka
4. Clerical Training School, Ndola

Relating to natural resources
5. Natural Resources Development College, Lusaka
6. Zambia College of Agriculture, Monze
7. Veterinary School, Mazabuka
8. Fisheries Training School, Sinazeze, Sinazongwe
9. Mwekera Forest Training School, Kitwe
10. Survey School, Mazabuka
11. Meteorological Training Centre, Lusaka
12. Meteorological Training Centre, Livingstone

Relating to community development and health
13. School of Hygiene, Lusaka
14. Medical Assistants' Training School, Lusaka
15. Government School of Nursing, Kitwe
16. Zambia Enrolled Nurses' Training School, Livingstone
17. Community Nurses' Training School, Kabwe
18. Public Health Laboratory Training School, Lusaka
19. Public Health Laboratory Training School, Kitwe
20. Urban Community Development Training School, Kitwe
21. Zambia Youth Service Training Centre, Kabwe*
22. Provincial Community Development Centre, Kabwe (used as national training centre for literacy workers)

Defence and security
23. School of Military Training, Ndola
24. Army School, Kabwe
25. Air force Technical Training School, Livingstone
26. Police Training School, Lilayi
27. Police Training School, Bwana Mkubwa
28. Police Telecommunications Training Centre, Lusaka
29. Prisons Training School, Kabwe

* These centres shift, and there are a number of others.

Works and communications
30. PWD Workshop School, Lusaka
31. Mechanical Services Headquarters School, Lusaka
32. Roads Department Training School, Lusaka
33. Department of Civil Aviation School, Lusaka
34. GPO Training School, Ndola
35. GPO Training School, Livingstone

Other specialized schools
36. Co-operative School, Luanshya
37. Income Tax Training Centre, Lusaka
38. Printing Apprentices School, Lusaka

General training institutions
A number of courses to train workers in various important fields of
the public services are arranged by:
39. Northern Technical College, Ndola (with other branches)
40. Evelyn Hone College, Lusaka

APPENDIX III

Tables relating to education, manpower and employment

Table 1. Government expenditure on education (all forms)

Year	£	Percentage of total government spending
1924	348	0·3
1934	26,000	3
1944	131,000	5
1954	1,100,000	6
1964	5,100,000	
1969/70	25,700,000	15

Source: Manpower Report, p 3.

Table 2. Literacy and sub-literacy, 1963

	Men	Women
Percentage of population with no schooling at all	52	82·1
Percentage with 2 years schooling or less	24·6	13·5
Total	76·6	95·6

Source: 1963 Census.

Table 3. Actual educational qualifications of persons in the civilian labour force with or in jobs requiring secondary education or above, 1965/6 and estimated demand in 1970

Educational qualifications	Africans	Non-Africans	Total	Estimated demand in 1970
Degree	150	3,499	3,649	5,600
Diploma or A-level	517	5,944	6,461	10,200
O-Level	1,516	11,965	13,481	23,400
Form 2	7,282	11,409	18,691	50,800
Less than Form 2, but in jobs requiring secondary education or above	12,015	1,853	13,868	—
In jobs requiring primary education or less	249,666	91	249,757	322,000
Total	271,146	34,761	305,907	412,000

Source: Manpower Report, pp 14 and 21.

NOTES AND REFERENCES

1. 1965 figures. See *Copperbelt of Zambia Mining Industry Yearbook, 1965*, Kitwe, Copper Industry Service Bureau, 1966.
2. *First National Development Plan, 1966–1970*, Lusaka 1966, p 21.
3. Figures at mid-1966. See *Manpower Report : A Report and Statistical Handbook on Manpower, Education, Training and Zambianisation 1965–6*, Lusaka 1966.
4. In Introduction to ibid. p iii.
5. Ibid. p 5.
6. Smith, Robert M., *Adult Education in Liberia*, Bloomington, Indiana, 1965.
7. This section owes much to discussion with colleagues at the University of Zambia, especially with Mr Harry Langworthy and Mr Trevor Coombe.
8. See, for example, Richards, Audrey, *Chisungu, a Girl's Initiation Ceremony Among the Bemba of Northern Rhodesia*, London 1956.
9. Gann, L.H., *A History of Northern Rhodesia : Early Days to 1953*, London 1946, ch. 20.
10. Davis, J. Merle (ed.), *Modern Industry and The African*, London 1933.
11. Jones, J., *Education in Africa*, New York 1922; Jones, J., *Education in East Africa*, New York 1925.

12. Information supplied by the Registrar, Evelyn Hone College of Further Education.

13. See Rotberg, Robert I., *The Rise of Nationalism in Central Africa : The Making of Malawi and Zambia 1873–1964*, Cambridge, Mass., 1966, especially chapters 5 and 11.

14. See Kimble, David, *A Political History of Ghana 1850–1928*, Oxford 1963, especially chapters 11, 111 and x111.

15. Department of Community Development Minute LIT/1. 15/6/67, Annexure 3.

16. Unpublished survey of 1,771 Government trainees. I am indebted to Mr Noak for permission to quote it.

17. See Anglo-American Corporation Training Development Unit Paper, *Survey of Educational Attainment of the Zambian Labour Force at Rhokana* (1966) which describes the testing of 8,024 volunteers at Rhokana. This Survey was conducted by Mr John H. Kemp, the Corporation's Group Training Officer, to whom I am indebted for permission to quote it.

18. From an unpublished report on training submitted by the mining companies to the Brown Commission of Enquiry into the mining industry, 1966.

19. Cripwell, K.R., *Teaching Adults by Television* (Salisbury, University College Faculty of Education Occasional Paper number 6, 1967).

20. *Manpower Report*, p 40.

21. Grenville-Grey, W. & Holliman, S.G., 'Training Zambia's Bankers', in *African Adult Education*, vol. 1, no. 1, June 1967.

22. Sir Albert Cook's papers, in the archives of the Uganda Society, Kampala.

23. Iremonger, S.A., *Life of William Temple*, London 1948.

24. Kaunda, Kenneth, *Humanism in Zambia* and *A Guide to the Implementation of Zambian Humanism*, Lusaka 1967.

25. *Report of a Conference on the Role of the University in Adult Education Training*, Lusaka, University of Zambia Department of Extra-Mural Studies, 1966.

26. Busia, Kofi A., *Purposeful Education for Africa*, The Hague 1964.

7. India

S.C. DUTTA

Before Independence

In the history of the adult education movement in India, which extends over at least seventy years, the last twenty years have been the most significant, for changes of far reaching consequences have taken place during this period. Not only has the movement expanded, covering a much wider population, but what is more, the concept of the role of adult education is today much broader than ever before.

In the early part of the century, adult education was synonymous with adult literacy and limited to imparting a knowledge of the three R's. In 1937, when the Congress Party came to power in several of the states and adult education began to receive recognition and encouragement, it still remained largely a movement for literacy and the production of literature for neo-literates; it was restricted in scope as well as in its coverage.

After Independence, a major shift of emphasis took place. The basis for this shift was laid at the fifth National Conference of the Indian Adult Education Association, which met in Rewa from 29 to 31 December 1947. The Conference at once reflected the revolutionary environment that Independence had brought into existence and its repercussions on the adult education movement. Its final resolution clearly differentiated between adult literacy and the new concept of social education, the term still used in official circles as a synonym for adult education:

'Now that power has passed into the hands of the people on whom must devolve within the next few months the responsibility for making grave decisions, this conference stresses the view that the need for adult education in all aspects of its programme was never greater in our land than it is today.

At present the people are confronted with new problems and difficulties and new social and moral urgencies. It is necessary, therefore, to re-interpret the function and develop further, through bold experimentation, the technique of adult education as the only means of equipping the Indian people for playing their part worthily in the democratic social order.'

Having thus invested adult education with a broad perspective, the Conference defined the new concept:

'Adult education is larger than literacy and literacy should not be regarded as the best or the inevitable starting point of adult education in the prevailing circumstances of the country.

Adult Education must aim at enabling the common man to live a richer life in all its aspects – social, economic, cultural, and moral. For this purpose, adult education must definitely envisage all adult centres as social centres, interested primarily in providing social, recreational and cultural facilities for the people and must endeavor to develop their powers of initiative, judgement and integrity as citizens.

While a great deal of emphasis will naturally be placed on the education of illiterates, adult education or social education, as newly termed, should not confine its attention only to that class but should be extended to cover various forms of "further" seminars, discussion groups, arts, craft and music clubs. People's Colleges and other agencies need to be developed in India in the light of her special need. In order to expedite the process of adult education and reinforce the appeal of the printed and the spoken word, it is essential to make the fullest use as far as it is practicable of the modern media of mass communication like the radio, the cinema, the press, the theatre, folklore arts etc.'

Perhaps the most notable development in the subsequent growth of the movement was the recognition by the Government of the urgency of regarding social education as a part of the normal provision of education. This need was made vocal for the first time in July 1949 when the Indian Adult Education Association submitted a memorandum emphasizing the demand for full-time workers in social education and pointing out that the lackadaisical efforts of amateurs were prone to do more harm than good. 'Programmes of Social Education', it was said, 'could not be developed by immature students just emerging from schools and colleges...much less by teachers in elementary and secondary schools, who are induced to divert an extra hour or their free time for a small monetary consideration.' The memorandum stressed, therefore, the need for training and the formation of a cadre of competent teachers, organizers and other grades of workers required to promote the movement on healthy and robust lines.

The memorandum also pointed out that all this called for a carefully conceived administrative sub-structure within the governmental framework : 'the enormous amount of additional work involved in the promotion of social education cannot be taken up by the Departments of Public Instruction as an appendix, as it were, to the work already on hand with the Department of Education nor should it be entrusted to bodies involved or affiliated with political works'. The memorandum therefore recommended the setting up of State Boards of Social Education and Departments of Social Education which would be independent both of the universities and the educational branches of the Government. The State Board, which was to consist of fifteen members nominated by the union Ministry of Education in consultation with the State Governments and by the voluntary agencies engaged in adult education, was to forge the requisite co-ordination between these various bodies.

Post-Independence

The post-Independence era in adult education has been thus characterized by the gradual acceptance of the concept of social education. The Central Advisory Board of Education at its fourteenth meeting in January 1948 expressed the view that the organization of adult education in India had become 'imperative'. Under the chairmanship of Shri Mohanlal Saxena a sub-committee was appointed, which recommended, *inter alia*, that greater emphasis should be laid on general education so as to enable every Indian to participate effectively in the new social order. It recommended that provisional Governments should provide funds for adult education and fixed targets for the removal of 50 per cent illiteracy within the next five years. At the fifteenth meeting of the Central Advisory Board held in Allahabad a new impetus to the movement was given by Maulana Azad, the then Education Minister, who called it 'Social Education' instead of Adult Education. The lead given by the CABE was followed by the Central Ministry of Education which entered into discussions with the State governments. Conferences and seminars were organized at various places and grants were awarded to the State governments and to certain voluntary organizations.

These were years of experimental probings to give shape and substance to the new concept which implied the general education of adults in a developing society in order to enable them, as members of their communities, to work towards achieving social, economic and educational development. Bihar tried to implement a broad approach through the agency of existing educational institutions. West Bengal, and later on Bihar, also emphasized recreational and cultural activities. Mysore, through its State Adult Education Council, kept close to the original concept in which literacy was the core of adult education but encouraged folk arts as instruments of a popular renaissance. Delhi, through its famous 'Education Caravans', relied on the lure of audio-visual aids to attract people to social education. Bombay kept close to literacy and libraries. Madras instituted a fairly sound library system. More significant, however, for the future development of social education was the pattern evolved in Mad Pradesh and the Etawah project of u p. Madhya Pradesh, where an exciting programme was launched, aimed at the all-round development of the rural masses without neglecting literacy. The Etawah Plan concentrated on projects which were directly relevant to economic development.

As a result of these various experiments and thanks to the promptings of the voluntary organization actively associated with the programme of adult education, Social Education found a place in the five-year developmental plans of the country. Provision was made for establishing literacy centres, community centres, libraries and Janta (People's) Colleges. Social Education was also made an integral part of the community development programme, defined as 'Community uplift through community action'. Social Education included literacy drives, the establishment of libraries, cultural and recreational programmes, the organization of exhibitions, youth activities, radio groups, community centres and women's welfare. Two social education organizers (one man and one woman) were posted in each development zone to take charge of the work. In addition, the State Governments adopted certain other schemes with the assistance of the Federal Government, e.g. the development of school-cum-community centres, intensive educational development (which included 5 model community centres, a library service and a Janta college) and the founding of State, Central and District Libraries.

During the period of the first plan, a sum of rupees * five crores was allocated to the various schemes of Social Education. 67 lacs of adult illiterates were enrolled in literacy classes and 35 lacs* were declared literate after successfully completing the course. 63,000 community centres, 454 social-cum-community centres and 55,000 youth clubs were established. In addition, 100 district libraries were opened or reorganized. Five social education Organizer's Training Centres were established for training field workers.

The Second Plan was more richly endowed, with 15 crores allocated to social education schemes. In addition to centrally based programmes expected to cost Rs. 49·76 lacs, an appropriation of 267·44 lacs was also made for State schemes. Besides the Union and State Ministries of Education, a number of other official agencies such as the community development departments, the Central Social Welfare Board, the Coal Mines Welfare Organization and the Army Education Corps also initiated a number of important ventures in their respective fields. Among the voluntary organizations the Indian Adult Education

* One rupee = 1s. 1d.; 1 crore = 10 millions; 1 lac = 100 thousands.

Association, the Mysore State Adult Education Association, the Bombay City Social Education Committee and the Library House, Lucknow, continued to play an important role in the implementation of various projects.

The Third Plan received still larger allocations. The Central Ministry of Education and Community Development along with the State Governments together allocated rupees 25 crores. Notwithstanding, the percentage of literacy, as revealed by the 1961 census figure, rocketed to 24 per cent from 12 per cent in 1941 and 17 per cent in 1951. Compared with the enormous and widespread attempt to eradicate illiteracy, progress had not been encouraging and the slow rate of advance posed new problems to be studied and solved.

In a world of rapidly developing knowledge of science and technology and the proliferation of new methods and techniques for increasing agricultural and industrial output, a country with 75 per cent of its population illiterate cannot advance very far. The illiterate can neither become useful and progressive farmers nor contribute effectively towards increased industrial production. 'The illiterate army cannot win a war, whether on the battle field or in industries or even in agriculture,' observed the late Mr Shastri on one occasion. Literacy, though not the beginning of adult education nor yet the end of it, is certainly an important something in between. It opens the door to knowledge. The skills of reading and writing are essential if the mass of the people are to gain access to the treasure hidden in books. Unless those adults who are primary producers and wage earners and whose efforts prompt the country forward in its march towards social progress are enabled to derive from books an understanding of their work, tangible results in the field of development cannot be achieved. National and economic development is, therefore, very closely related to the reading and understanding abilities of the adult population.

After 1961, therefore, adult literacy programmes were again accorded high priority. Various experiments on the basis of the whole village mass approach like the *gram shikshan Mohim* have been undertaken for the early eradication of adult illiteracy. Another school of thought favours a selective approach on the basis of professional groups and local community needs. Such experiments are termed as projects for functional literacy either for farmers or for industrial workers. Whatever the approach, the objective is the spread of literacy among as many illiterates as possible with minimum loss of time.

Vital role of voluntary agencies

Thus, one fact stands out clearly – Social Education has been tending to orient itself to goals which are of fundamental importance to a community wherein social change is crucial for further development. That change is all-pervasive and extends from a modification of the social structure to the renunciation of traditionally accepted modes and values. Social relationships and methods of production are both in a state of flux. The role of social education in this complex situation is becoming clearer – it must concentrate upon problems that hinder the process of social change. In other words, it seeks to subvert the status quo in which, to quote one of our former Presidents, Dr Radhakrishanan, 'a few have prospered on the shame and subjection of the many'. In place of the decaying social order, adult education attempts to build a society where equal opportunity for all to grow in freedom and plenty will be ensured. That being the objective of adult education, it does not need much argument to question the validity of the assumptions which have made adult education an official preserve. A movement which must inspire the masses to reconstruct the pattern of their lives can never be sponsored by an administrative machinery which India inherited from an Imperialist master. As against this trend towards official control, there is a growing volume of public opinion, led by the Indian Adult Education Association, which believes that voluntary agencies are a *sine qua non* of a dynamic democratic society.

Voluntary agencies enjoy certain advantages which are of positive help to adult education in so far as its ultimate purpose is concerned. For one thing because voluntary agencies are the projection of popular initiatives and enthusiasm, they can evoke a more sympathetic accord among people than the official agencies. And because voluntary agencies have to thrive solely on the confidence people place in them, they reflect popular sentiment more accurately and adjust themselves to popular needs more aptly. Whether or not Social Education will succeed in this task will depend upon the measure of insight brought to bear by workers and administrators.

The Universities

Twenty years' experience of national independence have caused Indian educators and planners to recognize two basic desiderata for adult education : first, universities and educational institutions must play a dominant role in its promotion and, secondly, a profession of adult educators must emerge in order to integrate adult education into the normal educational system of the country by conceiving education and learning to be a life-long continuing process.

Early in 1964, the Indian Adult Education Association held its Silver Jubilee Conference. After week-long deliberations that conference adopted the following declaration:

'Life-long learning has become the condition of survival in our age.

The integral place of adult education in the life of the people, therefore, brooks no argument any more. The schools, the colleges, the
public libraries and other organized institutions for various types
of adult learning, ranging from literacy to continuing education,
must be recognized as essential components of the provision for
education in the life of the people.'

The Declaration made it clear that knowledge was 'a growing dynamic force in the life of society the world over' – the traditional patterns
of thought and behaviour and old modes of administration and
government can no longer enable the citizens of today to prove equal
to the demands which the impact of technology and industrialization
make on the individual in this era of rapid change.

The Conference decided that a deputation of adult educators should
wait on the Union Education Minister. This it did on 24 March 1964.
The deputation urged the Minister to make a clear-cut statement of
Government policy on adult education and submitted a memorandum
which, *inter alia*, said, 'The Association is convinced that Adult Education should become an integral part of India's educational system
and of its overall economic and social plans, so that all men and women
have opportunities throughout their lives for acquiring, increasing
and renewing useful knowledge and skills, for active and fruitful participation in civic and cultural life and in social and economic development of the country.'

While calling for massive effort to liquidate illiteracy, the memorandum stated that a drive should be launched, 'first of all for the age
group of 18–35. Along with it, adult schools of 9 hours a week for the
age group 11–17, preparing them for a primary course in 12–18
months, should be set up. Along with these schemes of adult schools,
provision should be made for the production of literature for neo-
literates, and for setting up libraries in rural as well as urban areas.'

On the role of universities, the memorandum stated : 'The universities in other countries have assumed and are playing an important role
in the development of adult education in many phases. In India, surprisingly, this field lies almost barren. The evening classes, correspondence courses, extra-mural education, extension lectures, short professional courses and above all research into the problems of adult
education present opportunities to the universities for rendering
valuable service to the society.'

Believing that universities must play a dominant role in the promotion and development of adult education, the Association sent out
an appeal to the universities in India calling upon them to found departments of adult education. Rajasthan was the first university to set
up a full-fledged department of Adult Education. There it was felt

that Jaipur would serve as a model for others to follow once the apathy and opposition had been overcome of those academicians who are indifferent to and ignorant about the work of universities in other countries in the field of adult education.

Simultaneously, the Association began lobbying the University Grants Commission, which then had in Dr Mehta as its Chairman, an outstanding physicist and educationist of vision and imagination. With the support of the UGC and the collaboration of the University of Rajasthan, the Association convened a conference of Vice-Chancellors and university representatives at Bhopal in Central India. The four-day conference began on 5 July 1965. About a dozen Vice-Chancellors attended personally, and another dozen universities sent representatives. The Conference adopted a resolution enjoining the universities in India to 'establish Departments of Adult Education with a comprehensive purpose in order that their services might reach as large a section of the adult population as possible'. The Conference also adopted the following statement:

'The twentieth century has brought out the significance of knowledge as the vital element to sustain, nourish and enforce the civilization of man. It has also put into relief the fact that an individual's capacity for knowledge lasts as long as his health and vigour last. In the first quarter of the century we realized that learning can be life-long. In this third quarter we see that our very survival depends on making learning life-long.

The realization of the close connection of knowledge with civilization and survival has opened up a new perspective to the institutions in society concerned with knowledge. Among these the universities are pre-eminent. The creation of knowledge and the dissemination of advanced knowledge have for centuries been the function of universities. The present time has only added a note of urgency to this function and has provoked a rethinking of the ways in which the university discharges its function. One result of the rethinking has been to abolish the exclusive concern of universities with adolescence and youth. If the times demand that learning has to be life-long the universities must reach out to the adults in the numerous roles they play in society to help them to perform them with greater knowledge, i.e. with greater competence and vision. After World War II this new concept of the University has been accepted all the world over. The Indian universities too have acknowledged this with enthusiasm.

If the modern age has brought out the new importance of knowledge, it has also added to its meaning. We see it equally in the skill of the worker, in the competence of the manager, in the dream of the dreamer. And it is this knowledge, in the fullness of its dimensions, that modern universities have to purvey to men and women occupying various stations in life.'

The Conference further resolved to create an organization for promoting the cause of university Adult Education and appointed a seven-man committee to draft a constitution. Of these seven, four were Vice-Chancellors and the other three were secretaries, respectively of the Education Commission, the Inter-University Board and the Indian Adult Education Association. These committeemen met and drafted a Constitution which has now been accepted and has resulted in the formation of the University Adult Education Association. 43 universities have already joined hands to work for the movement. Actual programmes, however, have yet to take shape.

The present position of adult education work in the universities is as follows. Out of over seventy universities in India only three have established special departments, namely, Mysore, Poona and Rajasthan. Delhi University has a Directorate of Correspondence Courses and Continuing Education.

The Chancellor of Mysore University, the late Highness Sir Krishnaraja Wadiyer, then Maharaja of Mysore, declared at the very first meeting of the Senate after the establishment of the University in 1916 that:

'Our University will also be engaged in diffusing knowledge among the section of my people, who for various reasons may not be able to participate in the course and discipline approved for regular examinations. It is with this object that the scheme provides for the establishment of an Extension and Publication Department.'

Little was done, however, up to 1932, when the University Teachers' Association was formed and the work was undertaken by them. Regular extension lecture courses are conducted and subsequently published under the title of 'University Extension Lecture Hand-Book Series'. Their range is wide, covering topics on literature, philosophy, science, engineering, technology, medicine and public health.

The University of Poona began its adult education work in 1948 when it established a Board of Extra-Mural Studies. The work of the Board consists of popular lectures and the arrangement of summer schools, adult education courses and similar courses of instruction. The vastness of the population which it serves has caused it to adopt as a policy the establishment of extra-mural centres only in towns with a population of 10,000 or more. These centres are managed by small communities which operate in accordance with rules laid down by the Board of Extra-Mural Studies. The annual syllabus consists of short courses of three to six lectures, summer and winter schools for primary

AENB L

and secondary school teachers and other selected persons with similar educational qualifications, and Extra-Mural camps. The Board also publishes popular books and pamphlets. So far 17 books and 31 pamphlets have appeared.

The third university with a department of adult education is Rajasthan, which is receiving assistance from Canadian advisors. Established in 1963, the Department has arranged a number of lecture courses and has conducted a few research studies into adult education problems. The conception of the functions of the department in Rajasthan is wider than in Mysore and Poona Universities which confine themselves to the dissemination of knowledge through extension courses and publications. The University of Rajasthan intends to devote much of its attention to courses for professional groups and community leaders. From the academic session beginning 1967–8 it also started a one-year diploma course in Adult Education for adult education workers.

The financial assistance given by the U G C for extra-mural work has enabled a number of other universities to arrange programmes of adult education. The University of Delhi has an Extension Lecture Board which has been organizing extension lectures in different parts of the capital. From the current year the Extension Lecture Board has merged with the Directorate of Correspondence Courses which has been renamed the Directorate for Correspondence Courses and Continuing Education. This department has quite a large coverage and thousands of adults from all over the country are taking advantage of its correspondence facilities. Extension lectures continue as before.

It will thus be seen that the newly formed University Adult Education Association has a heavy programme on its hands and that much effort will be required before adult education programmes take root in all the universities.

Future prospects

I have been describing the main changes that are taking place in the field of adult education. What of the future? I can do no better than to quote from a vital document, *The Report on Social Education*, prepared by a study team constituted by the Committee on Plan Projects, Planning Commission, Government of India. The report affirms:

'It is necessary that Social Education must be carried on by a dynamic agency and should have adequate financial resources. This agency must reflect the urges of the people, should be responsible to them and thus be able to evoke sympathetic response from them. It should be flexible and be able to adjust its policies and methods of work to the rapidly changing needs of the people and the nation. It

should also be able to experiment with new ideas and be able to dis-
card programmes which have not yielded worthwhile results.'
and continues:

'We are of the view that only an autonomous agency can fulfill the
above requirements. We, therefore, recommend as follows:

1. A central Board of Social Education may be set up to advise on
   planning and execution of the programmes of social education,
   to co-ordinate them and to lay down standards at different levels.
2. The aims and objectives of the Board would be:
   (a) creating public opinion for social education,
   (b) encouraging formation of voluntary organizations,
   (c) taking effective steps to see that social education program-
       mes are adequately financed,
   (d) securing public participation,
   (e) laying down standards for qualitative improvement of the
       various programmes of social education,
   (f) encouraging the promotion of supporting services of social
       education, such as production of literature, carrying out
       research, training, etc.,
   (g) establishing co-ordination in social education work being
       carried on by different Ministries, State Departments, and
       voluntary agencies.
3. Similar Boards should be set up at the State, Taluka (District)
   and Panchayat (Borough) levels.
4. This Board should have independent staff capable of enthusing
   people for launching a movement which will not only bring
   light and learning to the people but will bring about a change in
   their way of life.
5. As a first step to the setting up of an autonomous organization,
   we would suggest that an Advisory Board on Social Education
   may be set up whose advice, by convention, should be given due
   weight and, if there are no insuperable difficulties, should be
   treated as binding on all concerned. This advisory Board could
   help in creating an order in the jungle of administrative *laissez
   faire* prevailing now in the country.
6. This Board may be constituted by the Ministry of Education in
   consultation with the concerned Ministries and State Governments. The Union Education Minister should be the Chairman
   of the Board. The Board should have representatives of the
   Planning Commission, of various Ministries of the Government
   of India dealing with social education, the National Council of
   Educational Research and Training, State Governments and
   Union Territories, important voluntary agencies of standing in

the field of social (adult) education, of the University Grants Commission and the Inter-University Board. Some prominent persons in the field of social education should also be nominated on the Board.

7. The Board should have a separate administrative machinery to be provided by the Ministry of Education. It should have a whole-time Secretary.

8. Besides, it should have a small study unit consisting of 3 – 5 experts who will survey the position from time to time and pose issues for consideration by the Board.

9. The Board should constitute separate Committee for dealing with such important aspects of social education as literacy, production of literature for neo-literates, promotion of libraries, etc. These committees should have the right to co-opt members.'

The above Statement relates to the organizational pattern suggested for the more effective and fruitful working of the movement. As far as programmes are concerned, a major shift in the pattern is now needed. With the new stress on linking literacy with functional competence and the development of abilities and skills for increasing production and earnings, the mass approach to literacy is neither desirable nor necessary. Literacy programmes ought to be conducted for selected groups of people and with a particular purpose in view. This will involve changes in organization, methods and techniques. The materials needed for implementing the programmes both for reading and for using as supportive services also have to be developed and produced.

The imparting of literacy skill has now to be project-oriented and accompanied by actual work. This needs greatly inherited skills and learning on the part of not only teachers but also supervisors. More vigorous efforts to produce literature, equipment and material and to train workers is also called for.

This is the shift that relates to programmes of adult education for technical-productions skills, whether on the farm or in the industrial units. These skills have to be developed in the adult farmers and the industrial workers. Beyond the category of adult illiterates, however, there is a large number of people that need continuing education for better prospects in their future careers. The establishment of regular evening schools or correspondence courses for continuing education provides the answer to their problem. This is another dimension in the scheme of Adult Education that calls for greater attention in the years to come.

The concept of life-long integrated education is yet another area to be pursued vigorously. It is felt that the concept is of special significance at this stage of India's development. The terminal concept of education is totally inadequate in the present social, economic, and technological context. In static societies, when a man's tasks in life and the challenges he faced conformed to a predictable pattern and a slow pace of change, the terminal view of education seemed all right. The equipment that education provided during adolescence and youth gave the limited foundations required to perform jobs, to take decisions, to determine social relationships and to seek self expression. Today, however, education terminating at a particular age and designed to be self-contained is a poor foundation for the future and does not give the stimulus that can last throughout a lifetime. It is an inherent limitation of the terminal view of education that whatever improvements in educational methods and institutions may be attempted (as they have no doubt been proposed and sometimes implementted), they cannot overcome this limitation.

The explosion of knowledge following discoveries, scientific inventions and the refinement of technology, is the primary cause of this inadequacy because much of the information gathered in terminal education soon becomes out of date. Other notable factors like the breakdown of traditions and customs, acceptance of parliamentary democracy, democratization of social and cultural life, increased availability of labour, movements of population, changes in the composition of the intelligentsia and the disappearance of religion as an educational force, have demonstrated the impossibility for the average man of leading a life without a chain of frustrations.

This is not all. The adult has to play many roles in his lifetime. He is a wage earner, member of a family, a citizen, a social being, and a seeker of inner and aesthetic satisfaction. In the past social and cultural values regulated men's conduct, behaviour, and activities through religion and customs. Today that framework is gone and regulation by political institutions and social codes touches only a fraction of man's personality. Should not education attempt to provide his moorings in this situation? But at present it seems powerless to do so since a system of terminal education cannot be a force for the integration of the various facets of the human personality.

Integrated education is thus a horizontal process to cover the various facets of a man's life and the spectrum of his interests, just as lifelong education is a vertical process comprising inter-related phases of pre-adult formal education in schools and colleges, and adult exposure to various kinds of training opportunities and a learning environment. The two are essential components of the one concept of lifelong integrated education. This new concept needs to be tried out in practice on a pilot project basis and we in India are asking UNESCO to move from theory to practice.

8. The Philippines

ARTEMIO C. VIZCONDE

History

Adult education in the Philippines has passed through several distinct stages in the process of meeting the problems and needs of the adult population to which the various changes that have taken place in the socio-economic and political development of the country have given rise.[1] These stages will be discussed briefly.

The inauguration of the Philippine Assembly in 1907 is an important landmark in the political history of the country. Act No. 1829, passed by the Philippine Assembly on 21 May 1908, provided for a system of popular civico-educational lectures to be conducted in the municipalities, principally in the barrios. On 4 December 1914, Act No. 2424 was passed amending Act No. 1829. This law placed upon municipal teachers responsibility for arranging lectures to be delivered on specified days of the week. The giving of lectures, however, suffered a lull between 1921 and 1932. On 18 February 1933, Act No. 4046 was passed providing for the holding of community assemblies. It also provided for the planning, control and preparation of lectures for the community assemblies. Thus, the community assembly movement was born.

After the inauguration of the Commonwealth of the Philippines, Commonwealth Act No. 80 was passed creating the Office of Adult Education. This Act enumerated, among other things, the duties of the Office, defined its objectives, and furnished funds for its operation. The aims of adult education as prescribed in this Act were 'to eliminate illiteracy and to give vocational and citizenship training to adult citizens' as an implementation of the Constitutional mandate which stated that '...the government shall establish and maintain a complete and adequate system of public education, and shall provide at least free primary education, and citizenship training to adult citizens'.[2] Adult education was carried on under the direction of this Office up to the outbreak of the Pacific War in 1941 and again immediately after liberation.

About a year after the inauguration of the Republic of the Philippines, the Office of Adult Education was converted, by virtue of

Executive Order No. 94, dated 4 October 1947, into a division of the Bureau of Public Schools. The newly created division was named the Division of Adult Education, later changed to the Adult and Community Education Division in order to reflect its expanded programme of activities. In face of new problems and needs, the Bureau had to redefine its aims. These aims, which reflect the philosophy of the adult education movement in the Philippines, are:

1. The immediate objective of adult education is the eradication of illiteracy and the promotion of better ways of life for those of the population who have not yet received the benefits of education.
2. The broader, long-range objective shall be the improvement of community life in all its aspects, through the provision of vocational, recreational, social, and other educational opportunities for adults to make themselves more efficient citizens.[3]

The emphasis laid on education for better living has led to the growth of indigenous practices involving the integration of child and adult education programmes. The expansion of this educational programme stems from the following concept of the community school:[4]

'The community school is one whose programme is aimed at promoting the optimumgrow th and development of the school child, giving basic education to the out-of-school youths and adults, and helping effect improvement in all aspects of community living.'

Recognizing the vital role of the community school in the total programme of community development, the Board of National Education made the following statement of policy:[5]

'The Board adopts as one of its basic policies the development of a sound, practical and continuing community school programme as a vital instrument for community development .The programme of the community school shall give special attention to the out-of-school children and youth who must be provided with at least fundamental education.'

In the light of the philosophy of the community school and of the policy of the Board of National Education stated above, the public schools serve as the machinery for the promotion of the adult and community education movement in the Philippines. The concept of the community school aims at the realisation of a tri-pronged objective – (1) promoting the optimum growth and development of the school child, (2) giving basic education to the out-of-school youths and adults, and (3) helping effect improvement in community living. With this concept adult and community education becomes an integral phase of the community school programme and, therefore, the public schools give equal emphasis to the implementation of each of the three objectives.

Programmes

In conformity with the aims of adult education, the Adult and Community Education Division of the Bureau of Public Schools offers two distinct but interrelated programmes, viz. (1) the programme on functional literacy, and (2) the programme on continuing education. These two courses cover the two main areas of adult education in the Philippines.

1. *Functional literacy* (*basic curriculum*). The functional literacy programme[6] includes the following subjects:

a. Reading and writing. This subject includes the development of the ability to read and write simple messages and brief personal letters and notes; to read and understand vernacular newspapers and easy reading books; and to understand the meaning and use of commercial and business instruments such as paper money, money orders, cheques, public advertisements, and notices. Emphasis is laid on legibility and the correct use of capital letters and punctuation.

b. Arithmetic computation. This includes simple arithmetic problems related to market deals, prices of prime commodities, cost of materials, products of farm and industrial business, household purchases and ordinary family transactions.

c. Health and sanitation. This includes the development of essential skills, practices, and attitudes related to home sanitation, such as proper installation and use of toilets, proper disposal of garbage, proper construction of drainage, better home arrangement, and closer co-operation in community health activities.

d. Citizenship. This includes activities that encourage the participation of the adults in community projects. It gives emphasis to the acquisition of basic knowledge about such matters as the obligations and duties of citizens, local ordinances and government policies, tax regulations, payments, peace and order.

e. Vocations and industries. This subject is intended to provide the adult student with essential knowledge of the vocations and industries available in the locality and to arouse in them a desire to engage in gainful economic activities.

The functional literacy programme is carried out through the organized literacy classes and very rarely through the 'Each-One-Teach-One' scheme taught by teachers and volunteer workers.

2. *Continuing education for adults and out-of-school youth*. The programme of continuing education is an extension service offered to out-of-school youths and adults, who wish to improve their ability or increase their competence in the vocational, social, and other fields of

human endeavour. The continuing education programme generally includes courses in the following:

a. Cultural or personal enrichment
b. Vocational development
c. Practical crafts
d. Health and safety education
e. Parent and home and family education
f. Civic and citizenship education
g. Women's education
h. Workers' education

That list of courses is far from complete and all-embracing. It serves merely as a guide to all adult education workers in curriculum building.

It is fully realised that no one adult education teacher can deal with all the courses listed, so that the need for a co-operative effort on the part of all responsible leaders in the community is imperative. Someone else may know better what instruction adults need in order to become better citizens.

In places where regular classes cannot possibly be organized, the continuing education programme may be conducted through study-discussion groups, seminars, workshops, and work conferences. Local resources and the services of competent persons in the government or private employment are liberally made use of. Veterinarians, agronomists, physicians, treasurers, and many others participate in the continuing education programme.

Methods

In promoting adult and community education, the Bureau of Public Schools resorts to the following approaches:

a. *Adult and community education through the school curriculum.* One of the most effective means of attaining the objectives of adult and community education is through the school curriculum. The curriculum approach is an attempt to effect changes in people's attitudes and way of life and improve community living through functional classroom instruction. The needs, problems, interests, and resources of the community as revealed by surveys are used to enrich the curricular offerings and vitalize the teaching-learning process. The knowledge, skills and abilities acquired by the pupils and students are carried over to the classroom work or studies. This process of gearing classroom experiences to the community strengthens the acquisition of the basic tools of learning. It also enables the learners to become active participants in the life of their community.

The curriculum approach is used effectively for adult and community education by involving the children, out-of-school youths, parents, and other adults in : (1) surveys of the needs, problems, interests and resources of the community which will serve as the bases of the objectives of the resource and teaching units; (2) the formulation and development of resource and teaching units; (3) the study of the solutions of problems considered in the resource and teaching units; (4) the culminating activities of the units which may include the formulation of plans for launching action projects in the homes and in the community; (5) the actual performance of the action projects in which knowledge, skills, habits, and appreciations developed in the classroom are called into practical use; and (6) the evaluation of the end-results of teaching-learning activities in which the participants experience thinking and working together as a practical lesson in the ways of democracy.

The curriculum approach is an effective way of causing co-ordinated interaction between school and the community and between the child and the adult. Community action projects become outgrowths of the classroom teaching-learning process, thereby strengthening educational experiences among the participants.

The curriculum approach as described above is an application of the following ideas which are basic in the implementation of the community school programme:

1. The children are continuously being given educational experiences in the school and in their homes and communities – utilizing as much as possible all the available human, technological, institutional, and material resources for the enrichment of learning activities. As the child participates more actively in home and community life, he acquires a sense of community living.

2. The adults are increasingly drawn into the planning of the instructional programme and other activities of the school based on the interests, needs, and problems of the community.

3. Direct and specific efforts are being made by the school in the person of its school staff, students, and pupils to encourage and help local inhabitants to play an active part in community education and development.

4. The community school builds the curriculum around the interests, needs and problems of the homes. Community surveys are made not only to enrich and stimulate classroom instruction but also to discover problems that may need immediate solution and promote awareness and concerted effort on the part of the community.

5. The community-school service programme is an out-growth of classroom instruction. It provides work experiences for the child-

ren and students in and out of school, thus promoting integrative activities between the school and the community.

b. *Adult and community education through the extension services of the school.* The community school renders extension services directly to the community for the improvement of community living. These services are in the form of (1) demonstrations, (2) community assemblies and forums, (3) study sessions, (4) organized literacy classes, (5) folk schools and evening classes, (6) mass education through audio-visual aids, radio broadcasts, etc., (7) library and museum facilities, (8) field trips and intervisitations, (9) barrio fairs, and (10) home industry centres. Such school-to-the-community services are usually rendered with the assistance of the various community agencies both public and private.

One alarming fact about Philippine education is the high percentage of young people who are out of school. According to the Swanson Survey Report, of 2,192,000 youths ranging in age from 13 to 16, only 392,768 are in either public or private secondary schools. In other words, 1,800,132 youths or 82·69 per cent of those who should be in the high school are not in attendance.

Various schemes have been tried by different agencies to provide education for the out-of-school youth. One of these is the opening of folk schools. Starting with only three folk schools which operated during the summer vacation of 1961 in Bayambang (Pangasinan), Gapan (Nueva Ecija), and Morong (Rizal), with an enrolment of 297 students, there were during the summer vacation of 1966 twenty-seven such folk schools with an enrolment of 1,871 students in 176 classes.

The folk schools are in session for nine weeks. These nine weeks coincide with the summer vacation period. Because the regular classes are not in session, the facilities of the school in buildings, equipment, and sites are available for the use of the folk school students. It has been reported that several students who completed the nine-week courses of the folk schools decided to continue their studies in the regular high school. Other graduates of the folk schools have started money-earning projects of their own.

Another approach to meet the problems of the out-of-school youth is the opening of evening classes. This provision is particularly made by the Division of City Schools in Manila. Several large high schools are offering the regular secondary school course to boys and girls who for various reasons are not able to attend the regular day classes. The general secondary curriculum of four years has been redesigned such that the required courses can be completed during the period of five years. Ten high schools offer these evening academic classes. These students range in age from 16 to 26 years old. In addition, five big secondary schools in Manila with well-equipped vocational shops are offering vocational and technical courses at night to the out-of-school youth. Among the courses offered are dress-making, foods and cookery, secretarial, hand and machine embroidery, automotive, sheet metal work, general electricity, stenography, radio electronics, men's tailoring, commercial arts and graphic arts, photography, and drafting. Other cities are following the example set by Manila. In these cities, there are also evening classes for the out-of-school youth. Among the courses offered are dress-making and nutrition.

c. *Adult and community education through working with local community organizations and service agencies.* Adult and community education is the concern of all. It thrives best when whole communities participate in the programme. Realising this fact, the community school creates opportunities to draw the people into the programme. One such opportunity is through community organization.

A decade of experience with community education led to the discovery of the 'little democracy' locally called *pook* or *purok*. The 'purok' is one of the functioning units of the community school. It is composed of closely associated households numbering from 20 to 50 families, who all engage in activities for their own good and advancement. The organization of each 'purok' is based on democratic processes. The scheme develops a sense of responsibility in group living and group action among the 'purok' members. Each 'purok' is organized for self-help. It is through the 'purok' organizations that communities are helped to discover their resources and bring to their attention the technique by which all citizens can be brought together to think and work out effective solutions to their own problems.

With creative leadership and the reasonable support and co-operation of other agencies, the 'purok' organization contributes significantly to the development of community living. Problem-study committees, composed of purok members, are created to study and resolve problems in connection with the promotion of literacy, economic productivity, good health, recreation, moral and spiritual values, and citizenship. Problems requiring services and technical aids from outside agencies are usually referred to existing agencies for action. A few of the agencies have representatives who serve as consultants and resource persons in the study committees.

Besides organizing puroks, the community school helps stimulate all the community agencies such as the PTA and barrio councils, as well as civic and religious groups, to participate in the promotion of the programme of adult and community education. Through such stimulation, favourable interaction and co-operation are made possible and the potentialities of each agency are drawn to co-ordinate and help lay out one integrated programme for the solution of some of the major problems of the community.

d. *Adult education through the radio*. Radio has been referred to as the university of the air for many of our people. Realising this, the Bureau of Public Schools conducts a radio broadcast in Philipino every Sunday afternoon from 5.45 to 6.00 p.m. over Stations DZRP, VOA, DZAS in Manila, and over Stations DYBU in Cebu City, DXRP in Davao City, and DZEQ in Baguio City.

The topics which are presented to the listening public in dramatized form cover four main areas of living – personal and environmental health, parent education, education for better citizenship, and education for better livelihood.

To utilize more effectively the educational radio broadcasts the organization of listening-discussion groups is encouraged. The home-room PTAS, school PTAS, 'purok' organizations and other organized clubs form such listening-discussion groups. The meetings are scheduled to coincide with the Sunday broadcasts, and immediately after each broadcast a discussion based on the subject matter of the broadcast is conducted. The success or failure of the radio broadcast as an educational activity hinges mainly on the interest and efforts exerted by teachers in organizing the listening groups, in providing strong motives for adults to listen to the broadcasts and in participating actively in the discussions that follow.

Beginning with the school year 1967–8 adult education through the radio has been expanded to include another course broadcast every Monday, Wednesday and Friday, from 4.30 to 4.45 in the afternoon. The course consists of 12 lessons and each broadcast is designed as a complete lesson. At the end of the series, all the adult students who listen to all the programmes and discussion sessions that follow each broadcast are awarded certificates of attendance. Courses offered are on Citizenship, Health, Food Production, and other subject matter of special interest to adults.

Administration and supervision of the programme

Since the conversion in 1947 of the Office of Adult Education into the Division of Adult Education, now Adult and Community Education Division, the programme has been greatly expanded and the number of staff correspondingly increased.

To carry out effectively the functions of the Division, four sections have been established, namely : (1) Promotion Section, (2) Leadership Training Section, (3) Research and Evaluation Section, and (4) Curriculum and Publication Section. Each section is headed by a section chief who is responsible for the working efficiency of the personnel and the accomplishment of the tasks assigned to the section.

The four sections of the Division perform the following specific functions:

A. *Promotion* (Literacy and Continuing Education)

1. Helps maintain direction and interest in the programme of adult and community education;
2. Helps upgrade the general level of education among the people, particularly the out-of-school youths and adults;
3. Helps promote socio-economic development through the promotion of:
   a. functional literacy,
   b. active citizenship,
   c. a better livelihood,
   d. health and sanitation,
   e. the socio-cultural aspects of home and community living,
   f. a better moral and spiritual life;
4. Helps stimulate and organize effective neighbourhood and international relations;
5. Helps promote community organizations and encourage the active participation of and close collaboration among government and non-government agencies for the promotion of adult and community education;
6. Works and co-operates with all the promotional divisions of the Bureau of Public Schools in the implementation of the total educational programme;
7. Devises techniques, methods, and approaches for the promotion of the education of the out-of-school youth and adults;
8. Utilizes radio and television and other mass communication media in the promotion of adult and community education; and
9. Assists all schools at different levels in formulating and launching a workable action programme of adult and community education.

B. *Training Section*

1. Assists teacher training institutions in developing a course in Adult Education that is practical and up to date;
2. Promotes in-service education activities for administrators, teachers and lay people and helps them acquire skill and competence in:
   a. organizing literacy classes;
   b. organizing other activities for adults and out-of-school youths and
   c. organizing parent and other adult discussion groups.

3. Works with other promotional divisions in upgrading the supervisory service of general office supervisors;
4. Helps develop professional and lay leadership for community education;
5. Trains adult education workers in the use of specific methods, techniques and approaches, and in the use of audio-visual equipment, etc.; and
6. Renders consultant service and technical assistance that may be needed in the field by both government and non-government agencies in the promotion of their leadership training activities.

c. *Curriculum and Publication Section*

1. Promotes the development of the curriculum for adults and out-of-school youths;
2. Helps evaluate reading materials for further improvement;
3. Draws from available researches data on different vocations as a basis for improving the curriculum offerings for adults;
4. Improves and up-dates old reading materials for adults;
5. Writes new reading materials of current interest for adults in the form of books, brochures, pamphlets, newsletters, etc.;
6. Writes and publishes materials for the professional growth of adult education workers;
7. Prepares teaching guides for adult education teachers;
8. Translates reading materials for adults in Philippine dialects, especially in the eight major ones;
9. Takes charge of printing and reprinting reading and instructional materials for adults; and
10. Keeps record of all office publications and prepares and administers plans of distribution of reading materials, teaching guides, and supplies for adults.

D. *Research and Evaluation Section*

1. Helps evaluate reading materials for further improvement;
2. Conducts researches on different vocations with a view to improving the curriculum offerings for adults;
3. Conducts surveys of and studies on local resources as a basis for the preparation of new materials to enrich adult and community education;
4. Evaluates old reading materials for adults and out-of-school youths;
5. Conducts studies on the problems of youth;
6. Devises instruments for the evaluation of youth and adult education programmes;

7. Initiates and conducts surveys to determine the extent and distribution of illiteracy among adults and out-of-school youth;
8. Devises and constructs literacy tests for adults to determine the extent of their proficiency in the 3 R's;
9. Evaluates accomplishment and progress on the implementation of the programme of adult and community education; and
10. Prepares statistics and data on various activities that have been undertaken in the pursuance of the programme goals.

Staffing

To ensure the effective implementation of the adult and community education programme in the field, community and adult education supervisors with the rank of division or city supervisors are assigned to provincial and city school divisions. They are responsible for the formulation, launching, implementation and evaluation of the programme at the provincial or city level. They supervise the different schools; conduct in-service education programmes on adult and community education for school officials and teachers; help in the organization of 'purok' and other community organizations; assist the barrio councils in planning and carrying out their development projects; foster close co-ordination among local agencies for the promotion of the total adult and community education programme; and help in the development and deployment of lay leadership.

In some provincial and city school divisions, adult and community education teacher-co-ordinators have been appointed in order to help implement the programme. They organize and teach adult education classes and promote adult education directly by : designing and developing adult education projects that meet the needs and interests of the adults and out-of-school youth; initiating and conducting researches and surveys and keeping up-to-date statistics on adult and community education; working with the barrio councils in organizing and holding community assemblies; assuming actual leadership in all aspects of the adult and community education programme; and demonstrating or helping to demonstrate accepted approaches, methods, and techniques in adult and community education. As co-ordinators they help develop, through effective public relations, harmonious relationships between the school and other community organizations and service agencies such as purok organizations, parent-teacher associations and women's clubs etc.; establish and maintain close co-ordination between the public schools and other agencies, both public and private, in promoting community development programmes; and help integrate and promote closer articulation of adult and community education with other levels of education –

elementary, secondary, and tertiary.

Through the Philippine community schools, all adult and community education supervisors, on the national and local levels, teacher-co-ordinators and teachers, are seeking to strengthen the curriculum and extension service programmes of the schools.

Finance

Commonwealth Act No. 80, passed by the Philippine National Assembly, created the Office of Adult Education and provided among other things the funds for its operations. Since 4 October 1967, however, when the Division of Adult Education became a division under the Bureau of Public Schools, the appropriation for adult education has been part of the annual budget of the Bureau.

In addition to the annual appropriations for adult education, local government agencies, civic, religious, and fraternal organizations contribute their share to the clubs; religious groups and masonic bodies set aside a portion of their funds for the operation of literacy classes. Purok organizations, barrio councils, and PTAS not only donate labour and materials but also give money to finance community development projects. All these community agencies contribute in no small measure to the support of the adult and community education programme.

Problems

The public schools have made a major contribution to the socio-economic development of the country through their adult education activities. Nevertheless, the programme is still beset with a host of problems, some of which are now considered:

1. *Finance*. Although the annual appropriation for adult education has been substantially increased since the Division of Adult and Community Education was made a part of the Bureau of Public Schools in 1947, the funds allotted to it are still considered very meagre to meet the problem of making literate over 5,000,000 illiterates. Added to this number of illiterates are one and a half million out-of-school youths between the ages of 14 and 17 who do not attend any secondary school. From this age-group come the juvenile delinquents who are increasingly a menace to present-day society. To these two groups should also be added the millions of adults who, despite their previous training, need to be given some form of continuing education in order to cope with the challenges posed by an ever-changing society.

Shown below are the annual appropriations covering a period of five years which have been available to the Adult Community Education Division for the operation of its programme:

1962–3	P417,859.00[7]
1963–4	426,964.00
1964–5	397,766.00
1965–6	397,766.00
1966–7	376,892.00

If one takes the highest appropriation of P426,964.00 in 1963–4 and divides it by the number of illiterates, the average appropriation per illiterate would amount to only a little more than P.08. This, indeed, is insufficient to meet the needs of the expanding programme of adult education.

2. *Staffing.* At present, thirteen school divisions do not have community adult education supervisors for lack of resources. Similarly, there are also no definite items in the plantilla for community adult education teacher-co-ordinators as suggested in Memorandum No. 22, s. 1966. The present ones are merely designated to serve in that capacity and do so on a part-time basis. For the programme to be effective, it is necessary to provide an adult and community education teacher-co-ordinator in every complete elementary school. To avoid too much financial strain on the government, this scheme could be introduced gradually starting first on the district level and later on in every school, until all schools have been allocated a co-ordinator.

3. *Reading materials.* The Philippines has eight major dialects and about eighty or so minor ones. To provide basic reading materials for the eight dialects alone will require, according to recent estimates, about P10,000,000.00. In view of the meagre appropriations for adult education mentioned previously, the problem is both gigantic and challenging, and further compounded by the fact that for purposes of educating adults the reading materials should be varied and frequently changed in order to reflect rapidly changing conditions in each locality.

4. *Communications.* According to the Census of the Philippines in 1960, most of the illiterates and out-of-school youth live in the rural areas. One reason why they cannot pursue their studies is the lack of mobility caused by bad roads. Thus, the conditions which encourage the acquisition of literacy skills are practically non-existent. For adult education personnel and voluntary workers, the lack of communications is a discouragement to penetrate remote areas which can hardly be reached even on foot. Unless the government becomes really serious about its programme of road and bridge building, specifically in the rural areas, this situation will continue greatly to hamper the full realisation of the objectives of adult education.

5. *Teachers.* Another problem caused by the multitude of dialects in the country is that some teachers assigned to the rural areas do not speak the local dialect and therefore find difficulty in establishing the

right climate for the promotion of a better relationship between the instructor and the adult students, who tend to regard their prospective instructors with suspicion and unease. The problem of human relations is further aggravated by the fact that most teachers are trained in English and think in English.

6. *Involvement.* Adult education is the concern of all. The school should not be left alone to carry out the objectives of the national and local programme. However, the resources of other agencies, both governmental and non-governmental, have not yet been as fully tapped as they should be and in several places the schools are still the only agencies educating adults.

Though adult education in the Philippines is beset with many problems, the public school system, on which the main responsibility falls, is nevertheless moving rapidly towards the realisation of a broader concept of adult education by helping to turn out patriotic citizens who are socially, vocationally, morally, spiritually, and physically efficient.

NOTES AND REFERENCES

1. Amado Agorrilla, *Adult Education in the Philippines*, Manila 1952, pp 1–5.
2. Section 5, Article xiv, *Constitution of the Philippines*.
3. *Report of the UNESCO Consultative Educational Mission to the Philippines*, Paris, unesco 1949, p 36.
4. *BPS Memorandum No. 89*, s. 1956.
5. Section 9, Article ii, *The Revised Philippine Educational Programme*.
6. Bureau of Public Schools, *Functional Literacy in the Philippines*, Manila, Bureau of Printing 1956, pp 56–57.
7. The peso is worth 2/- approximately.

9. The South Pacific Territories

KEVIN J. FLYNN

History

Some 20,000 islands dot the Pacific but the Ocean is so vast that a modern jet may fly for hours without ever sighting a single island. In the immensity of water the land area of the island is relatively small, being something less than half a million square miles, of which New Guinea accounts for no less than 90 per cent.

The islands of the south seas have never been the idyllic lands of fiction. There were already rivalries and bloody quarrels before the European whalers, traders, sandalwooders, black-birders and adventurers arrived to set *vavusa* aganst *vavusa*, village against village, and chief against chief for their own ends and to impose further strains on the traditional society. Diseases introduced from Europe also took their toll. It has been estimated that in the thirty years between 1875 and 1905 the Fijian population alone was reduced from some 200,000 to less than 90,000 people.

The European powers showed a general reluctance to undertake territorial responsibilities in the Pacific but the behaviour of their nationals could not be controlled without territorial authority and so the Pacific islands were distributed among them as cessions, annexations or protectorates. Though bringing some measure of order and security to the harassed islanders, colonial rule encouraged the growth of trade and the introduction of European customs. As the urban areas expanded and attracted people from the villages, so the villages themselves lost something of that social cohesiveness which had formerly made them resistant to social change.

Change came slowly however between the two world wars except where there were unusual circumstances, such as in Fiji where Indian immigrants developed a cane sugar industry. In the outer islands and remote villages, people lived much as they had for centuries. After the Second World War the rate of change accelerated. Many of the islands had been fought over – New Guinea, the Solomons, Gilberts, Marshalls and Marianas; the others, as bases for the Allied powers, saw the tremendous material power that could be marshalled for destruction. The social consciences of the more affluent nations, spurred on by the

United Nations, endorsed the expenditure of increasing sums of money on economic development, health services and education. More schools, agricultural and public health programmes, organized marketing and better transport began to change the normal pattern of island life.

The impact of the modern world on the South Pacific peoples was ably summarized by High Chief Sotoa in a paper presented to the Fourth South Pacific Conference at Rabaul in 1959. He cited the following changes in American Samoa as fairly typical of what was happening in the Pacific:

1. The extended family now aspired to raise standards of living in terms of money, clothing, radios, cars, refrigerators and other modern conveniences, rather than in ceremonial fine mats and the size of taro plantations.
2. Workers tended to move from villages to live in close proximity to places of employment, e.g. canning works. Problems of water and sanitation then arose in crowded and sub-standard living conditions.
3. Juvenile delinquency increased because children did not have the usual village chores to keep them busy. There was also less supervision when mothers worked.
4. Education tended to widen the gap between parents and children.
5. Individuals and families became more autonomous and resisted the communal authority with its demands on the person or family to share possessions.
6. The social security offered by the traditional social system for the aged, blind, helpless and orphaned tended to be regarded as a government responsibility.

The conference itself felt that change was inevitable and that steps should be taken to mitigate the effects of such change. The role of education was all important. Education in the Pacific began with the Christian missions and it is hardly possible to consider any aspect of educational practice without looking at their past efforts or their present influence on educational development.

It was coincidental that the invasion of the Pacific by Europeans took place about the same time as a missionary revival in Britain, for in 1796 the London Missionary Society, founded by Congregationalists, Methodists, Presbyterians and Anglicans, decided that its first band of missionaries should go to the South Seas. They came, of course, to Christianize the islanders and they also tried, with rather less success, to regenerate the Europeans for whose sins they sometimes paid with their lives. However, neither persecution, privation nor the active opposition of the traders blunted their persistence and by 1850 there was scarcely an island of any size that had not seen missionary endeavour by one religion or another.

Generally speaking, no dramatic success crowned their efforts, although from time to time the conversion of a chief was followed by the mass conversion of his people. Communication was the missionaries' first problem and they entered the field of education when, in addition to learning the vernacular themselves, they began to teach their metropolitan language to some of the early converts who showed a desire to preach the gospel to their brethren. These selected people, in addition to religious instruction, often learnt the rudiments of reading and writing as well and so the missionary became a teacher as well as a priest. This was only the beginning, for all denominations realised the importance of providing schools for the children since they could, by this means, more easily establish their religious beliefs and practices among the rising generation. Women's groups were also established, and although they had a strong religious bias, child care and homecrafts, particularly sewing, were usually introduced by the missionary's wife or a lay worker. As the need for churches, schools and living quarters grew, so did the necessity for tradesmen. The Pacific islanders were generally skilful builders in their own tradition but needed instruction in European techniques and this was and still is provided by on-the-job training given by mission carpenters.

While this sort of adult education – religious classes for adults, women's clubs and on-the-job tradesman training – was provided by the missionaries, the very fact that the churches entered the elementary and later the secondary field of education militated against any organized central control of adult education, for government control of education was by and large a post-war phenomenon and there were considerable difficulties inherent in establishing common standards and reasonably uniform levels of instruction when there were so many independent educational agencies operating throughout the islands.

In Papua-New Guinea there were, in late 1967, 82,304 children in government schools and 137,984[1] in non-government schools. Those in non-government schools could have been in schools conducted by any one of about 30 religious organizations. In Fiji there were, in 1965, 40 government schools in a total of 592 registered schools. The others were run by twenty-four different committees, church, company and other agencies.[2] In the British Solomon Islands Protectorate there were 6 government schools and 390 schools operated by other agencies.[3]

In such situations, common throughout the Pacific, the Education Departments were so busily concerned in co-ordinating the work of the agencies, as well as establishing secondary schools and teachers' colleges, that the development of adult education sections within the Departments was necessarily of late growth and the specific results of the practical Adult Education desired by the Fifth South Pacific Conference came from the extension work of Departments such as Agriculture and Public Health as well as from those which provided part-time and on-the-job tradesman training for local recruits.

The relationship between adult education and social change was considered by the Fifth South Pacific Conference, held at Pago Pago in 1962. In one significant resolution, the Conference recognized 'that for specific results the practical or demonstrative aspect of Adult Education should be strongly emphasized'.[4] This affirmation of the importance of adult education had been preceded by another resolution which set out in some detail those aspects of adult education which the Conference thought should be promoted in the territories. The resolution read:

'This Conference recognizes the tremendous importance of adult education in all territories. While appreciating that different territories will place emphasis on different sections, the Conference recommends the following lines for extending adult education work:
(a) Formal courses to further academic subjects;
(b) informal residential courses for married couples, with emphasis on practical work;
(c) courses, through the establishment of vocational schools where necessary, in technical and trade subjects, e.g. motor maintenance, radio repair, carpentry and building, sewing etc.;
(d) courses for particular needs, such as, for example, those of migrant groups in urban areas; and discussion groups for leaders;
(e) the development of activities by women's groups by making funds available to train their members in modern methods;
(f) the establishment of night classes for adult men and women, encouraging them to be able to read and write in their own and foreign languages;
(g) the exchange between territories of information on legislation related to organized adult education schemes;
(h) the establishment of classes where interested young men and women can meet together with older men and women (both locally born and from overseas but residing in the territories) to discuss problems relating to present democracy – civics, self-government and citizenship;
(i) the establishment of special classes in nursing schools where older and 'traditional' village midwives are gathered together

with younger wives and nurses, women teachers and other interested women, to discuss vital problems in childbirth, pre-
natal and post-natal care, food for mothers and other related
matters;

(j) encouragement in the use of library services by adult men and
women;

(k) encouragement of the interchange between territories of reference materials, periodicals, bulletins, etc., on subjects of mutual
interest.'[5]

Role of the South Pacific Commission

A brief outline of the work of the South Pacific Commission in the
region and the developing patterns in several territories will suffice to
illustrate the extent to which social change and economic development have dictated the direction taken by adult education in the Pacific.
The South Pacific Commission was set up in 1947 by the six governments responsible for the administration of island territories in the
Pacific: Australia, France, the Netherlands, New Zealand, the United
Kingdom and the United States. (After losing its territorial interests
in New Guinea, the Netherlands was, in 1964, replaced by Western
Samoa which had become independent in 1962.) The purpose of the
Commission is to advise and assist the governments and territories
within its area to improve the social and economic well-being of their
people. Direction is given to the work of the Commission by periodi-
cal meetings of delegates from the South Pacific territories who, in
conference, make recommendations which are later considered by the
Commissioners from the six governments meeting each October to
approve a work programme for the following year.

The wider aspects of adult education have more than once been de-
bated at South Pacific Conferences. The Second Conference, in 1953,
was particularly occupied with the role of women's organizations in
the Pacific societies. Recommendations stressed the need for territorial administrations to encourage activities directed towards the further
education of women, particularly the formation of women's clubs and
committees. The Conference also recommended that the Commission
facilitate the co-operation of women's organizations throughout the
Pacific by bringing them together to discuss problems of special interest, including maternal and infant welfare, the education of women
and girls, homecraft and women's organizations.

As a consequence of these recommendations and with the approval
of the Commission, a Women's Interests Officer was appointed in
1959 who visited territories over the next three years to assist in the
promotion, formation and organization of women's groups. In 1961 a

Women's Interests Training Seminar was convened in Western Samoa and training was provided in organizing and constructing programmes for women's clubs. The seminar emphasized the importance of training courses and was particularly interested in the establishment of a Community Education Training Centre. Such a centre began operations in 1963 at Samabula near Suva as a joint project of the South Pacific Commission and the Home Economics Branch of the Nutrition Division of the UN Food and Agriculture Organization. It was financed with the generous assistance of the Australian Freedom from Hunger Campaign, and the Government of Fiji provided buildings. The Centre has provided courses in Home Economics for teachers and in Home Economics for Community Work for field workers from the Pacific territories. The course is designed to train these future field workers to assist in the formation of women's organizations, to construct suitable work programmes for them, to evaluate and direct their work and generally promote an active interest in improving standards in homecrafts, child care, health, hygiene, sanitation and nutrition. Over thirty young women who have been through the courses are working full-time in adult education programmes in territories within the Commission's region. Their work receives the stimulation and encouragement of the FAO Home Economist when she visits territories as part of a follow-up programme. With the recent appointment of a Visual Aids Officer to the Centre greater stress will be placed on this aspect of communication in the training programmes for field workers and visiting groups which, from time to time, receive *ad hoc* training from the staff at the Centre.

Apart from the training offered at the CETC in Fiji, the Commission's Project Officers, based in Noumea, New Caledonia, provide and arrange training in Business Methods, Health and Hygiene, Language Teaching, Tropical Agriculture, Librarianship and in other fields consonant with the general aims of the Commission to promote the well-being of the island people.

Papua and New Guinea

The pattern of adult education in Papua and New Guinea is that appropriate to a developing country – on-the-job training for working adults both in private industry and government service, extension work by a number of government departments assisted by a Department of Information and Extension Services, training for community development, women's interests clubs and some evening courses offered at technical schools in the larger centres.

The Department of Education is primarily responsible for the education of children at primary, secondary and technical schools, which are producing qualified people in increasing but not yet sufficient numbers. Some sort of continuation programme is therefore necessary to raise educational levels and to train adults who are only partly skilled. For those who have left school for employment but remain anxious to qualify for better jobs in private industry or entry to the Second Division of the Public Service, the Secondary Correspondence School offers tuition to the Intermediate level, as well as instruction in apprenticeship subjects. This school will also arrange tuition with outside institutions where courses are not available in the Territory. Language courses in Malay and Motu, technical drawing, welding, car maintenance and homecraft subjects are also offered at night classes in technical schools in the larger centres where there is sufficient demand. English literacy classes are also available for people who have the opportunity to practise, and the need to use, English in their daily lives. The courses will include, as well as oral and written English, elementary mathematics and other studies for which there may be a demand in a particular area.

The proposed expansion in the adult education activities of the Department of Education will involve the appointment of Regional Adult Education Officers in a number of centres and the setting up of classes that will meet expressed local needs and utilize local resources. Practical skills needed in the area will be taught and literacy classes in the *lingua franca* of the area will be arranged if this is required as a step towards the learning of English. The programme will be co-ordinated with the extension work of other departments, churches and voluntary agencies and will proceed in close association with the activities of village councils and indigenous co-operative societies.

The Welfare Section of the Division of Social Services and Community Development in the Department of District Administration is especially active in arranging courses throughout the Territory. Some fifty Welfare Officers and Welfare Assistants arrange and conduct courses in Community Development, Women's Interests and Leadership. Some instances will illustrate the participation in, the subject matter of and the variety of these courses:

1. A Community Education Course in the Eastern Highlands District attended by ten married couples from an isolated area. During the course, visits were arranged to schools, aid posts, forestry nurseries and model piggeries.
2. A 'Better Kitchens' course in the Milne Bay District, attended by eight men, nineteen women, and seven schoolgirls during their holidays. The discussions covered the building of a kitchen, equipment, the construction of a Chula stove, the preservation of food, nutrition, hygiene and sanitation.

3. On Bougainville, the promotion of a girls' club whose activities include sports, games, music, folk dancing and sewing.
4. Three courses in Homecrafts in the East New Britain District. Sewing, cooking, dancing, sport, carpentry and home management were the most popular subjects but interest was shown in the Radio News Sessions and accompanying discussions on Current Affairs.
5. A six-month course, five evenings each week, for workers on a plantation in the Bougainville District. Oral English was taught and there was instruction and discussion on current affairs, hygiene, government, child welfare and family problems.
6. A Club Leaders' Training Course for over 20 people in New Ireland. Practical teaching sessions were held and at the end of the course most could give a simple lecture effectively and all could teach songs to a group.
7. A six-week course in Youth Work Training for teachers and trainee teachers in the Central District.
8. A Community Development Course in the New Ireland District attended by 78 people. So many wished to attend that the lecturers had to work in shifts.

These examples should suffice to show the direction and purpose of this sort of adult education. Three features deserve special notice:

1. The attendance of men and women and married couples at courses on homecraft and community development is significant. The men at first are rather diffident but soon participate naturally and with considerable interest. As in similar village societies, the women's position is normally inferior, but working together with the menfolk tends to elevate their role in the community.

2. Women's clubs have been operating in the territory for some years now and their number is increasing. At the same time, there would seem to be a greater possibility of their promoting and influencing the policies of village councils than there was with the older, narrowly based clubs.

3. The multiplier effect of the training courses is quite considerable. Those who have done the courses carry the acquired attitudes back into the villages and influence others. Many prove to be stimulating and effective leaders who assist in the formation of further clubs.

The Department of Information and Extension Services is active in the adult education field itself and it assists other departments in their extension work. It controls Administration Broadcasting Stations at Rabaul, Wewak, Daru, Kerema, Goroka, Mount Hagen, Bougainville and Milne Bay, from which programmes for the people are presented in English, Pidgin and vernacular languages. News and information programmes, music, field recordings and interviews are broadcast. Listeners' attitudes are ascertained through correspondence and there is an increasing field contact with village and urban communities to promote listening and the purchase of radio sets.

The Department's Extension Officers assist other departments such as Agriculture and Public Health with their programmes by carrying out field studies in attitudes and beliefs, advising on publications for extension work and writing texts for them.

The Division of Business Training and Management in the Department of Trade and Industry helps Papuans and New Guineans to set up and run businesses and some 300 co-operatives, which between them have over 120,000 members, about $A2·0 million subscribed share capital and an annual turnover of some $A7·0 million.

The Business Advisory Service, with officers in several centres and plans for expansion, gives advice to individuals, partnerships and companies while the Training Section arranges formal courses for directors, officers and employees of co-operatives and other indigenously-owned businesses. Courses are conducted by instructional staff at the Co-operative Education Centre at Konedobu and also at convenient centres in the territory. Books, pamphlets and instructional material are prepared with the assistance of the Department of Information and Extension Services. The Division of Business Training and Management, in carrying out these extension services which assist people to develop their own country, works in close collaboration with the field workers in Agriculture, Forests and Fisheries, and assists in the courses arranged by the Division of Social Services and Community Development.

Adult education in the Territory of Papua and New Guinea is the sum of the extension activities of voluntary agencies and a number of government departments. It is therefore not surprising that the Adult Education Council that advises the Administration is comprised of the Director of Education, who is Chairman, representatives from the Departments of the Administrator, District Administration, Agriculture, Public Health, Trade and Industry, and Extension Services, and from the Reserve Bank, the House of Assembly and the voluntary agencies. By and large it is intended to promote the economic development of the Territory and assist the native people to make the social change that they are attempting.

American Samoa

Another, and in some respects unique, programme of adult education is being developed in American Samoa. Here, formal education through Grades 1–12 makes maximum use of televised lessons which children watch for almost a third of their school day. The system was inaugurated in late 1964 and the programmes, which are prepared in an Education Resource Centre, are broadcast to consolidated schools through six VHF channels from a transmitting station on Mt Alava which towers some 1,600 feet above Pago Pago harbour.

At its inception this system of co-operative instruction making maximum use of television had at least two major goals:

(1) to raise the achievement levels of Samoan students to State-side standards as soon as possible;

(2) to raise the teaching competence of Samoan teachers by the development of a televised in-service teacher-training programme.

At the same time, it was realised that the control of a televised service gave the Government a highly effective method of reaching adults, not only in the remoter villages of Tutuila but also on neighbouring islands. This contact, besides assisting the people themselves, would familiarize them with the sort of educational process which their children were experiencing and help to avoid the dichotomy between school and home which so frequently occurs when the children of one culture are being educated in a new system belonging essentially to the culture of another society.

Three- to four-hour evening programmes, broadcast over two channels, may be watched in the consolidated village schools. They are designed to assist adults to become increasingly competent in the use and comprehension of English, to enable them to improve the standard of village living, to involve them in a system of government that is wider than that of the traditional village community, and to provide them with entertainment.

Children's films are shown but these are watched with no less interest by the adults who question the children about the English dialogue. Thus, while incidentally learning the language themselves, they have an active interest in their own children's progress. The entertainment section of the programme also includes a film or television series which is popular in the United States.

Government departments are required to present material illustrating their activities so that people may understand their functioning and purpose, but beyond this programmes are presented which specifically attempt to educate people towards a higher standard of village living. Thus the Department of Agriculture's television extension programme may demonstrate improved methods of taro and banana culture or illustrate methods of food preservation. The Department of Medical Services may present health education programmes ranging from dental care to the control of filariasis and elephantiasis. The Public Health Division may offer a Family Planning programme, explaining why it has been offered and where advice may be obtained. There is an up-to-date news coverage each evening which includes island and Pacific events as well as world news in both English and Samoan.

Naturally enough, the first years of televised education have been primarily occupied with the perfecting of techniques and programmes for formal education in the schools, but there is now a firm basis for an expansion of adult education that can reach every village on Tutuila and the neighbouring islands.

Fiji

The Annual Report for the Department of Education for the year 1965 (p. 10) stated that there was 'no formal scheme of Adult Education in the Colony'. Nevertheless, there was a Women's Interests Section in the Department which maintained contact with almost a thousand registered Women's Clubs. Courses, varying from one to seven days, were arranged in club organization, sewing, cooking and housewifery in all parts of the Colony. A ten-day course for District Leaders was also held.

The Derrick Technical Institute, which was opened in 1963, provided a number of trade courses for apprentices, as did Natabua High School. The Institute also provided extension courses in automotive engineering, boilermaking, plumbing and fitting, and machining, for experienced tradesmen who, through lack of training facilities, had had no earlier opportunity of undertaking recognized trade courses.

There were also extension classes for those interested in industrial or commercial subjects, and students who had by a narrow margin failed in the Cambridge Overseas School Certificate or the Fiji Junior Certificate Examinations could take subjects such as English language or literature, history, geography, physics, chemistry, mathematics, health science or book-keeping to complete certificates. Part-time courses were also given in English, Hindi and Fijian for those who wished to take these as second languages. Courses were also available at twelve other centres throughout the Colony so that, although there was, indeed, no formal adult education scheme, nevertheless there was a good coverage of those aspects of adult education appropriate to a situation of rapid social change and accelerated economic development.

Post-school training in Papua and New Guinea and the British Solomon Islands Protectorate

In any country moving from a subsistence to a cash economy there is a shortage of professional, administrative and technical personnel. The lack is made up, initially, by the employment of expatriate officers from metropolitan countries, but this poses problems of higher salaries and allowances as well as lack of continuity because of rapid staff turnover. To some extent the problem will remain insoluble until local officers with professional training and experience become available. However, in the lower echelons of public service and business, directed on-the-job training can provide indigenous officers who, while they may not be as well qualified academically as their counterparts in the metropolitan countries, are nevertheless equally efficient because of their local knowledge and specialized training. One finds, therefore, in the Pacific territories, that special emphasis is placed on in-service and on-the-job training both in government service and business.

Young people in Papua-New Guinea who aspire to become administrative clerks in the Public Service may be accepted as trainees if they have passed Form IV or at least studied in that Form. They are accommodated at the PNG Administrative College and for the first six weeks do their training there. After that they live at the College while working for their departments but are recalled to the College from time to time for special courses. At the end of the first year, some selections are made for a further year of full-time study, but the others continue training in their departments.

Patrol officers and assistant welfare officers in the Department of District Administration are also trained on the job. Male trainees for careers as welfare officers spend a year in the field with experienced welfare officers before doing the Stage I course at the Administrative College. Female trainees who possess a Form III Certificate likewise do 12 months on-the-job training before attending a one-year course at the Ahioma Women's Training Centre in Milne Bay. These young people receive training in establishing group activities, youth work, women's clubs and community development. Assistant broadcasting officers, extension officers and film directors similarly receive training in their own Department of Information and Extension Services.

Other departments do, of course, provide full-time training for cadets, e.g. the Department of Education for teacher-trainees at several colleges, the Department of Public Health for dental officers at the Dental College and for medical officers at the Papuan Medical College. Agriculture and Forestry are likewise studied full-time at Vudal and Bulolo respectively. But these courses differ only in degree from similar courses in metropolitan countries, being of the full-time academic type rather than the part-time, post-school vocational type.

On a more restricted scale, in-service training is also offered in the British Solomon Islands Protectorate for Extension Assistants in Agriculture, Fisheries Assistants, Co-operatives Inspectors,

Programme Assistants for the Solomon Islands Broadcasting Service and others.

The missions in the Protectorate offer a similar type of training for their job requirements. The Anglican diocese of Melanesia offers, for instance, apprenticeship pattern training in carpentry, marine, general and electrical engineering, boat building, navigation and printing.

Other territories

Most of the Pacific territories present a pattern of post-school education very similar to those already described. Women's clubs have been widely promoted and generally successful. Part-time vocational training has made up, in some degree, for the lack of those training facilities which are found in the developed countries, but literacy work for adults has not proved generally successful. It is admittedly difficult for any person to make the shift from his native language to another. It is doubly difficult for the villager, in his limited yet secure environment, to transfer from his own language habits to a metropolitan and sophisticated form of communication. There is motive enough to learn English for the youngster seeking a government clerical job, but little incentive for the older villager, who need not leave his village or seek employment elsewhere than in his garden.

However, as literacy has increased, so library services have become more significant and sought after. In New Caledonia and Western Samoa, mobile libraries bring books, pictures and information to remote villages. A similar service is being developed in French Polynesia. At Vila in the Condominium there is a Cultural Centre Library which provides books in both French and English. There are central libraries in Apia (W. Samoa), Noumea (New Caledonia), Suva (Fiji) and other large urban centres. In the smaller Territories services are gradually being developed. In Honiara (BSIP) for instance the Education Department is developing a library which has been assisted from time to time by donations of books from the British Council, which has also agreed to contribute handsomely towards the cost of creating a permanent library.

Besides the library service and women's clubs, in the British Solomons classes are held at varying levels in English, geography, civics and local government, painting, building and technical drawing, book-keeping, and typewriting. Most of these classes are conducted in and around Honiara itself.

In Western Samoa there is little formal adult education. The Society of Accountants provides classes in commercial and accounting subjects and there are also night classes which enable adults to study subjects for the General Certificate of Education as a qualification for promotion in their trades or professions. A local art class is conducted by a parish priest.

In Nauru adult education classes taken by expatriate teachers are held at the Teacher Training Centre. Most of those enrolled take Victorian (Aust.) Department of Education correspondence courses at Intermediate, Leaving or Matriculation level. There were, however, two classes of adult women taking sewing and cookery courses.

On the small island of Niue there are classes in the Niuean language for expatriate officers. There are regular screenings of educational films in the villages and a 'box' scheme gives a library service to outer villages from the small public library at Alofi.

The role of the universities

The extra-mural programmes of modern universities vary very widely. They may embrace correspondence tuition or evening classes which enable part-time students to gain degrees, or lectures, vacation schools and short courses in the fields of arts, music, creative writing, architecture, history, government or international affairs, all carrying no credits. A growing number provide professional refresher courses for graduates in law, medicine, accountancy, economics and other disciplines. It is, as yet, too early for the new universities of the South Pacific to have given much indication of the extra-mural programmes that they might follow.

The new University of Papua and New Guinea was, in its first academic year, concerned mainly with a preliminary year of studies for students who would begin their degree courses in 1968. An intense pre-occupation with setting-up exercises in building and recruitment leaves little time for extra-mural programmes, for which no department is at present provided. However, the Ordinance (No. 16 of 1965) providing for the establishment and incorporation of the university appears, in Part 11 Section 7(d), to have made ample provision for such activity. It provides that:

'7. The objects of the University include the following:
   (d) to provide facilities for university education throughout the Territory by the affiliation of educational institutions, by the establishment of tutorial classes, correspondence classes, university extension classes and vacation classes and by such other means as the Council deems appropriate;...'

The University of the South Pacific at Laucala Bay, Suva, Fiji, had begun its preliminary year in 1968 and is, at the time of writing, still in the planning stage. It is interesting, however, in respect of extra-mural studies to look back at the Report which recommended its

AENB N

establishment. In mid-1965 there were discussions between represent-atives of the British and New Zealand governments about suggestions which had been made for the provision of higher education in the Pacific, and following these a Committee under the Chairmanship of Sir Charles Morris, a former Vice-Chancellor of the University of Leeds, was set up. That Committee published a Report in 1966 which recommended that steps should be taken to establish a fully autono-mous University of the South Pacific as soon as possible. A special section in the Report recommended the inclusion of an Extra-Mural Department in the new University and the Committee's remarks left little doubt of the importance that they attached to its establishment, for they wrote in paragraph 182:[6]

'It will not be forgotten that university extension work of this kind can play, and should play, an extremely important part in the politi-cal and social education of the people at large, and especially of those thoughtful and active members of the public, all over the countries of the region, who do so much to form opinion. It is hardly possible to think of any possible beneficent influence which could be more important in assisting the healthy development of democratic and responsible government, both national and local. Without educational provision of this kind it is hardly possible for governments, political movements or public opinion to keep in step with the rapid pace of the times.'

The Committee also considered a proposal that the South Pacific Commission's Community Education Training Centre should be taken under the wing of the university and could make a most valu-able contribution to educational thought and practice in the region. Its place in relation to the Institute of Education, the Department of Extra-Mural Studies and the 'Secondary Teachers' College was left for later resolution.

Sir Norman Alexander, who was appointed Academic Planner for the new University in June 1966 by the Inter-University Council for Higher Education Overseas, saw Extra-Mural Studies as being com-bined with Education in an Institute of Education and Extra-Mural Studies and the SPC Centre as providing a Community or Social Wel-fare Training programme. He regarded its influence in changing the pattern and general standard of village life as being of profound im-portance.

In view of the provision made for extension work in the establishing Ordinance for the University of Papua and New Guinea and the ex-pressed interest in extra-mural studies of the University of the South Pacific, it would seem that these universities will exert a considerable influence on adult education work in the Pacific over the next decade.

It is possible also that consultation and co-operation will develop between the new universities and the Institute for Technical Interchange, East-West Centre, which works in close association with the University of Hawaii.

The Women's Career Development Section of the East-West Centre offers development programmes to the English-speaking women of all the Pacific territories over a wide range of subjects. In 1967 courses of approximately three months were offered in library assistantship, tools and techniques for teaching, business education, cosmetology, and music leadership. Longer courses were offered in business education (5 months) and waitress supervision, pantry and food cost control (9 months). Offers for these courses were made also to Malaysia, Indonesia, Vietnam, Taiwan, and the Philippines and Thailand.

Conclusion

Adult education in the Pacific is, then, very much what the Fifth South Pacific Conference wanted it to be – a practical form of post-school education giving specific results in terms of higher standards of living and increased technical competence. However, like any other sector of education, its effectiveness is very much controlled by the amount of finance and number of personnel available to it.

Until recently the economic returns from education were regarded as being rather intangible but researches have shown a fairly high correlation between educational investment and economic development, particularly in respect of secondary education. While universal primary education may be politically desirable the high drop-out rate, especially in remote areas, and the rapid disappearance of barely-attained literacy considerably reduce its returns. Now, while academic and technical secondary education in developing territories have had the blessing of the economists, little or no inquiry has been made as to the economic benefits that might flow from a higher investment in specific training programmes for adult men and women. In consequence, adult education in the Pacific territories has been something of a Cinderella in the competition for the limited funds available for education, and the development of Adult Education Sections within Departments of Education has necessarily been of slow growth.

There is also some lack of continuity in direction which results from a high turnover of expatriate personnel and recruitment difficulties. Instances could be cited where replacements for Adult Education Officers or Women's Interests Officers had taken up to a year to recruit.

There are also difficulties in communication, which make supervision difficult and prohibitively expensive. The Trust Territory of the Pacific Islands is a case in point. Here, there are some 2,000 islands scattered over 3,000,000 square miles of ocean. In spite of the difficulties, training sessions are held for leaders of women's clubs and in Yap classes were held in English, business machines, and food preparation. In Ponape there were adult education classes in sewing and handicraft, while in Palau adult classes in English were broadcast over the radio. With increasing technical improvement, television and radio may become the most effective means of communicating with adult groups in the islands and, indeed, the most important media of communication for education generally.

Despite the problems of finance, personnel and communication, much has been achieved in the Pacific territories by the extension activities of different government departments. Of all the developments perhaps the most significant is the increasing interest and activity in the women's clubs, for it is above all in the homes that adjustment must be made to the increasing independence of family units in a changing society.

REFERENCES

1. Ed. Dept. of Territory of Papua and New Guinea, *Journal of Education*, vol. 5, no. 2, September 1967, OUP, p 67.
2. Legislative Council of Fiji, Council Paper No. 27 of 1966, *Dept. of Education Annual Report for the Year 1965*, Govt. Printers, Fiji, p 3.
3. British Solomon Islands Protectorate, *Dept. of Education Annual Report 1966*, Honiara, BSIP, p 12.
4. *South Pacific Commission Pacific Forum : Report of Fifth (1962) South Pacific Conference by Secretary-General*, S.P.C. – 1962, p 63.
5. Ibid.
6. Ministry of Overseas Development, *Report of the Higher Education Mission to the South Pacific*, HMSO 1966.

10. The West Indies

REX NETTLEFORD

Introduction

When the Irvine Committee of 1944[1] recommended the establishment of a University College in the West Indies, it gave high priority to the programme of adult education that was to be undertaken by the College's Extra-Mural department. This was no accident : it was a necessity, for the fledgling institution was to be designed to serve the needs of Barbados, British Guiana (now Guyana), British Honduras, Jamaica, the Leeward Islands, Trinidad and Tobago and the Windward Islands. Since then the Bahamas and the British Virgin Islands have joined the University community. Geographically they add up to an archipelago scattered over distances not readily appreciated on printed maps. From Guyana located on the South American mainland to British Honduras in Central America is as far as Cornwall in England is from Newfoundland in Canada. This span presented psychological as well as communications problems and from the beginning the adult education wing of the University was charged with narrowing the gaps. It was a challenging and exciting assignment and Mr Philip Sherlock (now Sir Philip, Vice-Chancellor), the first Director of Extra-Mural Studies, gave just the leadership which was then needed. His knowledge and experience in the field of education, as well as his awareness of similar work abroad, particularly in the United Kingdom, proved invaluable. So also did his position as Vice-Principal of the new University College since it gave the adult education department a direct voice in the highest councils of the University and conferred on the Department a welcome prestige within the College and, more important, within the communities that it served.

The work today is no less challenging, partly because the gaps between the West Indian communities are in some senses as wide as or even wider than when the University started. The adult education programme of the University as a vehicle of West Indian unity suffered a severe setback when the federal experiment which received constitutional articulation in 1958 failed, following Jamaica's withdrawal by referendum from the Caribbean enclave. The adult education programme was here robbed of a major part of its frame of reference. It had assumed underlying unities tying together the sprawling region it was called upon to serve. Historical connections of slavery, a plantation socio-economic system and colonialism had provided a tidy perspective into which much that was called liberal education could be fitted. So had the nationalist fervour of the nineteen-thirties which had revealed all West Indians as brothers under the skin crying out for the right to control their destiny, the right to govern or misgovern themselves, the right to self-respect and individual dignity – the right, in a word, to self-government. The Federal experiment was seen as a means of realising this. But after 1961, the Extra-Mural Department was faced with the challenges of psychological and even structural re-adjustments to meet the new developments. By 1962 Jamaica and Trinidad were to become independent followed by Barbados and later Guyana, which had had only observer status in the old federation in any case. Guyana was herself to withdraw in 1964 from the University of the West Indies arrangements and form her own University. This was of course a challenge for the entire University, but the Department which acts as liaison with the outside communities felt the effects more immediately than others. The University itself has had to decentralize, setting up campuses in Trinidad and Barbados, and again the net effect on the adult education programme was to fragment it in order to meet the realities of the new situation.

Objectives

Against this background of change the Extra-Mural Department has betrayed weaknesses as well as strengths – admittedly more of the latter than of the former. This has been so because of its continued relevance in a society which still needs its services. The main objective of the Department continues to be the provision to adults and out-of-school youths in communities supporting what is now the University of the West Indies of an educational service which is efficiently organized so as to equip and assist them to make a continuing and increased contribution to the social, economic and cultural improvement of their own society. This definition is wide enough to cover the five categories of adult education enunciated by the Exeter Conference on the Comparative Study of Adult Education.[2] Experience has taught wisdom and the Department has become increasingly selective in its field of operation. It was with the benefit of this experience that the Department's staff at their 1967 Annual meeting crystallized what they called 'policy guidelines' which were considered necessary for the attainment of the objectives.[3] Among these were:

'(a) The Department should make full use of resources wherever they can be found. In the West Indies, resources of money and staff are extremely limited. Pre-planning, skilful budgeting and well thought out deployment of available full-time and part-time staff become central to departmental administration. With large distances to cover transportation costs become prohibitive. Lecturers and tutors are still engaged in Extra-Mural programmes as a labour of love and the fees paid are appreciably low even by West Indian standards.

(b) The Department should provide opportunities for those who cannot be served by established institutions. (So where governments' educational programmes are lacking, the Department may find itself offering "O" level work and even literacy classes since this is a pre-requisite for the higher level work of the Department. In the bigger territories like Trinidad and Jamaica, the University has withdrawn from areas adequately served by either government or private institutions. So in Jamaica the College of Arts, Science and Technology has taken over the Accounting Classes that were once organized by the University's adult education Department.)

(c) The Department should seek to provide appropriate educational in-service training for groups which exercise an important influence on the development of the societies in which they operate. (Civil servants, teachers, trade unionists, social workers, employers come to mind and are in fact an increasingly important segment of Extra-Mural clientele throughout the West Indies.)

(d) The identification of talent and potential and the provision of opportunity for its development should be the concern of the Department. (In the absence of adequate educational provisions, there can be much wastage of manpower resources through lack of exposure at an early enough age. Through courses the Extra-Mural Department (more correctly the Extra-Mural Tutors) are able to "spot" undeveloped talents and give help.)

(e) Since the Department is responsible for creating and maintaining a favourable image of the University in all supporting territories it must assume a role of leadership in all activities related to community development. (This is essential, particularly in the smaller territories with their shortage of skills and expertise. The University is a resource for advice on many aspects of national development. The obvious pitfall is that of not being able to fulfil the functions expected of a Delphian oracle. What is worse, however, is the University's adult educators attempting to be all things to all men and ending up being nothing to anyone.)'

Diffusion of effort has been avoided in the main since there have been 'centres of emphasis' as Cyril Houle,[4] the American adult educator, saw them in the late fifties. He suggested that these were:

'(i) to provide continuing educational opportunities for *the leaders and potential leaders of the society* (my emphasis)

(ii) to train the leaders of the other educational and social services

(iii) to carry on experimental efforts

(iv) to assist and teach those who are trying to achieve external degrees or other forms of advanced certification.'

The third emphasis affirms the commitment to creativity in the programme, a commitment bolstered by the needs of a shifting, developing environment and maintained by the quality and orientation of staff members in the Department. The fourth emphasis has taken on new significance in the past three years with the increasing awareness among adults all over the West Indies of the benefits of formal higher education.[5] With it has come an increasing demand for certification of efforts expended in seminars and courses. The old philosophy of preparing people not for examinations and certificates but for their own personal fulfilment and enrichment was a borrowing from British adult education traditions which, though still praiseworthy and even useful, does not meet fully the needs of today's West Indian ambitions. The emergence of the American idea of university extension seems inevitable in the future in this part of the world.

Structure and organization

Until this comes, the structure and organization and programme of West Indian University adult education will continue to reflect the cumulative experience since 1948 when the Extra-Mural Department was first established. The Department consists of a Director[6] who is responsible to the Vice-Chancellor, the academic and executive head of the University, for the development and direction of the Department. Since 1963 the Department has been placed within the structure of a newly-created Faculty of Education comprising the Department of Education and the Institute of Education which has umbrella activities for extension work in education throughout the region. (In the absence of any intra-University programme for the teaching of adult education in either undergraduate or graduate courses, the Extra-Mural Department has yet to realise an organic relationship with her sister departments. Future development in Extra-Mural work cannot possibly fail to reflect this need.) The Director of Extra-Mural Studies has a seat on the University Senate, the governing academic body in the University. He has responsible to him a Deputy, a number of Resident Tutors located in the different territories, and a number of Staff Tutors based on the Mona campus in Jamaica. There is a Resident Tutor in each of the following territories : British Honduras, Antigua, St Kitts, St Lucia, Dominica, Grenada, St Vincent and The Bahamas, while in Jamaica there are provisions for two such Tutors, one responsible for the corporate area of Kingston and St Andrew and another, who is based in Montego Bay, responsible for the northern and western section of the island. Extra-Mural Representatives work part-time in Nevis and the British Virgin Islands. Since 1964, Barbados and Trinidad have had 'Organizing Tutors', each directly responsible to the Pro-Vice-Chancellors of the two offspring campuses at St Augustine and Cave Hill. Recommendations on making the tutors in the cluster of islands known as the Leewards and Windwards directly responsible to the Cave Hill Pro-Vice-Chancellor in Barbados have not been taken seriously. The organization of adult education, however, followed the parent University in the process of decentralization. The adult education programme also has the services of an Administrative Assistant, an Accounting officer (both in the Director's office) and a clerical staff of eighteen.

Staff duties

Each Resident Tutor is responsible for developing a full programme of adult education in his own territory. In this he is advised by a local Extra-Mural Advisory Committee and works in fairly close relationship with the Government and other adult education agencies in the territory. The policy followed by a Resident Tutor is within the framework of the general policy of the Department, but the line of development varies from one territory to the next according to the special needs and background as well as to the special skills and capacities of Tutors. Besides his straight adult education duties, the Resident Tutor, in territories outside those with their own campuses (i.e. Jamaica, Trinidad and Barbados), undertakes representative tasks on behalf of the University and is responsible for maintaining a favourable image of the University with the Government and the community as a whole. He also acts in an advisory capacity either directly or through Governmental and quasi-Governmental Boards and committees on which he may be asked to serve. This gives him an *entrée* into areas of influence and affords him contacts important to the work in adult education. It also leads to problems, none of them insuperable but many of them tiring and tiresome – problems which demand the expending of valuable energy that could best be ploughed into the education of adults *per se*. One good example can be seen in the energies tutors must sometimes expend to maintain an 'absolute' neutrality in the face of rival political parties or factions, all of whom may be necessary to the success of the Tutor's work in any given territory.

The Staff Tutors are not altogether free from this type of challenge but they have more opportunity to concentrate on those areas of the work which have over the years developed as specialisms in the programme. The Tutors serve the entire English-speaking area, travelling out frequently from home-base at Mona to conduct seminars, participate in conferences and for consultation. At the present time, the Department has specialist Tutors in Creative Arts (a Secretary and a Staff Tutor in the Creative Arts Centre), Radio Education (a Supervisor of the Radio Education Unit), Agricultural Extension, Social Work and Labour Education (Director of Studies in the Trade Union Education Institute). They conduct courses, plan conferences, carry out research and advise Resident Tutors on syllabi and on the organization of their courses in the field. The work in Creative Arts, Radio Education, Social Work and Labour Education has become institutionalized over the past five years, each acquiring buildings and facilities for greater work in depth. This welcome development has brought unwelcome results like the shortage of staff and the decreased mobility of the Department's specialists. Resident Tutors are apt to feel that their programmes suffer subsequent neglect as a result of this development. The net advantages are probably to be seen in deeper work on an adult education basis, better facilities for in-service training for people like trade unionists, middle managers, social workers, and, soon, of creative artists. The development of these 'institutions' within the Department is changing its structure as well as deepening its adult education work in important areas which need it. The approach to the training of social workers, trade unionists, agricultural extension officers, aspiring performing artists and middle managers is approached from the view of teaching adults, the techniques used being consciously related to the participants' experience, special gifts and special limitations.

Of the nineteen tutors on the current establishment serving all territories including Trinidad and Barbados only three are not native West Indians. One of the 'expatriate tutors' is married to a West Indian and has settled in the island she serves. Another, a Continental European, has also settled in the island where she works. Of the fifteen, five are women. Five hold postgraduate degrees (one a doctorate) in fields ranging from Politics to Agricultural Economics. Six did their undergraduate work at the University of the West Indies (as did the Administrative Assistant after gaining professional diplomas in Psychiatric Case Work from London). Others are shared between London,

Toronto, Columbia, Tuskegee, Cambridge, Marburg-Lahn, Western Ontario and Edinburgh Universities. Postgraduate work was pursued at Oxford, Stockholm, Indiana and Columbia. Tutors on the Mona campus have managed to straddle internal and external student bodies. One Tutor teaches political theory and labour relations to under-graduates in the Departments of Government and Economics re-spectively. Another has conducted tutorials in English and History in the internal departments and the Staff Tutor in Social Work is a mem-ber of the Faculty of Social Sciences because of her supervisory work in the Certificate course offered in Social Work in that Faculty. This does not mean that there are joint appointments, there being little enthusiasm so far for such appointments. A former Resident Tutor is now Professor of History at the University of the West Indies and yet another is now a Lecturer in History. A former Staff Tutor in Indus-trial Relations is now an Economics professor in an American Uni-versity and a Staff Tutor in Creative Arts, who received a doctorate from Yale, now directs a Creative Arts programme in a New England College. Another Resident Tutor moved on to the U W I Department of Government as a Lecturer and now heads the Department of Government in Guyana's new University. Other Tutors have moved altogether out of the academic field into public life. A former Deputy Director first went on secondment to serve the Bahamian Govern-ment and was subsequently recruited into the Jamaican foreign ser-vice as a Representative for the Jamaican Government. A one-time Resident Tutor moved to the University's Registry, then back to Extra-Mural as Director, then went on secondment as his country's first ambassador to another West Indian territory, ending up as a Minister of State in the Jamaican Government. Another Tutor is now serving as his country's ambassador to the United States and the Uni-ted Nations. One ex-Resident Tutor now serves as Governor of one of the West Indian Associated States and actually conducts Law classes for the Extra-Mural Department in his gubernatorial mansion. The Creative Arts Centre's Secretary belonged to the post-war London school of West Indian novelists. By reasons of their skills Tutors are constantly called on to share in public duties by governments e.g. arbitration, commissions of inquiries, conferences (at home and abroad) and technical missions abroad.

The above career pattern demonstrates the potential of Extra-Mural staff both now and in the past. The variety is a source of enrich-ment for the work. But, as Houle pointed out, it can make the pro-gramme into a highly personal one, 'depending to a great extent on the influence and ability, and contact of...the particular Tutors'. Over-centralized bureaucratizing of the work becomes almost an impossibility in the face of so many 'personalities', who are in any case called upon to fend for themselves in places far away from head-quarters in order to make the programme work.

The programme

The nature of the duties of the Tutors as outlined above should give an idea of the programme of the Extra-Mural Department. It can be divided into two broad categories – first the *general programme* and secondly the *programme of the specialized areas of work*.[7] The general programme should be further broken down into the class programme, courses and seminars, and public lectures.

1. The general programme

The class programme. This has strong antecedents in the experience of British adult education as organized by the Workers' Educational Association. The myth of preparing adults for the sake of learning rather than for the practical uses to which such knowledge can be put has been of little practical significance in the programme.[8] The Depart-ment has been offering classes in subjects such as English language, English literature, French, Spanish, German, history, geography, economics, sociology, West Indian history, English history, consti-tutional history, mathematics, chemistry, physics, botany, zoology, interior decorating, agricultural accounting, accountancy, law, music and art appreciation.

In such territories as Antigua, Trinidad, Barbados, the Bahamas and more recently Jamaica, it has been noted that the demand for classes which lead to specific qualifications (e.g. the General Certifi-cate of Education) is much greater than that for classes offered mainly to provide a liberal education and which are therefore non-vocational.

In Barbados, where a Community College for sixth-form work has been started, the class programme has been greatly curtailed. In Jamaica and Trinidad, since the institution of evening classes on the Mona and St Augustine campuses, there is less demand for advanced qualifications from Extra-Mural resources. For example, classes for persons studying for London University external degrees have been obsolete for some time now. In the Bahamas it has been accepted in principle that Government-sponsored G C E classes will join forces with the Extra-Mural class programme. In the Leewards and Windwards, the needs are sometimes more modest.

There has been much debate concerning the levels at which Extra-Mural classes should be offered. The 1963 Antiguan Conference on Extra-Mural work in the Caribbean[9] recommended that although it may be necessary to offer classes at the G C E 'O' level standard, classes should not normally be organized for the purpose of satisfying the 'O' level examination. But a re-examination of the position has since forced the Extra-Mural Staff Conferences of 1967 and 1968 to offer the view that 'teaching sponsored by the Department of Extra-Mural Studies should not necessarily be limited to teaching above the standard of the G C E "O" level'.

On balance, it does appear that while ideally the University, both internally and externally, must concern itself with the higher intellectual levels of education, there are instances where for a variety of reasons there may be a demand for 'O' level teaching which is not being met – or at least fully met – by other local agencies. In such circumstances the Extra-Mural Department has felt itself obliged to fulfil such a demand and in practice Resident Tutors have actually pursued this line.

It has been suggested that in territories like Jamaica, Barbados and Trinidad in which there are other agencies offering part-time tuition, the Department should no longer offer academic classes as it has been doing since its inception. However, in Jamaica and Trinidad registrations for classes over the past year do suggest that the Department is still meeting a demand which is not being fully satisfied by the other agencies operating in this field. It still remains true that many of these classes, meeting generally only once per week, do not provide that intensive 'cramming and coaching' which is reported to be the case elsewhere. For this reason, students are encouraged to do as much work on their own as is possible and even to use reputable correspondence courses from abroad, especially from the United Kingdom.

Languages, particularly Spanish and French, still attract students out of general cultural and intellectual interest. Contact with Latin America and with the French islands of Martinique and Guadaloupe has sharpened interest in these two languages among adults in different parts of the West Indies.

Courses and seminars. It may be argued that this area of the Department's work has been most successful and useful. Courses have been offered in a variety of subjects including public administration, local government, agricultural extension, human rights, social work, the teaching of poetry, teaching of modern languages, teaching of chemistry, teaching of general sciences, industrial relations, psychology, archaeology, anthropology, business management, drama, dance and adult education methods. Conferences have been held for many magistrates, farmers, social workers, literacy teachers, drama producers, labour leaders, political leaders, hotel workers, taxi-drivers and youth leaders. Some of these have been in-service training courses, while in some instances employers have sponsored the attendance of their employees. This has been particularly true of the business administration courses and the trade union training courses.

One pattern which has been followed is for the Extra-Mural Department to sponsor a particular seminar or training course until a suitable agency emerges which can take over the responsibility. 'Suitable agency' has in the past meant the internal department of the University itself. So public administration and social administration were nursed by the Extra-Mural Department until internal departments were instituted for the granting of professional diplomas and certificates in the subject.

Whatever happens in the future it is clear that the Department must continue to make available a Citizenship Education programme,[10] for which there appears to be great demand in most of the contributing territories. Supplementary work by the Radio Education Unit has been a conscious activity of the Unit.

It has also been suggested that more courses (or classes) should be offered for teachers (mainly non-graduate), dealing with the content of some of the subjects which they are required to teach. Such a programme would have to be very carefully planned and structured with the collaboration of the Institute and Department of Education within the University.

Public lectures. The Department's Public Lecture programme has been one of the most dynamic and successful parts of its programme. Resident Tutors outside Jamaica have long used it as a way of introducing internal lecturers to the communities they serve. Single lectures have been most frequent but specific themes are sometimes pursued in a series of lecture/discussions over periods of from 4 to 8 weeks.

The Citizenship programme, which was established under a Staff Tutor in Political Education between 1961 and 1963, was conducted on this basis in most of the territories as well as in rural Jamaica. Usually, topics covering the Federation, constitution-making and the meaning of independence drew enthusiastic response all over the Caribbean in the early post-Independence period in the case of Jamaica, Trinidad and Tobago, Barbados and Guyana. In the case of the Associated States the same thing occurred during the period leading up to the talks in London which granted the new status.

At best the public lectures are a means of establishing contact between an inquiring West Indian citizenry and the University. But the danger that inheres in this is the threat of the programme falling into the tradition of 'sermon-tasting' which is strong among any highly religious and politically conscious populace. Some Tutors have been known to express preference for sustained concentration through courses and seminars. Yet public lectures continue to be popular and are a very good outlet for visiting lecturers and professors to the territories.

It is also a service on which other adult education agencies in the community can draw and the Extra-Mural Tutors often find themselves recommending lecturers for a variety of topics requested by voluntary organizations and professional bodies. The system operates well for rural Jamaica where the Extra-Mural Department works in close collaboration with the Library services. In the past it has kept a University presence in districts outside Port-of-Spain, Trinidad (including Tobago) and it has helped to bring Belize, the capital of British Honduras, nearer to the hinterland of that country. All over the West Indies the public lecture is found to be useful in getting the University to focus attention on public matters of moment, sometimes even involving public controversy with the established order.

2. *Specialized programmes*

As has already been mentioned, there has been a tendency during the last few years for work being done by our Staff Tutors to become more specialized and institutionalized. Thus buildings have been provided for social work, radio education, trade union studies, and more recently the creative arts. This has resulted in the Staff Tutors concentrating on working at their own Centres. The facilities are, however, normally available to students from the entire Caribbean. More than ever the University's adult education programme must concentrate on training the trainers who will act as leaven back in their own communities.

Social work. This is centred at the Social Welfare Training Centre, which is on the Mona Campus. A four-month social work course is offered at the Centre with practical work done either in Jamaica for non-Jamaicans or in Puerto Rico for Jamaicans.

UNICEF provided twenty of the scholarships awarded in 1967. Of the other three participants two were given scholarships by the Council of Voluntary Social Services in Jamaica and one by the Sugar Producers' Association in Guyana. The categories of workers from which participants have been drawn have been very wide, ranging from professional social workers to agricultural extension and public health officers. These courses appear to be meeting a very real demand in the Caribbean and will continue for a few years yet. A reference library in social work is now being established with the assistance of funds from UNICEF. The Social Welfare Training Centre has served as a residential adult education centre, since, when available, it has been used by a variety of organizations for residential courses or seminars in subjects such as home economics, local government and basic school teaching. The programme is directed by the Staff Tutor in Social Work who also acts as a Warden of the Training Centre in all aspects of its work. The Department of Sociology collaborates with the Staff Tutor in organizing programmes and the Staff Tutor maintains strong international contacts in her field.

Trade union education. The Trade Union Education Institute has achieved considerable success both in terms of the academic standards attained and its general acceptance by the trade unions of the region. This latter achievement is particularly significant in view of the great rivalry which exists between trade unions in many of the territories.

The core of the Institute's training programme is one-month courses usually held three times per year. Participants are mostly drawn from the voluntary leadership of the rank of chief delegates, but the smaller unions often send their general secretaries or their assistants. The syllabus has been designed to assist in developing in trade union leaders a capacity for critical and analytical insight into labour management problems, and to see their role and functions within the context of a developing West Indian society.

In assessing the regional role of this Institute it must be borne in mind that both Guyana and Trinidad have established their own 'Labour Colleges', but the TUEI's Director of Studies maintains close contact with trade unions and labour educators all over the Caribbean. In addition to teaching, the Institute has encouraged research into relevant topics. The documentation of the history of Labour and Industrial Relations Affairs has also commenced. The Institute has begun the publication of a series of booklets which will be of value to the trade unionists of the region. It also runs courses in industrial relations for middle managers and joint labour-management seminars in industrial engineering and related subjects. It is headed by a Director of Studies who is advised by a committee appointed by the Vice-Chancellor and chaired by the Director of Extra-Mural Studies. The committee includes union leaders and University teachers, as well as representatives from the Ministries of Labour and of Education. The staff is mostly part-time and drawn from labour, management, government and the Faculty of Social Sciences.

Radio education. The Radio Education Unit of the Department of the West Indies plays a double role – public relations work for the University and adult education work in both live and recorded programmes. The situation is complicated by the lack of money for extended radio work. Since the end of the financial year 1963/4 the Unit has operated solely on a grant from the University, as its second Foundation grant, which expired in that year, was not renewed.

By contrast with the Eastern Caribbean neither of the two radio stations in Jamaica carry R E U programmes free of charge. Uncertainty about the financing of these programmes has affected the character of such work – the Unit being compelled to produce 'public relation' programmes rather than 'educational' broadcasts which depend for their effectiveness on continuity and design.

Recently the radio unit has been considering whether to expand its work by making available taped material for group discussion both in a 'Listening Post' type of programme and as a supplement to class-room work, especially at the University Centres now being established. The Supervisor of the Unit has assisted with courses on the use of radio for education and information and in schools broadcasting. It can hardly be overemphasized how much the Radio Education Unit requires extra funds in order to maintain, let alone expand its work.

There has been some talk of establishing a 'Communications Centre' at the U W I of which the Radio Education Unit would become a part, but this proposal has not yet got beyond the stage of preliminary discussions. The West Indies possesses a strongly oral tradition in its communication process. Knowledge rooted in experience is richly stored in a bulky archive of tape-recordings of views, opinions and facts by persons who have lived through and have helped shape some of the most important years of modern West Indian development. Some of them have even helped to shape the communities as they are now known. These records are invaluable as primary and secondary sources for research. They serve as means for the adult citizen to keep abreast of developments in his community and to put them into perspective. The Unit is rather strong on the social sciences, the creative arts, Caribbean folklore, and branches of the natural sciences, introducing into the University community what the North American scholars now refer to as oral history.

Creative arts. With the establishment of a Creative Arts Centre, the entire character of the creative arts programme is likely to be altered significantly. But as the Centre is less than a year old it is impossible at this stage to make any definitive statements concerning its use. Prior to the establishment of the Creative Arts Centre there was a Staff Tutor in the Creative Arts based on Trinidad and one based on Jamaica. One of them has expressed a preference for short intensive courses rather than the longer, termly courses. These shorter courses require much careful preparation beforehand either by the Resident Tutor or some other locally interested persons. There is little doubt that at least in some territories the Extra-Mural activities in the creative arts have stimulated much local interest in the field and in the best situations, as

AENB O

in the Leeward Islands, have produced active local groups, some functioning independently, others working under the sponsorship of the Extra-Mural Department.

The Creative Arts Centre has hung exhibitions, staged performances in drama, dance and music, as well as provided a base for West Indian creative artists living both in and outside the West Indies. It promises to be the major bastion of a lasting ideal of adult education anywhere – that is education for self-fulfilment 'aimed primarily at learning for the sake of learning'. It is sited on the Mona campus and invites the fullest possible participation of students and the rest of the campus population. In this it can act as a bridge between town and gown, a necessary bridge in a developing country which is suspicious of all institutions having connotations of traditional élitism. The Creative Arts Centre is searching for new financial resources which will enable it to institute a varied and concentrated programme which will expose the University community as well as the community at large to the work of writers, painters, sculptors, musicians, choreographers and dancers, playwrights and actors.

Agricultural extension. This area of our programme was started as a result of a grant from Esso Standard Oil SA (Jamaica) Ltd. to the University to undertake a project for training staff officers of the Jamaican Agricultural Society. This has so far resulted in residential courses as well as guidance and leadership in field activities.

One wonders to what extent this activity marks the beginning of further involvement of the University in agricultural extension as has happened in certain other countries. The programme is restricted to Jamaica where there is a strong and viable agency – the Jamaican Agricultural Society – capable of doing such work with help from the University. The Department actually organized the early courses in Agricultural Extension many years ago in collaboration with the JAS and the old International Co-operation Administration of the United States. The Faculty of Agriculture in Trinidad conducts its own extension programmes though the emphasis is on technical rather than social aspects of farm and rural life. British Honduras, Barbados, Trinidad, Antigua, Dominica, St Lucia and Grenada are current beneficiaries of the Faculty's programme.

Publications. As part of the programme the Department aims at publishing journals, pamphlets and books as necessary supplements to its general programme. The most successful publication has been *Caribbean Quarterly*[13] which includes articles on matters of Caribbean interest reflecting either original research or informed comment on Caribbean matters. The editor is the Director of Extra-Mural Studies, who is advised by an Editorial Board. This magazine has an influential if a not particularly large circulation. It is in great demand by libraries and certain other agencies overseas.

There has been some criticism of *Caribbean Quarterly* mostly on the grounds that its format is antiquated and that it does not have any clear-cut editorial policy but tries to be all things to all men and in doing so means little to anybody. There are a number of improvements, from the format to the quality of articles, which ought to be made in *Caribbean Quarterly*, but it must always be borne in mind that the Department of Extra-Mural Studies as a University institution has to be concerned with the advancement of knowledge. The provision of a suitable publication with a high academic standing, in which members of the Department and other scholars of the region may publish, is an important contribution to the Department's role as an organization for advancing knowledge.

Other publications include a series of 'Caribbean Plays', which has been very useful to local drama groups throughout the area. Two other attempts at publication, 'Caribbean Affairs' and 'Public Affairs Pamphlets', have not fulfilled their initial promise.

Occasionally Resident Tutors may produce publications designed mainly for the territories which they serve. For example, a recent series in Trinidad, 'The Anatomy of the Constitution' in St Kitts, 'Bahamia' and 'The Community and the Offender' in the Bahamas.

In addition, the Trade Union Education Institute publishes a series of pamphlets on Labour and Industrial Relations, and is in the process of producing occasional papers based on depth research into different aspects of West Indian labour relations.

Finance

One may well ask how are all the above activities financed? The University pays the salaries of all the academic and non-academic staff in the Department. It also provides a grant for the development of the work in each territory, though this grant is never adequate and supplementary allocations are often made by governments either for specific courses or as general grants for the overall programme. The principle will find greater practical application when University Centres, signifying more boldly 'University Presences', are fully established in territories without campuses. Local government authorities have also been known to make grants for work in specific local government districts.

There are important aspects of the adult education programme which are not financed by the University at all. Radio education existed for five years on a substantial grant from the Nuffield Foundation. Trade union education has had capital and recurrent expenses paid for by the USAID (the Government of Jamaica will bear most of the costs after 1969). Social Work is financed in large part by UNICEF (its capital grant comes from the Jamaica Government) and the creative arts have had the benefit of a capital grant for buildings from the Calouste Gulbenkian Foundation as well as from an anonymous Canadian donor, while recurrent expenses are paid in part from a grant by the Jamaica Public Service. Further income comes from more modest benefactions as well as from fees, which are very small.

The variety of sources of income produces some problems of financial administration for academic and administrative staff in the Department. The problems are sometimes increased by the fact that supervision by remote control is second best. Procedures have however been refined[12] over the past five or so years to oil the machinery into better running order. The University Bursary is in constant touch with the Department and has built up what is seemingly a genuine understanding of the financial demands of an adult education programme. The appointment of a clerk in charge of Departmental accounts was a welcome development in 1961. Idealistic tutors have themselves learnt to relate expenditure realistically to budget forecasting. Yet 'virement' is an often-used word in correspondence between Director and tutors, since programme allocations are made on the principle of self-financing projects and are therefore never adequate. Opportunities for expansion are often thwarted by this inescapable fact. On the other hand, enthusiasm can make the worst of itself, and financial strictures have also served to help the Department to state its objectives and pursue them with some rigour. The net effect is that there are never enough funds for adult education in the West Indies.

Special problems

A number of special problems emerge from much of what has been indicated above. Some are problems having to do with the University in general. Others are more specifically Extra-Mural.

The sprawling little empire of just under 4 million people presents administrative problems. The decentralization of the University into three major campuses has eased the burden on Headquarters since the Barbados and Trinidad campuses now have to direct their own Extra-Mural sections. But this keeps Grenada still three air-hours from Mona, Jamaica. In any case, plans for the establishment of University Centres in the territories will intensify the work, not lighten it, and problems of co-ordination will most certainly present themselves. The virtues of autonomy and initiative in decision-taking are sometimes cancelled by uncertainty resulting from there being no sign of clear-cut policy decisions about important aspects of programming and funding. The University sometimes cannot commit itself where expenditure of large amounts are involved. It depends itself on Government grants which are not there merely for the asking, and the mechanics of getting budgets and requests through University grants committees and Council takes time. Furthermore, as a regional institution the University as a whole is particularly vulnerable in the face of conflicting ambitions among governments of territories. The scare resulting from the break-up of the federation can be seen on the UWI. In its effort to readjust to the new situation the University seems hard put to making hardline decisions at times and the Extra-Mural Department sometimes suffers as a result. The recent establishment of a Caribbean Area Free Trade Association (CARIFTA) augurs well for the future, and the regional security of adult education will probably be restored sooner than expected.

The turnover of directors [14] in the Department has been fairly high over the past five years, and though the Department has suffered less than could be imagined (the work has actually deepened and expanded in many areas during this time), the appointment of a permanent incumbent to co-ordinate the work and give it new dimensions will deserve early consideration. There is no doubt that the Extra-Mural Department is changing; the Director will need to understand the changes and transform their effects into instruments for further creativity.

Then there is the question : should the Department of Extra-Mural Studies continue to be a part of the Faculty of Education or should it be on its own? In 1963 the Department was placed in the Faculty of Education because it was felt that it could co-operate and participate directly both inside and outside the UWI in the programmes of the Department and of the Institute. Another reason was to make it quite clear that the Department of Extra-Mural Studies is an integral part of the University. The first of these objectives has scarcely been achieved. Although there has been much cordiality and sympathy among the members of the Faculty, there has been no organic link, except at Faculty Board level, between the work of the Department of Extra-Mural Studies and that of the two other members which comprise the Faculty. One wonders, therefore, whether it would not be better for the Department to be on its own and have its own direct representation in all councils of the University, or whether there should be a Faculty of Extension comprising the Extra-Mural Department and all other University Extension agencies. The problem will probably be solved when, with the development of programmes in the University Centres in territories outside of Jamaica, Barbados and Trinidad,

Faculty members will find a real need for working together in areas of mutual interest.

The relationship with other departments in the University sometimes becomes a problem in many places, including the United Kingdom. In the West Indies as elsewhere, the Extra-Mural Department has suffered from both the snob attitudes as well as the admiration of internal colleagues. The real problem is of a different kind, however. There has been a growing tendency for internal departments to develop their own extension programmes. In many instances this is essential. Both the Department and Institute of Education must have staff deployed throughout the Caribbean. So must the Faculty of Agriculture and Department of Government (Public Administration). Colleagues in the natural and physical sciences have been doing important work among science teachers in secondary schools all over the West Indies. Naturally lines cross and Extra-Mural Tutors are frequently ignored in the planning of courses and conferences taking place in the territories they serve and in which they are University representatives. The 1967 Extra-Mural Staff Conference asked that the University make it clear that 'The Department of Extra-Mural Studies was the department responsible for Extra-Mural teaching'. This role could be reinforced in practical ways by close liaison between departments on the different campuses and the Director and the Tutors involved. Heads of Departments in the Faculty of Education will naturally get the best results by working together, particularly in such areas as subject-matter development for teachers (trained and untrained) and co-curricular activities like creative arts and citizenship education.

The University Centres

Such co-ordination is going to be vital when the University Centres are finally established. The 1963 Antigua Conference shared with the Cato Committee [15] and the Houle Report the view that a physical symbol of the University in each territory was an urgent necessity. Many political leaders also pressed for this in response to the regional uncertainties that followed not only the earlier break-up of the West Indies Federation but also the subsequent failure of the attempts at uniting the 'Little Eight' territories. The anxiety about getting value for money among some of the contributors to the University is understandable enough but the non-viability of mini-universities scattered all over the region had to be brought home to many nationalists. The establishment of University Centres, based on the work of the Extra-Mural Department, seemed the logical answer to most needs. The financing of the construction of the Centres is to be from a Canadian

Government Grant, matched by grants from local sources including the Governments of territories concerned.

It is now necessary to give some thought to the content of activities which could be offered in these Centres in addition to the usual Extra-Mural programme already discussed. In some territories there has been a request that the University Centre should become a part of a complex of higher education, including teacher training facilities and a technical college. There is also a demand in some territories for the teaching of first-year undergraduate courses. A corollary of this is that the University would give credit for such work done externally. Then, there is the problem of finding a sufficient number of qualified Tutors and eligible students to make the effort worthwhile. At one staff conference it was strongly felt that any such local tutoring would have to be supplemented by any or all of the following aids : taped material, radio programmes, staff assistance, assistance of internal staff for vacation courses, library facilities and correspondence courses.

Thus it will be seen that before this very considerable effort is made it must be demonstrated that there are a reasonable number of interested students and enough qualified tutors. There has been a suggestion that a pilot project of teaching at this level should be launched in a very limited way in Antigua and Dominica, where it has been reported that the necessary criteria exist, even if in a restricted academic area.

From 'Extra-Mural' to 'Extension'

One major implication of University Centres is the intensification of formal aspects of University adult education, particularly in the sense of the University adopting a credit system which would include (a) credits for courses organized by the Extra-Mural Department towards degrees and (b) credits in non-degree courses, such as social work and industrial relations, for University Certificates and Diplomas, bearing in mind the important fact that courses taken for external credits would have to be the same or along similar lines as those required for courses taught internally, the following considerations would have to be borne in mind:

(a) Tutors would be needed to prepare teaching materials, to direct the students' study and reading, and to mark and comment on written material submitted by the students.

(b) Even in instances where suitable local tutors could be found, much supplementary work by internal staff members would be necessary.

(c) Such supplementary work could be supplied through intensive vacation courses and correspondence courses. But internal departments might decide that they would need more members of staff before they could contribute to these correspondence courses.

(d) It would have to be decided whether to place the administrative machinery necessary to co-ordinate and direct the credit courses in the Department of Extra-Mural Studies or in the Registry or elsewhere.

These difficulties are not insurmountable, but University Senate committees must come out strongly in support of a programme like this. Many who may have been concerned with costs in relation to available teaching and supervising staff in the territories have been won over, and a paper on the subject is in preparation for full-scale discussion in Senate. But the idea of 'credit' is, one suspects, too 'American' a device to fit into the strongly British pattern which has taken root in West Indian University adult education. The device is already in operation in the Faculty of Natural Sciences for internal students. The Extra-Mural Department could benefit from its extension to work in the University Centres.

For after twenty years the Extra-Mural enterprise needs this new dimension, upon which much of the future structure and role of University adult education will hinge. First, it should be admitted that the work that it has developed throughout the Caribbean is valid and must be continued. In any case, there is no turning back on areas that have been institutionalized on the Mona campus, for social work, trade union education and creative arts, even if integrated into the programme of internal departments, *will by their nature continue to demand attention outside the walls of the University.* The Resident Tutors (as academicians, organizers, advisers, consultants, and University representatives) will naturally have to continue in these multiple roles in most of the territories. The conception of University Centres was never intended, it would appear, to lead to the abolition of the duties connected with these established roles. But it is in the establishment of these Centres that change is likely to come in the work of Resident Tutors and the general work of the Department.

The question of what is to be done in the University Centres is one that has been exercising the Department's mind since 1963. The areas of activity for each Centre foreshadowed in 1964 in a progress Report on University Centres still hold. The lack of information as to how they should be implemented merely underscores the assumption that each territory will have to evolve its own programme based on felt needs and special circumstances. A close examination of the suggested areas reveals that the University Centres are specifically expected to continue the work already in progress in the Department. Such work covers (a) 'non-examination courses in subjects such as Citizenship,

Politics, Education, International Affairs, Caribbean Studies, *and others of special relevance to the area*' and (b) '...training programmes of varying periods in selected fields [with] emphasis [being] placed initially in public administration, social work and community development, and the creative arts'. The phrase 'intensive training...' is actually used in the Progress Report. Already intensive work is being done in these fields through the internal department of Government (in Antigua) and through the Extra-Mural Department (Social Welfare Training Centre and Creative Arts Centre – Mona Campus). The availability to University Centres of resources concentrated in the last two will naturally require systematic planning in the future programme of the Department.

The other two areas of activity specified in the Progress Report point to *new areas* which are of deep concern because they have far-reaching implications for the Department's future work if these areas are at all taken seriously by the University. They are:

(i) '*Examination courses* designed to fit into the framework of the University curricula and to give some preliminary training for degree courses', and

(ii) '*Extension work* of the professional schools of the University such as Agriculture, Medicine, Education and Engineering.'

One should here add public administration, social work and industrial relations. The phrase 'preliminary training for degree courses' seems specially included to facilitate the sixth form work that is much needed in many of the territories.

The new dimension that calls for serious attention is that of Extension work, vis à vis Extra-Mural work. By this is meant work that is a literal extension of the disciplines of internal departments in the University. This implies the organization and structuring of courses for credit in line with the degree and certificate structure of the UWI. Correspondence courses, 'booster' seminars, student potential, qualified teachers and adequate supervision of students, the credit system – all come to mind. But many Tutors are already aware of these factors and have taken them into consideration in assessing their territories' capacity to cope with a University credit course.

The student potential is most likely to be found among teachers and civil servants : this intensifies the anxiety to see closer collaboration develop between the Institute and Department of Education and the Extra-Mural Department. St Kitts and Antigua have undertaken formal surveys into student potential in those territories with encouraging results. The need for *specialist staff resident in the territories* is a very real one. There is provision for staff members based on the different campuses to travel to University Centres in other territories. But where permanent resident specialist staff is concerned this would probably have to be a charge on the Treasury of the Government of the territory concerned. This method of fulfilling territorial needs is being increasingly adopted by some territories, notably Trinidad and Tobago, Jamaica and Barbados. If inability to pay full costs is pleaded by the territories of the Windwards and Leewards then a formula could probably be worked whereby governments of these territories make joint grants earmarked for this kind of work in their territories, making this special staff interchangeable. There is something already in operation like this, for example, the grant covering the Institute of Education and the grant to the Trade Union Education Institute. In any new development of University Centre work along lines suggested above Resident Tutors will need as much academic help as is possible. Some of this will be provided on a part-time basis by qualified personnel resident in the territories but the security of another permanent colleague would provide the confidence and efficiency that will be necessary. The presence of a Staff Tutor in Public Administration in Antigua could only have strengthened the University's adult education work as well as the University's image. Institute of Education personnel working in Eastern Caribbean territories may well be integrated into the Extra-Mural Tutor's programme much more than has been done up to now. Or, to put it another way, the University programme in each territory should be conceived as parts of a whole so that some sense of cohesion can be given to the idea of a 'University presence' which is the dream of leaders in territories without campuses.

If this new dimension of intensive Extension work is accepted then it seems that for the foreseeable future, particularly during the period of the 1969–72 triennium, the Department should restructure itself where necessary to meet the needs, and the role of the Director would be more easily defined in terms of the new developments.

Evaluation

Despite what would seem to be an 'occupational commitment to optimism' on the part of the staff of the Extra-Mural Department, no one has been smug enough to ignore the need for periodic evaluation and reassessment of the work in adult education. In 1958, Sir Philip Sherlock, the first Director of the programme, invited J. Roby Kidd of Canada to do a full-scale inquiry into the work of the Department.[16] Descriptive rather than analytical, Dr Kidd's report put between covers important and useful facts and figures on how the Department went about its business. That report was to form an invaluable background for Professor Cyril Houle of the University of Chicago who came a year later and reported yet again on the work of the Department. Before that, in 1954, Dame Lillian Penson had led a team of visitors to the University and had reported, *inter alia*, on the work in adult education. So in fact did the Cato Committee made up of West Indian and British leaders, in 1958. All the evaluators spoke enthusiastically in praise of the work of the Department. The Penson Committee recognized 'evidence of a contribution of high academic standards and realisation of the special circumstances and requirements of the various territories of the West Indies, to be found in Extra-Mural work.' The Cato Committee acknowledged the University's 'anxious concern to serve the West Indian community by the wide dissemination of learning and study in a variety of subjects' and reaffirmed its faith in the work of the Extra-Mural Department. Kidd's careful documentation of the Department's activities is itself an expression of his regard for the work that was done. Houle went further by not only praising the excellence of the staff and work in general but also pointing out shortcomings which hampered the work, particularly in the matter of administrative arrangements.

Added to all this has been the constant review by members of the staff itself. Self-criticism has been more than a pastime with tutors, however, and the annual staff conference instituted by Acting Director Rawle Farley and continued by Visiting Professor S. G. Raybould of Leeds. H. L. Wynter and Hugh Miller were to serve as forums for re-examination and self-appraisals. The crisis of the University has been in a real sense the crisis of the Department. Questions of the relevance of the institution to West Indian life and charges of the University being an ivory tower of colonial élitism, to name just two things, have all been squarely confronted in the work of the Department. The work has also constantly faced the threat of diffusing itself too much in order to meet the needs of the scattered populations it serves. But as the Penson Committee said 'it is perhaps in its own interests that the Department should have to work to a fixed limited budget, sufficient to meet its expenditure on its permanent staff and minimum central activities and overheads, since this compels it to be selective in its work and to make every effort to transform its separate activities into self-financing operations'.

Yet the effort to do just this has sometimes served to deprive the work of other things as important. The field of adult education as a discipline quickly comes to mind. Despite the wealth of experience gleaned over the past twenty years in the Department no systematic codification of it has been done in adult education terms. The appointment of a Staff Tutor in Adult Education, following on the Houle recommendation, did not result in definitive work since the incumbent was soon to be put in charge of other priorities concerned with the day-to-day operations of the Department. Not all tutors in the Department have felt that Adult Education has a sufficient subject matter or is sufficiently rigorous to constitute a separate discipline. Yet one Resident Tutor pursued diploma work in the field and another is currently on leave in Canada pursuing a doctorate. The Department did, however, design blueprints for a post-graduate course in Education. Perhaps the uniqueness of West Indian experience must await postgraduate researchers who will be sufficiently stimulated to isolate the principles which have governed that experience so that a body of teachable material can be produced as incentive for further work.

The Extra-Mural Department has naturally identified the activity as one essential to the growth of a people and has consciously given leadership over the years to adult education agencies all over the Caribbean, especially in social welfare, labour co-operatives and agriculture. In 1952 the Department spearheaded an international seminar on Adult Education and in 1959 the Resident Tutor in Jamaica arranged a follow-up. But although its leadership in the field has been dynamic, the Department has never given the impression that it wishes to hold sway. This has helped to maintain the necessary climate of goodwill and interest such as the United Kingdom Extra-Mural work had from the W E A at the turn of the century. Extra-Mural programmes are invariably presented 'in collaboration with...', or in joint sponsorship with, one or more of the going adult education agencies in territories throughout the West Indies. It accounts for the wide voluntary participation in the programme and helps to explain why so much can be achieved despite the lack of funds.

For the work of the Department can claim some achievement. Most of the major creative artists in the West Indies in the post-war period have received a fillip from Extra-Mural work. Hundreds of civil servants, public leaders, including prime ministers, premiers and ambassadors, and labour leaders participated in early Extra-Mural programmes as students or teachers or both. The other thousands who have attended workshops, seminars, courses, conferences ranging from a day to six months are not mere statistical entities but living men and women now contributing to West Indian life. For many years the University meant 'Extra-Mural' to most West Indians outside Jamaica, where the University was originally sited. The Penson Committee felt it was 'fair to recognize that the Department, by the very nature of its work and by the representational functions of its tutors resident in each of the seven territories, had made an invaluable contribution to the general public relations of the University as a whole, and that the financial investment made in this work cannot be judged wholly in terms of its technical qualities'.

It is by the qualitative measure of its contribution that the Department is most fairly judged. Some of its achievements defy quantification, though one must not deny the usefulness in knowing that in St Vincent in year X, for example, enrolment for classes rose by 200 per cent over the previous year. Indeed the rigorous keeping of records has not been a strong point of the Department's work and though more recently positive steps have been taken to ensure that usable records are at hand for comparative study and for reassessment exercises, it will be some time before the full effect of this is felt.

This probably accounts for certain criticisms that are sometimes levelled at the Department. One such criticism is that the Department does not build up a statement of major objectives nor does it list priorities for future expansion should resources become available. This is not altogether the case. The 1963 Antigua Conference did formulate a list of priorities, though the more valid criticism that there has not been a thorough follow-through cannot be gainsaid. Priorities have emerged and the Department has found itself in a surprisingly receptive mood to cope. The Social Welfare Training Centre, the Trade Union Education Institute, the Creative Arts Centre have all developed naturally out of the Department's work in the training of social welfare workers and community development officers, in the training of labour leaders, and the stimulation of the arts, particularly drama, dance, music and painting, almost from the beginning of the Department's life. These are not things grafted on to a dying institution, rather they sprang out of the fertility of the early work started. The newly-consolidated programme needs to be contained in a slightly different structure where Resident Tutors in the field can feed wholesomely on the work of these specialized agencies. But not all tutors and not all territories will have a 'felt need' for social work training or labour education or even creative arts in large doses. The obvious answer would be that tutors should be realistic and offer what the University Extra-Mural Department *can* offer. But any such simplistic approach to the solution of the special problems of the territories is likely to negate the Tutor's work.

The criticism that the recruitment, induction and training of staff members is largely a matter of chance and opportunism is still valid. There have been improvements in approach since Cyril Houle made the criticism, but Extra-Mural work, uncodified and protean, is left to reveal itself to many a tutor rather than be studied in the abstract. Problems are avoided by the instant spiritual connection tutors seem to make with the work. Those who have found it too taxing in its many-sidedness and uncertainties have resigned without much ado. Many others have remained, and there are some who seem committed to making it a life-service.

The physical facilities of University Centres will ensure greater continuity for many aspects of the programme all over the West Indies. It may even help to knit together the many adult education agencies which have sprung up in the field since Extra-Mural began. The limitations of the programme are still not understood by many well-meaning public leaders who support the programme, and Tutors will always be faced with the vagaries of compromise between making their work a commonplace ingredient of community service and attempts at bringing to the community intellectual excellence, which is the job of a University adult education agency.

The goal is all the more important in a West Indian community which has no strong intellectual tradition, where the rationale of existence turned on commercial profit for far too long, and where, as hewers of wood and drawers of water, most people had their thinking done for them elsewhere. In this respect the adult education programme of the University of the West Indies must be strengthened not weakened, for the 'best' is yet to be achieved.

The Department has the good fortune to have a staff comprising people with a great sense of dedication and an idealism that happily is not often used to blind them to realities. It is a highly self-critical staff, sometimes impatient with the slow rate of change where change is necessary, but never falling prey to incurable cynicism. Most of them have a good deal of energy and better still an understanding of the kaleidescope of issues which concern us daily in West Indian life. The issues in the end all turn on the over-riding need for an uprooted people with varied backgrounds and with new responsibilities following on the transfer of power to find themselves in the context of a rapidly changing world dominated by technology and torn by myriad contradictions. In many ways the West Indies is a microcosm of this wider world experience and this gives to the work of West Indian adult education a certain sense of immediacy that it might otherwise have lacked.

The work may need to be tightened up and given sharper focus in the wider framework of West Indian adult education but it can never flourish if bound by a straitjacket of inflexible administrative procedures and spiritless pedestrian policies. For the task is still to educate for nationhood, or rather to help translate the formal transfer of power into positive and substantive action by West Indians who see themselves as citizens of a modern world. The work in adult education remains at heart then a creative exercise – disciplined indeed, but never lacking in vitality and never to be deprived of the spirit of discovery which must be its dynamic motive force.

NOTES AND REFERENCES

1. In 1943 the Secretary of State for the Colonies appointed the
Asquith Commission to inquire into Higher Education in the
colonies. The West Indies Committee of the Commission, known as
the Irvine Committee from the name of its Chairman, Sir James
Irvine, Vice-Chancellor of St Andrews University, was appointed in
January 1944. Its recommendation of the founding of a University
College (in special relationship with London University) was
accepted by West Indian governments – 'West Indian' refers to
English-speaking communities in the Caribbean (see *Historical
Introduction*, University of the West Indies Calendar 1968/69, also
Article on The University College of the West Indies by T. W. J.
Taylor, *Caribbean Quarterly*, vol. 2 no. 1).
2. See *The Exeter Papers : Report of the First International Conference on
the Comparative Study of Adult Education*, p 9ff.
3. Through annual conferences off-shore tutors are able to meet with
colleagues on the Mona campus, to hammer out difficulties and
delineate guidelines for operation back in their own territories.
Through this device they manage to have direct contact with the
officials in the Bursary, who clarify points of financial administration, as well as with the Vice-Chancellor, Registrar, and officers in
charge of entrance examinations, since Resident Tutors act as representatives of the University in territories that have no campuses.
4. See C. O. Houle, *Report on Adult Education in the British West Indies*,
Centre for the Study of Liberal Education for Adults 1960.
5. As can be seen in the number of students which has grown from
the original 33 at Mona in 1948 to a total of 3,614 spread over three
centres, Mona, St Augustine and Cave Hill, at the beginning of the
1967/68 academic year.
6. The following have served as Directors in the Department:

1948–60	Sir Philip Sherlock
1958–60	Dr Rawle Farley *Acting Director*
1960–61	Professor S. G. Raybould *Visiting Director*
1961–63	Mr H. L. Wynter
1963–64	Mr G. E. Mills *Acting Director*
1964–65	Mr A. A. Thompson *Acting Director*
1965–67	Mr Hugh Miller
1967–	Mr R. M. Nettleford *Acting Director*

7. See Annual Reports of all Tutors.
8. The tables on pp 209–11 indicate numbers participating in the
Extra-Mural programmes. In Extra-Mural jargon 'courses' refer to
formal classroom instruction with lecturer-student relationship –
'seminars' to discussion of a chosen topic with or without formal
lectures or papers. This category includes workshops – practical
activity such as research or technical instruction being implied. In
class programmes the term 'effective attendance' means the numbers
of students who attended 70% of the classes offered in any course.
9. The Antigua Conference met in St John's, Antigua, in September
1963 following the request of the Council of the University, at its
meeting in June 1963, to consider and report on the detailed organization and future of university extension work in the smaller

208 « *Rex Nettleford*

territories and the staff requirements in view of the extension of
university facilities at Mona, St Augustine and Cave Hill and the
recommendations of the Appraisal Committee.

10. The Citizenship programme was given impetus first by the establishment and then by the dissolution of the Federation between 1958
and 1961. The gaining of Independence by the bigger territories and
of Associated Statehood by the smaller provided further impetus for
courses, seminars and public lecture discussions on citizens' rights,
responsibilities, structure of government, nature of constitutions
and the meaning of Independence. In Jamaica and Guyana extra-
mural groups took active part in constitution drafting and gave
their recommendations to 'founding fathers'.

11. 'Recurrent expenses of the University are met by contributions
from the following : Antigua, Bahamas, Barbados, British Honduras,
British Virgin Islands, Cayman Islands, Dominica, Grenada,
Jamaica, Montserrat, St Kitts-Nevis-Anguilla, St Lucia, St Vincent
...' (See *Historical Introduction*, University of the West Indies Calendar
1968/69.)

12. This was done largely under the direction of Professor S. G. Raybould of the University of Leeds who was Visiting Director in
1960–1. Further organization was done by Mr H. L. Wynter who
had had experience as a senior university administrator.

13. Started by Sir Philip Sherlock, the first Director, there are 14
volumes to date. It has over the past six years moved its headquarters from Trinidad to Jamaica. Editorial management is normally done by the Department's Administrative Assistant.

14. See note 6.

15. In 1957 the Standing Federation Committee of the West Indies
appointed a Committee to review the policy of the University
College of the West Indies and to report on future policy under the
Chairmanship of A. S. Cato. The Committee reported in January
1958.

16. J. Roby Kidd, *Report on Adult Education in the British Caribbean.*

SCHEDULES FOR NOTE 8

Class Programme

Territory	1963–4		1964–5		1965–6		1966–7	
	Total enrolment	Effective attendance	Total enrolment	Effective attendance	Total enrolment	Effective attendance	Total enrolment	Effective attendance
Antigua	229	—	321	—	1,036	609	942	564
Barbados	606	373						
British Honduras	166	133	138	31	204	72	183	77
Dominica	237	158	274	—	404	—	420	158
Grenada	169	101	260	114	269	236	266	213
Jamaica	706	365	1,457	1,012	1,238	258	388	128
Montserrat	243	198	248	199	319	252	437	303
St Kitts/Nevis	75	64	159	148	131	107	72	64
St Lucia	910	467	539	272	303	131	336	133
St Vincent	178	—	357	198	215	112	456	302
Trinidad and Tobago	1,235	855	6,833	4,463	11,375			
Creative Arts (Jamaica)	112	87	132	112				
Bahamas					563	279		
Total	4,866	2,801	10,718	6,549	16,057	2,056	3,500	1,942

Source: Annual Resident and Staff Tutors' Reports

Public lectures

Territory	1963–4 Public lectures	1963–4 Total app. attendance	1964–5 Public lectures	1964–5 Total app. attendance	1965–6 Public lectures	1965–6 Total app. attendance	1966–7 Public lectures	1966–7 Total app. attendance
Antigua	37	1,096	19	770	12	—	20	1,992
Bahamas			7	950	9	700	4	—
British Honduras	13	1,502	11	907	26	2,897	19	1,176
Dominica	14	440	19		18	1,535	12	1,125
Jamaica	79	4,555	83	5,876	23	1,502	25	1,665
Montserrat	7	—	17		10	606	5	505
St Kitts/Nevis/Anguilla	31	1,120	41	3,527	35	2,229	25	2,158
St Lucia	23	2,026	17	1,382	18	1,218	15	1,464
St Vincent	none held		21	1,305	36	3,295	18	1,455
Trade Union Education	none held		none held		18	1,115	8	263
British Virgin Islands	1	65	none held		none held		not available	
Trinidad	17	577	19	1,780	23	1,645	not available	
Grenada	15	1,085	7	335	none held		8	1,690
Total	224	12,466	251	16,832	228	16,742	159	13,523

Source: Annual Resident and Staff Tutors' Reports

Courses and seminars

Territory	1963-4 Courses and seminars	1963-4 App. attendance	1964-5 Courses and seminars	1964-5 App. attendance	1965-6 Courses and seminars	1965-6 App. attendance	1966-7 Courses and seminars	1966-7 App. attendance
Antigua	5	95	13	—	8	—	6	182
Bahamas			6	209	12	449	4	300
British Honduras			10	210	12	348	19	358
Dominica	9	492			3	150	5	89
Grenada	9	726	7	228	8	254	none held	
Jamaica	16	581	31	1,615	22	1,490	16	518
Montserrat	2	105	1	60	7	208	1	30
St Kitts/Nevis	2	71	4	334	8	466		
St Lucia	7	243	13	420	10	472	5	181
St Vincent	2	50	5	158	6	214		
Social Welfare	32	1,111	40	1,740	65	1,836	48	1,580
Trade Union Education			13	335	10	416	6	143
British Virgin Islands	2	82					1	
Trinidad and Tobago	6	113	3	125	1	175		
Radio Education	4	150	none held		none held		none held	
Total	96	3,819	148	5,490	171	6,303	110	3,381

Source: Annual Resident and Staff Tutors' Reports

11. *Spanish-Speaking South America*

J. W. WENRICH

Introduction

On considering the field of comparative education G. Bereday recently observed : 'There is a need for greatly expanded and vastly more discerning studies of the Latin American countries, an area painfully neglected in North American scholarship.'[1] What he said of education in general is even more true about adult education in particular. This essay is an attempt to provide no more than an introductory review of the system of adult education in South America, with examples drawn from Bolivia, Peru and Ecuador, three Andean countries with large Indian populations. Brazil and the Guineas have been entirely excluded because they differ so markedly from the rest of South America. Though Bolivia, Ecuador and Peru must be differentiated from the other Spanish-speaking countries, they share with them the common problems of growing nationalism, economic development, and political stability. The types of adult education to be considered will be : literacy programmes; community development; agricultural extension; university extension; military civic action; and labour and industrial education.

The term adult education as used here will not be limited to formal, publicly-financed programmes administered through ministries of education. As a consequence, many of the programmes to be reviewed may not be described by their organizers as adult education. In almost every instance, the ministry or department officially responsible for education in South American countries has little to do with most of what will here be classified as programmes for adults except for literacy campaigns and some vocational training. Paradoxically, many of the programmes are *publicly financed* but administered by other agencies or ministries. It is virtually impossible to quantify programmes of adult education in Latin America with any degree of reliability.

The most salient characteristic of adult education in Spanish-speaking South America is its direct relation to the general problem of socio-economic development. There is an increasing realisation that even programmes of literacy are directly involved in total national development and must be adequately integrated with primary economic goals.

Most types of adult education activity receive financial support not from a ministry of education but from another ministry or international agency or from private sources such as the Catholic Church, philanthropic foundations and industry.

The problem of literacy

A recent study of adult education activities in Latin America undertaken by the Adult Education Association of the USA has pointed out that the highest priority areas have been literacy education and community development.[2] Governmental concern about literacy was first formally expressed at the second Inter-American seminar on specific education problems, sponsored by the Organization of American States in 1949. This Conference, held at Rio de Janeiro, was dedicated exclusively to literacy and adult education.

Illiteracy has been and still is one of the fundamental social characteristics of Latin America. According to the last comprehensive world statistical survey on illiteracy, compiled by UNESCO in 1957, over 40 per cent of the adult population in all Latin America was illiterate.[3] South America at that time had an estimated 67 million adult population, of which some 42–44 per cent could neither read nor write. This proportion varies significantly from country to country. For example, recent estimates suggest that illiteracy in Bolivia is at about the 60–65 per cent level.[4] But the level among the Aymara and Quechua Indians in Bolivia, comprising half to two thirds of the population, was estimated at 81–83 per cent in 1950.[5]

The Pan-American Union, first on its own and then as Executive Secretariat of the Organization of American States since 1948, is committed to literacy education. The Alliance for Progress, chartered at Punta del Este in 1961, set as one of its two main educational goals the elimination of illiteracy by 1971. The United Nations, in its General Assembly Resolution 1677 of December 1961, called upon UNESCO to review the whole problem. Subsequent studies resulted in new pilot programmes. In Spanish South America, Ecuador has been the focal centre. Ecuador has an illiteracy rate roughly equivalent to Bolivia's and approximately as large an Indian population. Under its National Plan for Adult Education and Literacy, prepared in 1964–5 with the help of UNESCO technicians, Ecuador has designated three pilot zones for intensive literacy campaigns.[6] These zones are related to economic priorities and the educational programme will be tightly integrated into the overall development plan. The goal of the pilot programme is to provide literacy training or basic education to some 40,200 adults in 1,270 centres spread throughout the three zones.[7] Ecuador is financing approximately 60 per cent of the costs of the programme and the UN

Development Programme, through UNESCO, is providing the rest. The results may prove quite significant for the rest of Latin America, but particularly for the other Andean Indian nations, Peru and Bolivia.

The literacy problem in Bolivia, Peru and Ecuador is compounded by the national language problem. Richard Patch estimates that 38 per cent of the Indians in Bolivia speak only Aymara, and 52 per cent speak only Quechua.[8] The question immediately arises whether to teach people to read in their primary language or in Spanish. On pedagogical grounds many missionaries, including the Wycliffe Bible Translators, Inc., advocate the former. Correspondingly, for political reasons some communists and leftists advocate teaching in the Indian languages alone, holding that to teach in Spanish is a bow to colonialism and the ruling oligarchies.[9] The Bolivian Commission for the Integral Reform of Public Education in 1953 decided that instruction would be given in both Spanish and the Indian languages.[10]

Bolivia's achievement in overcoming adult illiteracy has been limited. Periodic governmental and Church-sponsored campaigns receive favourable publicity and some support from university students. One analysis claims that the government's ten year campaign against illiteracy, begun in 1956, had reached 60,000 people by 1964.[11] But the same report admits : 'Thus, the adult level of literacy has been raised somewhat since 1950...from 30 per cent to 37 per cent, due primarily to the average annual increase in primary school enrolments of 7 per cent.'[12]

One interesting innovation in the majority of the Latin American countries has been the radio literacy schools, the *escuelas radiofonicas*. The radio literacy programmes began in 1949 in Colombia with the founding of *Accion Cultural Popular* (ACPO) as a private foundation of the Catholic Church. By 1963, similar radio schools had been founded in fifteen Latin American countries and these countries established the *Confederacion Latinoamericana pare la Educacion Fundamental Integral*.[13] Bereday claims that 'The schools by radio run by the *Accion Cultural Popular* are the most singular achievement of Colombian education and its major claim to fame'.[14]

The basic educational components of the radio literacy programmes are radio cells or centres in rural areas where villagers gather to listen to one-hour educational programmes from a station sponsored by the Catholic Church. While the programmes are chiefly related to basic literacy training, they are also concerned with the practical application of education, as well as moral and religious training. The students listen to a broadcast and then study for an additional hour or more with tutorial support from an *auxiliar* or helper, who is usually a young person aged 18–25 with at least a primary school education. The stations themselves are frequently run by a missionary order of priests, such as Maryknoll or Jesuit. Examples of such stations are : Radio Sutatenza in the Colombian Andes, Radio Altiplano at Penas on the Bolivian Altiplano, Radio Santa Maria at Santo Cerro in the heart of the Dominican Republic, or La Voz de Nahuala, Department of Solola, Guatemala.

One of the big problems with respect to literacy education is that of evaluation. An extreme illustration of the gravity of the problem comes from the anecdote about the late Dominican dictator, General Raphael Trujillo, who decided that everyone in the Dominican Republic should be literate. Thus, under threat of imprisonment or worse, all the *campesinos* were required to learn how to write their names and one hundred per cent 'literacy' was briefly achieved !

Beyond the problem of evaluation, adequate staff, materials and facilities are lacking. Sponsors of literacy programmes have various ends in view, for example, political propaganda or religious proselytism, which may or may not aid the process. Ladislav Cerych has pointed out an additional difficulty : 'Because in many instances the acquisition of literacy has not led to any improvement in standards of living or social status, many people who have become literate have not only, like those who have gone back to school and then been afforded no opening, lapsed back into illiteracy, but have also suffered from a sense of frustration which has been economically, socially and politically disastrous.' [15]

It is probably safe to assume that there will soon be a strong continuing interest in literacy throughout Latin America. But more and more it will be related to economic development plans and seen less and less as an end in itself. Ricardo Diez-Hochleitner summarizes the prospects : 'Again I would say that the need for literacy programmes is too evident, too much on the surface of the total problem, and the pressure too great to resist, But now, gradually, the whole idea of literacy as an instrument, as a tool, a very essential tool, which we certainly want to encourage, is being accepted ; but the need to provide skills to give these adults a chance to contribute to the social and economic development of their country effectively is now being recognized more and more.' [16] Meanwhile, though a great deal of lip service is paid to literacy education by public officials, educators, citizens' groups and the organized church, progress has been slow.

Community development

The major emerging form of adult education, particularly in the poorer Spanish American countries, is community development. In Latin America, the two classic examples of community education began only about fifteen years ago. Yet in those fifteen years, community development programmes have been initiated in most of the poorer Latin American nations, perhaps in large part due to the efforts of various UN agencies, the OAS, the US Agency for International Development, the Peace Corps, and volunteers from other missionary and private agencies. While always adapted to national conditions, community development is essentially a foreign import.

The United Nations provided the initial impulse for community development in Latin America. The *Centro Regional de Educacion Fundamental pare la America Latina* (CREFAL) was established in Patzcuaro, Michoacan, Mexico, on 9 May 1951, by UNESCO with support from the Mexican Government, the OAS, WHO, ILO, and FAO.[17] It has developed for leaders from all over Latin America a nine-month training programme in community development which combines theory and practical training in nearby communities. Its major contribution is not so much the change in Patzcuaro, but the training of hundreds of leaders who have returned to their own countries to begin community development programmes.

In contrast, the Vicos Project in Peru, undertaken by a study group from Cornell University, was a case study in social change. Vicos is an old *hacienda*, owned by the Peruvian Government and located some 250 miles north-east of Lima. The 300 Quechua families (roughly 1,850 Indians) living on the total 35,000 acres (of which roughly 7,000 acres were arable land) were virtual serfs of the *patron* to whom the Government leased the land.[18] In 1952, Cornell acquired the lease to Vicos and began an educational-technical assistance programme to break the cycle of poverty, illiteracy and traditional folkways established and perpetuated for hundreds of years. It was essentially a 'do-it-yourself' agrarian reform and social change programme, based on education, under the auspices of a foreign university. One of the project directors noted : 'It was assumed from the very beginning of the project that, without a carefully designed programme of education, both formal and informal, it would be impossible either to establish or perpetuate whatever changes were proposed, in ways of work or of thinking.'[19] Formal education programmes were begun, technical assistance in agriculture and home economics provided, co-operatives formed and local leadership strengthened. By 1957 sufficient progress and self-growth had taken place to allow the transfer of the hacienda lease from the Cornell Peru project to the community of Vicos itself. Cornell continued to supply technical assistance to Vicos, but did not supervise or control the project. While Vicos has been used frequently as an example of successful community development in Indian South America, it was a small and intensive project and, therefore, perhaps

not really suitable as a prototype for national community development systems. Nevertheless, it did set a favourable precedent.

Community development in Bolivia is perhaps more typical of the
rest of Spanish South America than is Vicos. As an institution, the
Oficina de Desarrollo de la Comunidad (Community Development Office)
is a relative newcomer to the Bolivian scene. The initial impetus came
from a survey made by the Agency for International Development in
the summer of 1964. Based on information from the survey-feasibility
study, a seminar was conducted in La Paz in January-February 1965
for representatives from various ministries, international organizations and the interested public. Out of this grew the new programme.

The philosophy of the Bolivian community development programme is essentially no different from that in other countries : 'The
goal is more than a series of episodes embodied in concrete physical
achievements. Success in these, important as they are, is less important than the qualitative changes expressed in enlightened attitudes
and relationships which increase the capacities of villagers to help
themselves achieve goals which they come to determine responsibly
for themselves.' The programme aims, for example, at greater literacy,
improved health, and more productive agriculture, but its prime goal
is concerned with what happens to the minds and capacities of the
villagers in the process of achieving them. [20]

The Bolivian community development programme began in three
provinces of the Department of La Paz, all located at the north end of
the *altiplano*, two of them bordering Lake Titicaca.[21] The first group of
personnel was trained and in the field by August of 1965. In less than
two years the operations had extended to approximately 1,848 communities, reaching an estimated 1,250,000 people or roughly 40 per
cent of the rural population.[22] The key element in the community development programme is the *Trabajador di Desarrollo de la Comunidad*
(TDC), or village level worker. TDCs are local *campesinos* (Aymara,
Quechua or mestizo) who go through an intensive five-month training programme and then return to work in five to ten villages in their
home province. In some cases, Peace Corps Volunteers have also been
used as TDCs. The job of the TDC is to stimulate other *campesinos* to
analyse their problems and seek their own solutions. The TDC helps
them organize a community council (by whatever name) and channel
their efforts into self-help projects. The TDC is a resource man in
matters requiring limited technical knowledge and a link with expert
assistance when more involved technical advice is called for. So far, a
total of 255 TDCs has been trained and placed in the field.[23]

The organizational pyramid in the community development operation extends upward from the TDC to a TDC Supervisor for every

eight to ten TDCs. Supervisors report to an Area Operations Office, which covers one or more provinces. The Area Operations Offices are responsible to the *Instituto de Colonizacion y Desarrollo de la Comunidad Rural* (Institute of Colonization and Rural Community Development) in La Paz. It is under the joint executive control of an inter-ministerial board composed of the Ministries of Agriculture, *Asuntos Campesinos* (Peasant Affairs), Public Works, Public Health and De-fence, all of which furnish technical support to the Area Operations Offices. More financial support for the administration of the pro-gramme has been supplied by the US Agency for International De-velopment than by the Government of Bolivia, but all projects must have at least 50 per cent support in kind or in finance from the village residents. According to one report, nearly 900 projects have been undertaken at the village level, with the community support or 'local cost contribution' averaging 69 per cent.[24] It should be noted that such figures are open to question since much depends on how the cost of the contribution of land, labour, and locally available materials is cal-culated.

The problems facing community development in Latin America are manifold. First of all, community development programmes pur-port to be instruments of education and major social change, when in fact they frequently are merely mechanisms for mobilizing some ele-ment of self-help in small public works projects. Pressures from inter-national agencies and the national government for 'success' statistics in concrete terms may tend to reduce the positive adult educational value. Another problem area is the lack of financial support and adequate technical resources to respond to community needs. Thus, community development may only serve to stimulate and then frus-trate rising levels of aspiration. A further tendency to paternalism is sometimes observed. While the essence of community development is to decentralize decision-making about local improvements and to involve the people at the grass-roots level in decisions that most direc-tly affect their lives, some government administrators have a propen-sity toward authoritarian control; community development then be-comes just another central government programme. A final problem is the lack of specialists in community development. Community de-velopment has frequently been a favourite category to classify foreign 'experts' who lack expertise in any other field. It is similarly an open target for local lawyers and liberal arts graduates who are looking for easy *entrée* to the political arena.

Community development is no panacea, but it has a legitimate role to play in adult education in developing countries, particularly in Latin America, which shares our common Western civilization heritage. It will require a firm commitment from Latin American governments, not just financial backing from the Agency for International Development. With the correct emphasis, as education not public works, community development may have more potential than any other current adult education effort, especially in the poorer South American countries with large Indian populations.

Agricultural extension

The Co-operative Agricultural Extension Service is one of the oldest and most successful forms of adult education in the United States. Dating from the Smith-Lever Act of 1914, it has doubtless been instrumental in the transformation of the North American countryside. It is administratively unique in that it unites the federal government, the state government and the land-grant colleges in the service of the people. It combines research and experimentation with extension education. The concept of a 'county agent' in a certain sense is the prototype for the village level worker in community development. The Agricultural Extension Service has been largely transplanted in most of the Latin American countries through direct bi-lateral US assistance. Former county agents and state supervisors, especially from the states on the Mexican-US border where bi-lingualism is common, have been some of the most effective technical experts that the Agency for International Development and its predecessor agencies have sent to Latin America. Working through the local ministries of agriculture, they have succeeded in establishing replicas of the North American programme in most of the Spanish-speaking South American countries.

Adult education methods developed in the United States have in general been transplanted without significant change. Experimental agricultural stations have been established; farmers' clubs, homemakers' clubs and youth clubs have been formed; technical publications and advice are freely given; teaching demonstrations and formal short courses are sponsored; and pilot projects ranging from trench silos to antiseptic animal baths are undertaken communally.

As in the US system, the extension agent is the key element in Latin American programmes. One author estimated that in 1964 there were 4,000 paid agricultural extension agents in Latin America.[25] In Bolivia there is a central agricultural extension office for each of the nine departments. Though the reliability of any quantitative data must be viewed with reserve, AID's report in 1963 that the Bolivian Agricultural Extension Service was aiding 330,000 Bolivian farmers was encouraging.[26]

Programmes of agricultural extension have made many advances in

Latin America, but there are still many problems to be overcome. The principal one is how to obtain qualified personnel to work at the local level. There are not nearly enough trained agriculturalists to fill the available positions. Unfortunately, the graduate of a university programme in agriculture, who is called an *ingeniero agronomo*, frequently has higher expectations than merely serving as an extension agent. He usually wants to work in the Ministry of Agriculture and to avoid getting his hands dirty. For him, agriculture is often just another mode of entry into politics. As a result, the extension agent is commonly a *perito agronomo*, i.e. a graduate of a technical agricultural secondary school. Efforts have been made to increase the number of *ingenieros agronomos* and to upgrade the technical capacity of the *peritos agronomo*. In this regard, the most notable institution currently operating is the Inter-American Institute of Agricultural Science at Turrialba, Costa Rica.[27] Agriculturalists from all over Latin America have graduated from courses of varying lengths and types at Turrialba.

Another problem has been the difficulty in getting Latin American governments to assume financial responsibility for the agricultural extension operations. Typically, governments in receipt of aid have expected foreign assistance to continue to support operational costs even when the service has been established.

Given the decrease of food production relative to world population growth, it is likely that agricultural extension will continue to play a major role in adult education in Spanish South America. Moreover, such technical assistance is integral to the successful implementation of the agrarian reform which is so ardently sought in all Latin America. Because of past success in a crucial area, it is probable that both the US Government and the Latin American governments will continue to support agricultural extension.

The universities

The typical Latin American university was created in the image of Paris or Bologna rather than Oxford, Cambridge or one of the German universities. As a result, for nearly four centuries the orientation of the Latin American university has been primarily philosophical and reflective rather than towards applied research, public service or the provision of extension instruction. Some aspects of the pattern began to change with the reform proposals outlined in Cordoba, Argentina, in 1918. The now famous Manifesto of Argentine Youth of Cordoba to the Free Men of South America of 15 June 1918 touched off a university reform movement in Latin America which to this day has not run its course. The two chief aspects of the proposed reform were university autonomy and student/alumni representation on the university and faculty boards of control. While some of the demands made by the students were unreasonable and have since led to virtual anarchy in some South American universities, others were fundamental if the universities were to play a role in national development. In the last of their twelve demands, the students proposed a 'close tie-up of the university with national problems and extension of university instruction and consultative services to the people'.[28] Unfortunately, this proposal was one of those least implemented. However, there are notable exceptions and the trend seems to be in favour of increased university involvement in national development. Harold Benjamin, in the most recent and thorough study of higher education in the Americas, concluded that the universities of southern Spanish America 'are generally developing their extension and community-service programmes'.[29] For example, the community development type programme undertaken by the Belaunde government in Peru, called *Cooperacion Popular*, was strongly supported by students from almost all the universities. Under the name *Cooperacion Popular Universitaria*, university students formed technical teams to spend their summers in the countryside providing assistance to rural dwellers. In 1964, nearly 1,000 students participated in this programme.[30] In Chile, all universities have extension departments, as do several universities in Argentina, Uruguay, Peru and Ecuador.[31]

In Bolivia, the universities are the major centres of culture and most of them provide some sort of consultative support to development efforts. For example, the University of Juan Misael Saracho in the small town of Tarija (population approximately 20,000) purchased a radio station and provides cultural programmes for the surrounding area. It also furnishes a service of soil analyses and dental laboratory tests at cost for the residents of the area. The University of San Andres in La Paz operates a special 'people's university' named after an Aymara hero, Tupac Katari, which 'operates a four-year political labour institute leading to secondary school baccalaureates, a three-year technical trade and agriculture institute leading to certificates of expertness, a two-year institute for training teachers in eliminating illiteracy leading to the title of literacy teacher, and a school of fundamental education in reading, writing, and other elementary school subjects'.[32] The *Instituto Tecnologico Boliviano* (Bolivian Technological Institute) was initially created by the MNR government and administered by the Ministry of Education. After the 1964 revolution it became part of the University of San Andres. While most of its work has been in the traditional technical areas of higher education, it may become more involved in extension-type programmes under the University.

There are significant problems in the university extension field in Spanish-speaking South America. One of the major problems is the active involvement of both students and faculty in party politics. This frequently leads the universities to become hotbeds of insurgency rather than centres of community service or extension teaching. There is a tendency towards status-seeking in the effort to develop the traditional faculties of law, medicine and philosophy rather than agriculture, engineering technology and the secondary professions. University students also need to be reoriented toward national development rather than self-centred personal aggrandizement.

The prospects for university extension in adult education in South America are good, provided that there is a decrease in partisan political involvement and an acceptance of more responsibility for socioeconomic development. The university is the major potential source for new programmes in liberal education for adults, a field at present virtually undeveloped. If current experiments in *colegios universitarios* can be based more on the US community college pattern, the university could become the principal leader in adult education. Harold Benjamin concludes : 'In Latin America many universities are now recognizing this function clearly for the first time and are rapidly developing extension programmes, service institutes, and research agencies directed toward regional problems. In the next thirty years, extension services of these kinds will expand more rapidly in many countries than will the regular academic programmes and will become a principal concern of higher education.'[33]

Military civic action

The Armed Forces in both developed and developing nations often provide one with the best examples of intensive adult education. In a matter of months or even weeks adult males are expected to learn entirely new skills and patterns of behaviour. Not only must the recruit be educated to fit in with the military frame of reference and structure of authority, he must acquire new motor and cognitive habits related to job skills such as firing a machine-gun, reading a topographical map or operating radar equipment. The modern army thus becomes one of the major educational institutions in society.

In developing countries the army also serves as an institutional mechanism of social mobility for the peasant. Theodor Shamin has pointed out that 'The modern army of mass enlistment is one of the few nation-wide organizations in which the peasantry actively participates. The segmentation of the peasantry is thereby broken...The army provides him with a hierarchical institution through which he may rise as a leader and be trained for this position. Even where some national organizations are represented on a rural level, the army generally provides the peasant with the framework for the most active participation. Moreover, the experience gained in the army service acts as an important influence on the villagers. The ex-serviceman by his new experience tends to become a leader and a channel through which outside influences reach the villagers.' [34]

The world-wide popular conception of the military in Latin America has to do with the frequency of the military *coup d'état* or *golpe de estado*. The most unpleasant aspects of contemporary Latin American history are associated with military men like Trujillo, Peron, Batista, Somoza, Perez-Jimenez and Stroessner. And until recently the Latin American *campesino* has largely viewed the army from this point of view. During the last six years a new conception of the role of the Latin American military has begun to emerge : Civic Action. The basic idea is to harness the human and organizational resources of the army for developmental purposes. Civic Action has two primary goals : (1) to instil a spirit of community service in the army and (2) to create respect for and confidence in the army on the part of the people. Part of the impetus for Civic Action has come from the revolutionary-insurgency training activities of the Castro Cuban government, in that the Latin American military is beginning to realise that efforts must be made to help the masses achieve social progress or the army will be forced to wage a continual military campaign against guerrillas. Hence, since 1961, US Military Missions throughout Latin America have also attempted to stress the Civic Action role of the army.

Civic Action training programmes include teaching recruits how to read and write, how to apply basic tools, how to improve agricultural production, and how to apply basic public health and first aid measures. Then, working with local villagers, army units assist in the development of socially desirable projects, such as potable water systems, secondary roads, rural schools, literacy campaigns, and pest and rodent extermination. In many ways, Civic Action is a form of community development.

Civic Action began in Bolivia in 1961 on a pilot basis. By the November 1964 revolution, through the combined efforts of the local people and the armed forces, supported by the US Military Mission and the Agency for International Development, the results were reasonably impressive : some 140 rural schools were constructed; training programmes for *campesino* soldiers were begun on twelve army farms; 4,200 kilometers of rural roads were improved and maintained; and several miscellaneous projects of land clearing, bridge construction, and latrine construction had been finished. [35]

All these physical results obviously did not instil a complete spirit of civic service or obedience to civil authority in the military; in 1964 they elected to carry out a *coup d'état*.

The major problem with Civic Action is that the military have not fully accepted the concept of dedication to social progress and national development. Many projects are undertaken solely for political or propaganda purposes. However, the significance of Civic Action is not really in the physical projects accomplished, but rather in the educational experience of the *campesinos* who are involved either as village volunteers or as soldiers. Returning soldiers not only bring back those skills which Shamin pointed out, but they have seen social progress in other villages during their military service. In addition to skills in leadership and weaponry, they usually have learned some other type of developmental occupation which will be useful to them in their community.

Given the Latin American tradition of support for armies and the continuing threat of Cuban-supported insurgency, it is likely that military adult education, particularly as it is manifested in Civic Action, will continue to be a salient form of adult education in Latin America. Military education will probably be particularly important in the socio-political integration of indigenous peoples in the Andean Indian countries of South America.

Workers' education

Trade and industrial unionism is a growing force throughout Latin America. So far its involvement in adult education has not followed the liberal tradition of the Workers' Educational Association in England, but rather the pragmatic approach of the AFL-CIO in the United States. Most education programmes sponsored by trade unions are directly related to problems of syndicalist organization, functioning and management. There is also a strong emphasis on the formation of co-operatives and savings and loan associations.

Labour education in Spanish South America has been strongly supported by foreign trade union groups. The American Institute for Free Labour Development (AIFLD), the overseas arm of the American AFL-CIO, sponsors training institutes in most of the Spanish South American countries. The *Organisacion Regional Interamericano de Trabajo* (ORIT), the Western Hemisphere affiliate of the ILO, also sponsors trade union education programmes. The Federal Republic of West Germany, in conjunction with a committee of Catholic bishops, has furnished support for labour training in several Latin American countries, but primarily in Chile through an organization known as DESAL (the Spanish initials for 'Latin American Socio-economic

Development').

Industrial education has been relatively neglected in Spanish South America, particularly in the Indian countries. Whatever low calibre industrial education has taken place until recently has been sponsored by ministries of education through vocational training schools and institutes. However, the increasing need for manpower education in industry has caused the emergence of several new apprenticeship programmes. Three good examples in South America are : SENATI (*Servicio Nacional de Aprendizaje y Trabajo Industrial*) in Peru; SENA (*Servicio Nacional de Aprendizaje*) in Colombia; and INCE (*Instituto Nacional de Cooperacion Educacional*) in Venezuela.[36] The apprenticeship system is frequently financed by a payroll tax on industrial firms and managed jointly by representatives of industry, government and labour.

Labour and industrial education has operated within narrow parameters so far. Latin American unions are usually entrenched in partisan politics, with each party having its own union structure. No attempt has been made to use the labour or industrial framework for broader programmes of adult education, with the single exception of the co-operatives movement. The trend for the future seems uncertain.

Conclusion

This brief essay has attempted to review the most salient aspects of adult education in Spanish South America, particularly as exemplified in Bolivia. In addition, in several countries there are ongoing training programmes for adults in several areas which we have not covered : in public administration, public health, public safety and civic leadership. Much of this comes under the category of political development. We have not considered the programmes of colonization and resettlement, which have large adult education components. These programmes are particularly prevalent in the Andean countries of Bolivia, Peru, Ecuador and Colombia. The long-range economic implications of these colonization projects, moving people from the Andean highlands into the less populated and more fertile interior, involve adult education in the most pragmatic terms. Another area is the upgrading of the level of rural education through intensive, short-term adult teacher training courses. For example, Bolivia was recently attempting to provide such training for 1,000 uncertified rural teachers each year. The development of co-operatives, mentioned briefly in conjunction with labour education, is another facet of adult education.

On the other hand, many forms of adult education found elsewhere in the world are generally lacking in Spanish South America. Week-

AENB Q

end, evening or short-term residential programmes in liberal education are virtually non-existent. Very little work is done in group
dynamics or sensitivity training. Few educational programmes are
available for adults in the areas of international affairs, scientific or
technological development, or even civic education. Libraries, except
in a few universities, are generally small and inadequate. No real
attempt is made to develop library extension education programmes.
One of the most promising US institutional patterns, the community
college, has not yet really been tried in South America.

It has been shown that while adult education programmes in Spanish South America are usually publicly financed, they are not administered by ministries of education. Yet they form an essential part of the
total education picture. Moreover, if violent revolution in that area of
the world is to be avoided, the prognosis for adult education is good.
Social progress and national development both require planned change
in human behaviour and attitudes, which by our definition is adult
education. From this review it is evident that adult education programmes in South America are, and will continue to be, integrally related to the process of socio-economic development. More than just
the future of adult education hinges upon their success.

NOTES AND REFERENCES

1. G. Bereday, *International Yearbook of Education*, Geneva 1963, vol.
   XXV, p 43.
2. 'AEA of the USA', *Study of Adult Education Activities in Latin America*
   (Report for 1 July 1965 – 31 December 1965, under AID Contract
   AID/LA 205), mimeograph, Washington, D.C., 1966.
3. UNESCO, *Illiteracy at Mid-Century*, Paris 1957, p 13.
4. Carol Stover and Joseph Allessandro, *Bolivia : Education Profile*,
   Washington, D.C., AID Mimeograph 1966.
5. Direccion Nacional de Informaciones de Bolivia, *Bolivia : 10 Anos
   de Revolucion*, La Paz, Burillo y Co. 1962, p 79.
6. Robert Mathias, 'Literacy and Ecuador's National Development
   Plan', in *School and Society*, v.95, no. 2287, 4 February 1967, p 85.
7. Ibid.
8. Richard Patch, 'Bolivia : US Assistance in a Revolutionary Setting',
   in *Social Change in Latin America Today*, New York 1960, p 113.
9. Jorge Ovando, ibid. p 151.
10. Robert Alexander, *The Bolivian Revolution*, 1958, p 85.
11. Stover and Alessandro, op. cit. p 8.
12. Ibid.
13. Manfred Nitsch, 'Fundamental Integral Education : Radio Schools
    in Latin America', in *Comparative Education Review*, vol. 3, Dec. 1964.
14. Bereday, op. cit. p 154.

15. Ladislav Cerych, *Problems of Aid to Education in Developing Countries*, p 88.
16. Ricardo Diez-Hochleitner, 'Educational Planning', in CER, op. cit. p 52.
17. Lloyd H. Huges, 'CREFAL : Training Centre for Community Development for Latin America', in *International Review of Education*, vol. ix, no. 2, 1963–4.
18. Allan R. Holmberg, 'Changing Community Attitudes and Values in Peru : A Case Study in Guided Change,' in *Social Change in Latin America Today*, p 79.
19. Allan R. Holmberg, op. cit. p 89.
20. Oficina Central de Desarrollo de la Comunidad, *Programa Boliviano de Desarrollo de la Comunidad*, p 9.
21. Oficina Central de Desarrollo de la Comunidad, op. cit. p 17.
22. US Agency for International Development, *National Rural Community Development Program in Bolivia*, p 7.
23. Ibid.
24. USAID, op cit. p 7.
25. Fernando del Rio, 'Agricultural Education in Latin America and Its Promises for the Future', in *Phi Delta Kappan*, vol. 45, Jan. 1964, p 206.
26. US Agency for International Development, *Alliance for Progress in Bolivia*, 1963, p 13.
27. Earl Jones, 'An Analysis of Inter- American Adult Education Programmes', in *Phi Delta Kappa*, vol. 45, Jan. 1964, p 189.
28. Harold R. W. Benjamin, *Higher Education in the American Republics*, 1965, p 53.
29. Ibid. p 83.
30. Secretaria nacional de Informacion y Coordinacion del Desarrollo Comunal, *Una Political para el Desarrollo*, 1965.
31. Benjamin, op. cit. pp. 83–4.
32. Ibid. p 84.
33. Ibid. p 207.
34. Theodor Shamin, 'The Peasantry as a Political Factor', in *The Sociological Review*, Mar. 1966, p 21.
35. Adolofo Velasco, Oficina de Accion Civica, *Informe*, 1966.
36. Franciso Cespedes, ibid. p 45.

12. Convergences

ALAN M. THOMAS*

Confusion of terms

For some time now the language of comparative national development has been producing increasing discomfort amongst its users. In the period when the word 'underdeveloped' was used to describe largely rural agricultural societies with large populations, low incomes and low *per capita* production, the discomfort was to a large degree political. No country, people, or leading élite likes to endure for very long the invidious title of 'underdeveloped'.

The shift to the term 'developing' in order to safeguard self-respect has not helped very much. If some countries are to be described as developing, then what are the others? While a sort of international blindness has tolerated this nomenclature, it has not concealed the fact that most people still believe, and act as though they believe, that there are two groups of countries. Both parties to this international word-game know this reality, despite ritual acknowledgements to other criteria that may alter the relative positions of the two types of country.

One of the dangerous results of the division is that some countries and their representatives find themselves consistently in the role of donor-teachers whereas others are consistently cast as beneficiary-learners. This is a serious state of affairs that must be altered if we are ever to attain an adequate international equilibrium.

But what if we were to take the language used at face value? Suppose we assume that all countries are developing, that they are developing in different areas and in different directions at different speeds. Let us suppose further that there are various criteria for evaluating this developing process and that the result of applying such criteria is to locate countries at different levels on different scales. That this may represent naive and gratuitous generosity on the part of citizens of rich countries who are more than adequately housed, fed and secured for the future can be granted. But the attempt is more than

*For four months in 1968 Dr Thomas acted as a visiting consultant in a number of African countries under the terms of the Commonwealth Aid Scheme.

merely generous, it is a form of self-protection. Canada may not be regarded as something other than a 'developing' country. If it is, it is unworthy of interest. However, if Canada may be termed a 'developing' country, then how can the word be applied to all countries? Only if the notion be accepted of many possible routes for development and many criteria. Development is not a straight line from poverty to comfort or affluence, as we are certainly discovering. Nor is it an inevitable climb up only one ladder. Suppose, for example, that so-called Western civilization was suddenly to enter a neo-religious period in which salvation, holiness, self-purification, and humane collective values were to become of all-consuming significance in place of those that now dominate. In the light of some of the present discontents and the self-exploratory activities and language of Western youth, it is not a wholly improbable eventuality. Which countries or societies would then be regarded as developing in either the current distorted use of the word or the descriptive one? If such a change were to come about, surely it would be by accepting the aid of current technology rather than abandoning or combating it? Would the currently advanced countries, measured in technological terms, become the more humane and holy ones, or would those that seem to have been able to maintain religious traditions while still grappling with the new sciences, industries and technologies?

None of us can know the answer to these queries, but it is possible that a consideration of adult education in several countries – the purpose of this book – might throw some light on the question. The approach here, however, is somewhat different from the approach in other chapters. Usually, culture in the full sense of the word is examined in order to separate out the institutions and practices of adult education. Unstated assumptions about the value and purposes of adult education inform comparative analysis, which in turn is generally governed by the assumptions about development already discussed. In other words the growth and range of adult education are examined implicitly as a factor in the support of economic development.

The general acceptance in Western countries of the belief that education, and increasingly adult education, is an investment leading to economic growth has recently been challenged by Robert Hutchins. In *The Learning Society* Hutchins argues that the only convincing evidence supports the opposite view. Instead of a rich and flourishing educational system leading to a rich and flourishing society, Hutchins points out that the reverse appears to happen – rich and flourishing societies create rich and flourishing educational systems. Attempts to prove the opposite have not yet been conspicuously successful.

With this in mind, the attempt will be made to explore in a comparative way manifestations of adult education in a group of countries, namely Canada and to a lesser extent the United States, and East and Central Africa, with a view to asking what these manifestations suggest about the possible development of these countries, rather than asking the more usual question of how does adult education support accepted development goals ?

'Learning' not 'Education'

It will assist clarification, perhaps, if we dismiss the term adult education, at least temporarily, and fall back on what is the more fundamental and genuine activity or function, namely 'learning'. Learning is what individual human beings do; it is an activity in which they engage. Whatever society or groups may do to arrange that predictable sorts of behaviour will be acquired by individuals, young and old, the individuals in question must engage in learning if the collective or group 'educational' efforts are not to be wasted. Learning far exceeds the limits of education, for all sorts of things are learned by human beings both individually and collectively that were not planned as an educational endeavour. In the English language, at least, the various contemporary uses of the words 'education' and 'learning' may leave this seemingly arbitrary definition open to debate, but the words do mean separate things and to use them in this way at least makes for some clarification.

Human beings learn, that is the quality of being human. In differing degrees they learn all their lives long. 'I shall be very well educated by the time I'm dead', grumbles Saul Bellow's Herzog. Therefore, a good starting point for any comparative study of education is to pose the question : how have different societies responded to the basic fact that their populations can and do learn?

There are a number of ways of responding to the question. The first is to exercise the maximum conscious direction of this potential, that is, to organize around those most intense biological stimuli to learning – passage through puberty, marriage, birth, and death – and to leave the rest of life's activities subject only to institutional or environmental factors. The opposite response is to try to subject the entire life span to a variety of controlled experiences so that no result is knowingly left to chance. The third approach, which by and large is the most common in Western society, is to organize intensively some aspects of individual lives, and to leave the rest to private and opportunistic direction.

When we speak of self-conscious organization of and for this potential for learning, we are of course speaking of 'education'. All societies organize this potential for learning to a greater or lesser extent. It would, indeed, be instructive to examine Western history with a view to estimating the differing degrees of organized learning that different societies have thought to be necessary. Certainly the last century, the period during which national concern for development has increased, has largely been a period of the steady extension of organized educational endeavour over ever-greater areas of individual lives. Nevertheless, the general pattern throughout the West and particularly in North America has been to concentrate heavily on the education of children, that is, on the early period of the individual life span, and only gradually and haphazardly to extend the organization to later periods.

While this may seem hardly more than a statement of the obvious, it presents an immediate and obvious distinction between the present circumstances of learning in Canada and in the East and Central African countries. The almost exclusive concentration on the education of children and youth to be found during the past century in Canada and the usa, buttressed by the compulsory attendance laws, the vigorous separation of children from parents for purposes of 'education', and the creation of vast 'public' educational administrative systems, has placed any other form or period of learning in special and ambiguous positions, to say the least. The destruction of any continuity in learning and, consequently, in living, is already painfully obvious. The growing use of the phrase 'continuing education' is a frail if determined attempt to combat the results of one of the most powerful and unquestioningly virtuous movements of the nineteenth century. The ideology of this movement perhaps reached its peak in the late 1930s in the United States with the publication of Courtz' pamphlet *Dare the Schools Build a New Social Order?* A whole theory of social change had been erected in the belief that the concentration of education on the early stages of learning is entirely efficacious. The Second World War dealt a serious blow to this optimism, and while the institutional elaboration of the belief has continued to work itself out, the ideological thrust has suffered nothing but reverses. What happened to it was simply that it became increasingly obvious that whether the schools 'dared' or not, the matter of courage, was not the point. What has been increasingly subject to doubt was whether they could, a matter of function.

In contrast, many of the less-well-developed countries in conventional terms have not been able, for a great variety of reasons, to concentrate so excessively on children. The result is much less separation of the child and adult in terms of learning, though fewer individuals may be engaged at any time in the educational process. The thread of continuity associated with learning is stronger and more habitual than it is in the heavily-industrialized countries. A second aspect of this is that the rigid separation of children from adults for purposes of learning is much less severe in the African countries in question, as in almost all of the less-developed countries. There are several possible reasons for this as well as a good many arguments about its virtue or lack of it. It is however interesting that a pronounced trend in the industrialized countries is to return to 'family' learning opportunities for the solution of certain social and educational problems that seem to yield to no other effort.

It is being suggested that 'learning' and 'education' can be separated from each other in any society in a useful way. While any 'educational' enterprise to be worthy of the name must engender or at least direct 'learning', there is a good deal of learning taking place outside of and independent of the official system or systems of education. That this is true, even where it is most intensively organized or applied as is the case of the education of the young in Canada, has been one of the main arguments of Marshall McLuhan. What the young learn from the external electronic environment outside the school competes vigorously and occasionally destructively with the planned environment within the school.

It is possible to hypothesize that learning in any society always outdistances education, and that rather than being a singular creative force in any society education is always accommodating itself to what is already being learned outside. This seems particularly true of adult education, where the relative absence of organized application gives us a much clearer view of what the environmental stimulants to learning have been and still are. That is what adults in any of the countries have been stimulated to learn as a matter of mere survival, as distinct from what any one or any self-conscious organization attempted to teach them.

The Canadian experience

Canada has been dominated from the outset by two overwhelming demands on human adaptation : learning-pioneering and immigration. The pressure of an alien environment that had to be mastered not merely to produce wealth and comfort but simply to permit survival has dominated the lives, the literature, the art, and the learning of Canadians. The adaptations of basic social groupings, as for example in Farm Radio Forum, co-operatives, and the like, to solve primitive questions of learning can be found in any common theme of Canadian history. The adaptation of formal institutions of learning to these basic adult needs followed as universities, interestingly enough, were established across the country. West of the City of Winnipeg they developed versions of the American-originated 'land-grant' colleges. The adaptation was natural because the circumstances were the same. Because these problems seemed totally unique to all those who experienced them, the settling of the continent of Europe was after all about 900 years away, there arose a particular concept of learning among Canadian adults. It was a mutual affair. There were few acknowledged experts or specialists. No one else's historical experience was either superior or even relevant; all were in it together. Teaching and learning were easily exchanged, often with some educational administrative assistance but only very slowly with defined expertise. This 'mutuality' which presumably gave rise to a good deal of the vocabulary of North American adult education, where the word 'leader' is often preferred to the word 'teacher', has provided a dominant atmosphere for informal adult education in Canada which is now struggling for continued existence. It most likely provided the basis for a sense of movement about which we shall say more later.

The second major impetus to adult learning was immigration. By the standards of European agricultural productivity the country was empty. By most standards of productivity and support it is still empty with a mere 20 million people. The land to be filled and the movement of alien adults, as adults, first into the empty agricultural spaces, and now into the cities, has continued for 300 years. It is not possible for an adult from Slovakia, Holland or Italy to settle in Canada alongside a native Canadian adult or another immigrant adult from somewhere else, without having to engage in fundamental learning. In the nineteenth century he faced a physically alien environment with totally different agricultural practices; in the twentieth century perhaps a more familiar urban environment, but with much greater environmental pressures to change, of which language is perhaps the most oppressive one. The formal schools quickly, or at least superficially, Canadianized the children, who brought new pressures to bear on their parents. In this process churches played a dominant role in providing a subtle and effective informal environment for learning. What also emerged was the ethnic-group, a half-way house which the immigrant had to alter himself merely to enter, and which then helped him with further adaptations so he might eventually leave it. Very little investigation of these learning experiences has been undertaken in Canada, but there can be no doubt that they are invaluable examples of institutions of 'learning'.

Perhaps the terms 'pioneering' and 'immigration' may be used interchangeably, for in both cases the adult as an adult has faced a totally alien environment, one physical and one human or social. Not all survived. Nor are the results very sure. A continuing aspect of this whole area is of course the present conflict between French- and English-speaking Canadians. What is interesting is that one argument recently used to persuade English-speaking Canadians to make necessary adjustments is that a bilingual, bicultural society gives an immense stimulus to learning.

The final theme, industrialization, is shared in common with other countries in all stages of development. The first industrial revolution came to Canada in phases and to different areas at different times. The necessity for adults to learn increasingly complex manual then intellectual skills has been imposed increasingly on Canada as it has on all other countries. The initial response in both Canada and the United States was to try to anticipate these demands, not by establishing facilities for adults to learn them, but to incorporate them in the pre-adult education of children. The 'Manual Training' movement, which grew steadily in the United States from the early 1920s, later reached its zenith in Canada in the 1930s, after fighting involved battles with the university-dominated curricula of the secondary schools. Canada responded by creating two distinct systems of education, each branching out of the secondary schools where theoretically all children attended by law until they were sixteen. But it was merely a stop-gap. Delayed to a degree by the Second World War, the full implications began to appear in the 1950s when it became all too obvious that the explicit preparation of children could not accommodate the occupational effects of rapid industrial change. Formal schooling became extended upward into various sorts of two and three year colleges, and universities multiplied, but far more important, a third whole new response to learning was created on a lavish scale in private industry itself. The chronicling of this growth in the United States by Harold Clark could be matched in range if not size in Canada during the same period. A whole new self-conscious response to the demands of learning, with different goals, different administrative practices, different staff and training had emerged in Western industrial societies. There has yet been very little theoretical appreciation of the fact that a large new segment of learning has increasingly been subjected to organization.

Before moving to a comparable examination of African societies, it is important to notice where the most exciting new learning might be said to be occurring. With the necessary application of automated industrial processes, the demand for conventional forms of labour has decreased. While nothing like a golden age of leisure and guaranteed annual incomes has yet emerged, intimations of greater degrees of discretionary leisure are to be found everywhere. Shorter working hours, earlier retirement, postponed entry into the labour force, longer vacations, all indicate a relaxed demand by conventional work. It is also true that the family and the church, the other two institutional mainstays of Canadian society, have also relaxed their demands. To be sure, formal continuing education has partially filled this gap, but a creative area is to be found where adults are facing available time unorganized either by traditional institutions or by trained habitual expectation. The results may be observed in increased political activity, the elevation of consumer problems to matters of considerable political importance, the growth of new social groupings, perhaps performing for these immigrants in time the same function as the ethnic group performs for immigrants in space, and a variety of other phenomena. Attempts to organize this area under the title of recreation or planning for leisure have so far been of slight avail, except by the engines of commerce, because this sort of activity is not subject to the ethics or administrative practices that have organized learning in societies dominated by work. This is the fascinating area in North America learning and where to look if any important convergence is to be found with African societies.

The African experience

One has to be careful in using historical parallels to examine learning as it has manifested itself in African societies. There is a tendency for the Western observer to think as though history began with the colonial period and there had been an uninterrupted sequence of predictable events leading to independence. The great problem here is that it is precisely in those areas ignored by colonial historians and of largely negative interest to the colonial administrators and even missionaries, that important learning of the sort we have described in Canada was taking place. Learning in the entire pre-colonial period may yet turn out to have been the significant element in the newly emerging Africa, except to acknowledge Professor Bown's comment that there are many 'institutions' of continuous learning to be found in all varieties of African culture.

The major task of the African after the onset of the colonial period was to learn how to deal with the invader and occupier. The literature of colonialism, technical as well as evocative, is full of the means by which this learning was undertaken and the price paid for it both by those who succeeded as well as those who failed. In examining the potentially positive side of this learning, that is the adaptation to health practices, technical cultivation, certain methods of government and administration, arts and the like, what is immediately clear is that this learning was never mutual in the way it was in western North

America. The colonized had not moved from out of their own environment. What the occupier brought was something that he knew and the African must learn. It was not, except under rare circumstances more apparent in recent times, a shared concern. This in part accounts for the formal rigidity with which the educational system of the colonial powers was imposed and accepted in African societies. There was little sense of its being adapted to suit the African society and its people. The colonizer, after all, knew the secrets of success, of power, of wealth. All that was left to the African was to learn what those secrets were. The General School Leaving Certificate, the ultimate goal for an African at any age, became the symbol of that achievement.

As the African did not move in the sense that the migrant population of Canada and the United States had moved, there was little of the identifiable general stimulus to adult learning that North America experienced. Because the colonizers were relatively few in number and African populations were large, the impact of the colonizer was felt less widely and more slowly. Whatever learning was indigenous to African tribal society in all its immense variety presumably continued down into periods of independence. The formal systems for the young, as we have already pointed out, gained a much slighter grip on the African population in terms of numbers, at least in the sense that they were confined to children and must be completed in uninterrupted sequence. There is an acceptance of education continued over an entire life-time among influential African leaders and functionaries that Western countries can well admire.

Independence movements have obviously been by far the predominant stimuli and shapers of adult learning in Africa. To overcome the colonial power with his own logic and his own political skills, parties had to be organized, political skills learned and massive schemes of public participation undertaken. In a way it is fair to argue that what was being undertaken was the creation of an African 'public' with all of the political, economic and social implications involved. The 'movement' seized imaginations, captured wills and prompted learning to the extent that nothing had before – or since. While the struggle for the emerging 'public' still goes on, it is apparent that a great deal of the individual commitment has declined since independence was achieved and with it the common learning. Indeed in Zambia, President Kaunda's 'Humanism' as represented in his *A Humanist in Africa* letters to Colin Morris, suggests genuine ambivalence with respect to how far he wishes to go in the creation of a 'public' which is seen as distinct from 'tribal Society'. His argument is that some of what is learned as a member of the public is undesirable in Zambia. In Tanzania, the ascetic example set by President Nyerere suggests the attempt to restore or maintain the enthusiasms engendered by the movement for independence, though the full connection with the potential of learning has yet to be made.

Following independence, the second major thrust has been, of course, the 'Africanization' of the various government and technical strata. This has involved not only the assumption by trained Africans of posts originally held by members of colonial governments, but the creation of entirely new positions and occupations relevant to and necessary for a self-consciously developing country. It also meant some changes in basic attitudes, since the learning acquired by Africans in order to deal with colonial governments was in some respects thoroughly inhibiting in the operation and direction of their own societies. However, since there was no time to wait for a generation of trained children to become adults, and no way to train them if the adult society remained untrained, all African countries established a wide range of specialized training institutions and colleges to produce the skilled administrators and technicians a modern government must have. For obvious reasons appointments to posts were often made with training to follow. The notion that any job of any significance is inextricably associated with periods of rigorous training, usually in residence, is generally accepted by most government employees. At the same time, the unremitting pressure exerted by African governments on private industries, particularly large ones like banks and mining companies, has produced a variety of industrial training programmes of a general and specialized nature, which are part of the planned educational enterprise in most African countries in a way they are not at all, or only latently, in Western countries.

Like Western societies the countries of East and Central Africa support a great deal of organized planned adult learning which is not described or identified as adult education. Almost every Ministry maintains one or more specialized adult schools, almost always on a residential basis, but designated as community development, youth brigades, police training, management development and the like. For this reason it is very difficult to assess just how much is being invested in adult learning or how extensive the activities are. Miss Bown acknowledges this in her estimate of the expenditures of the Zambian government on adult education or training. On the other hand, the Board of Adult Education in Kenya indicates that 1966 was the first year that any substantial investment was made in 'adult education' and by this they meant almost exclusively literacy since Kenya has an enormous variety of specialized adult schools. The administrative problems of locating adult education if only by defining it properly seems the same in African countries as in the West. The administrative history of adult education in its travels from department to department has the same nightmarish quality nearly everywhere. Perhaps all this does is to attest to the infinite variety of adult learning, and to the need for reform in our nomenclature.

The final general stimulus to adult learning usually confined to discussions of underdeveloped countries, in fact almost as a definition, is of course literacy. In one sense of the word now growing in use it could be argued that the fundamental stimulus to all learning is to acquire and maintain sufficient literacy with respect to the surrounding environment to survive. Thus one speaks of economic literacy, social literacy, literacy in communications of various kinds, and so on. Certainly in new attempts at dealing with deprived adults in Canadian society it is impossible and impractical to separate the various sorts of literacy involved except perhaps intellectually. Presumably this is what the new UNESCO schemes for 'functional' literacy really mean. What is very difficult to decide is whether the urge to be literate in the narrow sense of the word is really a mass stimulus to learning or a persistent demand placed on adult populations by a relatively small number of successful people who equate individual and national success with the ability to read and write. The success and failure of literacy programmes in the last hundred years would suggest something less than a mass movement in the sense in which we have been talking. The demand for literacy skills of the narrower sort does not seem yet to have stemmed from the bulk of the population. It may do so yet, but the nature of functional literacy is changing so fast as to make one sceptical. Nevertheless, large literacy campaigns are the most extensive mass adult education programmes that African governments have embarked on, and they have developed around them groups of able adult teachers and organizers who may prove to be great resources for any other educational enterprise.

Leisure in East and Central Africa is to a great extent the enforced leisure of unemployment or under-employment. A country like Canada simply could not or would not be able to support the degree of 'discretionary time' to be found in Kenya or Tanzania, for example. Whatever its cause, however, it is discretionary time and the overwhelming problem of these countries is how to utilize its potential. Various 'Harambee' schemes in Kenya match voluntary efforts in other countries. At the same time, it is arguable that the African has learned and continues to learn how to use such leisure, and what work is available to him, in a very different way from the Canadian. In a capital-intensive society the tendency is to move away from the use of human beings. Persons at work are reduced first to roles or functions, which are simplified, and then a machine is designed to perform their functions and they are driven from their occupations though not from the economy, since increasing productivity facilitates the separation of income from conventional work. The point of this is really the nature of the process rather than the result. The overwhelming attitude is based on the gradual and inevitable reduction of human contact at work, and the reduction of the need for human responses. We learn less and less from other human beings, about human beings, as human beings, until we come to the phenomenon of leisure, which without the productivity-oriented roles, functions and purposes, is suddenly overwhelmingly human in a dangerously unstructured way. This as we have already pointed out is the new frontier of enforced learning. In labour-intensive societies, no such constant reduction of the human element is possible, however desirable it may seem to be. More human contact is required; more learning is demanded between human beings. One should hasten to add that this does not always result in something desirable, since human responses are subject to the full range of good and evil possibilities. But the responses are in human terms, and the attitudes and institutions that exist for organizing these responses, not entirely dominated by work, are worth examining from an industrialized point of view. To return to an earlier comment, it may be here that the usual roles of teacher and learner can be reversed between countries, and some mutuality established.

Parallels

We have argued that the extent and variety of forms of adult education are one set of criteria for examining development. To do so, it has been further suggested that the separation of learning, the more inclusive term for adult education, from the specialized organized response is by far the most satisfactory way to begin the comparison. We have tried to identify those major areas of stimulation to adult learning in the two groups of societies, so as to see what might be learned from each other, and what the future holds. In both sets of countries we find similar ingredients in terms of organized education, though with different weight placed on them. We have also suggested that in each combination there are appearing some advantages, which hopefully will raise questions about active imitation of one set of countries by the other. Obviously, President Nyerere's break with industrial traditions as indicated in *Education for Self-Reliance* is a wholly admirable and sensible analysis and proposal. His arguments, it would seem, hold the key to a true system of continuing education and support for learning.

Clearly one of the tendencies to be found in the Canadian experience is that of mutuality – a tradition now struggling for existence, but which may be re-expressing itself around problems of leisure. One wonders where and the extent to which this mutuality already exists, or can exist in African societies. Where it does exist, Africa will find itself.

Clearly, too, the argument here put forward is that support for indirect or direct learning is a humane and unquestioned value for any society to pursue. None of the societies examined has in fact arrived at the point at which it might be said to be providing adequate support. There is no overwhelming evidence to suggest that such support is necessarily a concomitant of conventional forms of development. While the tradition of movement associated with adult learning in Canada and the United States remains temporarily obscure and confused, its absence so far in Africa is a disturbing phenomenon. But perhaps it is already manifesting itself under some new and splendidly African disguise.

Select Bibliography

BIBLIOGRAPHY

Bown, L., *A Preliminary Bibliography of African Adult Education* (University of Ibadan 1967)

GENERAL

Balogh, T., 'Misconceived Educational Programmes in Africa', in *Universities Quarterly*, vol. xvi, no. 3, 1962

Batten, T.R., *Communities and their Development* (London 1957)

Bereday, S.Z.F., and Lauerys, J.A. (eds.), *Educational Planning* (London 1967)

Busia, K.A., *Purposeful Education for Africa* (The Hague 1964)

Clark, Harold F., *Classrooms in the Factories* (Rutherford, N.J., 1958)

Coles, E.T., *Adult Education in Developing Countries* (London 1969)

Courtz, George S., *Dare the Schools Build a New Social Order* (John Day pamphlets, no. 11, New York 1932)

Curle, A., *The Role of Education in Developing Societies* (London 1961)

Dumont, R., *False Start in Africa* (London 1966)

Grefell-Williams, *Some Experiments in Radio in Underdeveloped Areas* (Paris 1950)

Harbison, F., and Myers, C., *Education, Manpower and Economic Growth* (London 1964)

Hely, A.S.M., *New Trends in Adult Education* (Paris 1962)

Hughes, I., and Tso, Priscilla (eds.), *Universities and Adult Education in Southeast Asia* (Hong Kong 1964)

Hunter, G., *Education for a Developing Region : a study in East Africa* (London 1964)

Hutchins, Robert M., *The Learning Society* (Toronto 1967)

Kaunda, Kenneth D., *A Humanist in Africa* (London 1966)

Kimble, D. and H. (eds.), *Adult Education in a Changing Africa* (Achimota 1955)

Lewis, L.J., *Perspectives in Mass Education and Community Development* (London 1955)

Liveright, A.A., and Haygood, N. (eds.), *The Exeter Papers* (Boston 1968)

Liveright, A.A., 'Conference on University Adult Education in Africa', in *International Journal of Adult and Youth Education*, vol. 14. no. 2, 1962, pp 101 – 6.

McLuhan, Marshall, *The Gutenberg Galaxy* (Toronto 1962)

McLuhan, Marshall, *Understanding Media* (Toronto 1965)

Pauvert, J.C., 'La Lecture publique et la culture populaire', in UNESCO : *Les Bibliothèques publiques en Afrique* (Paris 1953)

Pauvert, J.C., 'La Formation des leaders locaux', in *International Review of Community Development*

Prosser, Roy, *Adult Education for Developing Countries* (Nairobi 1967)
Raybould, S. G., 'Adult Education and Social Change in the Common-
wealth', in *Universities Quarterly*, vol. 12, no. 4, 1958
Raybould, S. G., *Adult Education at a Tropical University* (London 1957)
Read, Margaret, *Education and Social Change in Tropical Areas* (London
1955)
Thut, I.N., and Adams, D., *Educational Patterns in Contemporary Societies*
(New York 1965)
UNESCO, *Report of the Conference on African Women and Adult Education
held in Dakar* (Paris 1963)
UNESCO, *Literacy and Education for Adults* (Paris 1964)
UNESCO, *Final Report of the Regional Conference on the Planning and Organisa-
tion of Literacy Programmes in Africa, Abidjan, 1964* (Paris 1964)
Widstrand, C. S., *Development and Adult Education in Africa* (Uppsala
1965)

JOURNALS

African Adult Education
ASPBAE Journal
Community Development
Comparative Education Review
Indian Journal of Adult Education
International Journal of Adult and Youth Education
International Review of Education
Journal of the International Congress of University Adult Education
Women Today

ETHIOPIA

Brooks, K.G., 'Literacy in a Developing Country', in *Australian Journal
of Adult Education*, part I, vol. vii, no. 2, pp 5–10, part II, vol. viii,
no. 1, April 1968, pp 14–21
Central Statistics Office, Imperial Ethiopian Government, *Statistical
Abstracts 1966* (Addis Ababa, Artistic Printing Press)
Central Statistics Office, Imperial Ethiopian Government, Various Re-
ports on Urban and Rural Surveys (published in English 1966–7)
Haile Sellassie I University, Extension Bulletin 1955/67 (mimeographed
– English)
Imperial Highway Authority, *Annual Report 1965* (Addis Ababa 1965)
Imperial Board of Telecommunication of Ethiopia, *Annual Report 12th
year 1964*
Imperial Board of Telecommunication of Ethiopia, *Telecommunication in
Ethiopia, An Historical Review 1894–1962* (Addis Ababa)
Inquai, Solomon, 'The University and Adult Education', a paper pre-
sented at the Ethiopian University Teachers Association Conference on
The Role of a University in Developing Countries, 22–5 February 1967
Korten, D.C., and Frances F., 'Ethiopia's Use of National University
Students', in *Comparative Education Review*, vol. 10, pp 482–92
Ministry of National Community Development and Social Welfare,
Awasa Community Development Training and Demonstration Centre (Addis
Ababa, Central Printing Press 1968)

Ministry of National Community Development and Social Welfare, 'The Role of the Village Level Worker in Community Development' (Amharic, unpublished 1963)

Ministry of National Community Development and Social Welfare, *Implementation Report of the Second Five Year Plan* (Addis Ababa 1966, mimeographed)

National Literacy Campaign in Ethiopia (Addis Ababa 1965)

UNESCO, *Literacy and Education for Adults* (1964), pp 52–3

YMCA, *The 16th Annual Report 1966–67*

GHANA

Adali-Mortty, S., 'Adult Education and International Understanding in the Gold Coast', in *Adult Education* (UK), vol. xxxviii, no. 1, 1955

Du Sautoy, P., *Community Development in Ghana* (London 1959)

Griffin, Ella, 'Popular Reading Materials for Ghana', in *International Journal of Adult and Youth Education*, vol. xv, no. 3, 1963

Jones-Quartey, K. A. B., 'Adult Education and the African Revolution', in *International Journal of Adult and Youth Education*, vol. 13, no. 4, 1961, pp 198–203

UNESCO, *Literacy and Education for Adults* (Paris 1964), pp 62–3

INDIA

1. *General*

Airan, J. W., *Climbing a Wall of Glass : Aspects of Educational Reform in India* (Marak Tales 1965)

Sargent, Sir John, *Society, Schools and Progress in India* (London and New York 1967)

Sassani, Abdul Hassan K., and Barzdukas, D. K., *Selected Bibliography of Books and Pamphlets on Education in India* (US Office of Education 1961, p 14)

Siqueira, T. N., *Modern Indian Education* (Oxford 1960)

2. *Particular*

Daniel, S., 'Working Amongst Women in Uttar Pradesh', in *Community Development* (Sept. 1957, p 79)

Dutta, S. C., 'Trends in Adult Education in India', in *International Review of Education*, vol. 12, no. 2, 1966, pp 197–202

Dutta, S. C., 'New Experiments in Adult Education', in *International Journal of Adult and Youth Education*, vol. 14, no. 3, 1962, p 34

Dutta, S. C., *New Dimensions in Social Education* (New Delhi, Indian Adult Education Association 1962)

Dutta, S. C., *New Trends in Adult Education in India* (New Delhi, Indian Adult Education Association 1966)

Dutta, S. C., ed., *On to Eternity*, vols. 1 and 2 (New Delhi, Indian Adult Education Association 1959 and 1965)

Gore, M. S., 'Training for Rural Social Work at the Delhi School of Social Work', in *Community Development*, Sept. 1960, p 93

Hodge, P., 'Social Education Centres', in *Community Development* Dec. 1962, p 24

Indian Adult Education Association, *Life-Long Learning for Survival* (New Delhi 1964)

India, Planning Commission, Committee on Plan Projects, *Report on Social Education* (New Delhi 1963)

India, Planning Commission, Education Division, *Report on Gram Shikshan Mohim of Maharashtra* (New Delhi 1964)
India, Ministry of Education, *Report of the Education Commission 1964–66, Education and National Development* (New Delhi 1966)
International Co-operative Alliance, *Education and Voluntary Movements* (Delhi 1965)
Kahir Abdul, 'Staff Training Centre Village Aid', in *Community Development*, Sept, 1960, p 101
Kidd, Bruce, 'The Rajasthan Project', in *Continuous Learning* (Nov.–Dec. 1966)
Municipal Corporation of Delhi, 'Urban Community Development in the Delhi Pilot Project', in *Community Development*, June 1962, p 85
Murthy, B.S., 'Village Volunteer Force', in *Community Development*, June 1963, p 76
Naik, J.P., *Elementary Education in India : The Unfinished Business* (London 1959)
Peers, R., *Adult Education* (London 1958)
Rajasthan, University of, *Continuous Education at the University* (Survey Report 1965)
Rajasthan, University of, and Indian Adult Education Association, *University Adult Education* (Jaipur 1965)
Rege, K.B., *Magnitude of Illiteracy in India : 1961–81* (mimeographed, New Delhi, Department of Adult Education, NCERT 1967)
Singh, Sohan, *Social Education : Concept and Method* (Bombay 1964)
Styler, W.E., *Adult Education in India* (Bombay 1966)

IVORY COAST

Foure, P. *Experiments in Fundamental Education in French African Territories* (Paris)
Marcomer, S.A., *La Radio éducative en Afrique noir : la Cote d'Ivoire* (Paris 1966)
Pauvert, J.C., 'Tendances actuelles de l'éducation des adultes dans les états africains d'expression française', in *Tiers Monde* (Paris 1961)

KENYA

Mwendar, M., 'Adult Education through Radio and TV', in *Community Development*, Dec. 1963, p 13
Pittard, M., 'A Kenya Farmers' Training Centre', in *African Adult Education*, vol. 1, no. 2, March 1968, pp 19–24
Ross, F.E.U., 'The Training of Leaders for Community Development in Kenya', in *Overseas Education*, vol. xxv, no. 1, 1953
Wiltshire, H.W., 'Adult Education in Kenya : A Fresh Start', in *International Journal of Adult and Youth Education*, vol. 15, no. 2, 1963, p 73
Young, T.R., 'Adult Literacy in Kenya', in *Overseas Education*, vol. xxxi, no. 1, 1959

PHILIPPINES

Agorilla, A.L., *Adult Education in the Philippines* (Manila 1952)
Bernardino, V., *The Philippine Community School* (Quezon City 1958)
Bureau of Public Schools, *Leadership Training for Community Education* (Manila 1957)
Bureau of Public Schools, *The Philippine Folk School* (Manila 1962)

Bureau of Public Schools, *Seminar on Fundamental and Adult Education* (Manila 1952)

Bureau of Public Schools, *Functional Literacy in the Philippines* (Manila 1957)

Publications of the Adult Education Division, Bureau of Public Schools:
Adult Education in the Philippines, 1961
Adult Education the Concern of All, 1960
Evolving a Curriculum for Adult Education, 1957
Philosophy and Concept of Adult Education in the Philippines, 1961

SENEGAL

Cisse, B.M., 'Animation Rurale, Senegal's Road to Development', in *Community Development*, vol. 15, no. 2, 1964.

Fougeyrolles, P., Lowe, F., and Valadon, F., *L'Education des adultes au Sénégal* (Paris 1967)

Gueye, M., 'The Education of Women in Rural Areas of Senegal', in *International Journal of Adult and Youth Education*, vol. xiii, no. 14

SOUTH AMERICA

Note: With the possible exception of the study undertaken by the Adult Education Association of the USA there has been no comprehensive analysis of the aggregate activities in this field in Latin America.

Adult Education Association of the USA, *Study of Adult Education Activities in Latin America* (Washington 1966). Mimeograph edited report of a study conducted under contract with the US Agency for International Development.

Benjamin, Harold R.W., *Higher Education in the American Republics* (New York 1965)

Center of Latin American Studies, *Viewpoints on Education and Social Change in Latin America* (Lawrence 1965)

Cerych, Ladislaw, *Problems of Aid to Education in Developing Countries* (New York 1966)

Cortwright, Richard W., 'Adult Basic Education in Latin America', in *International Review of Education*, xxii, no. 2 (1966) pp 176–83

Del Rio, Fernando, 'Agricultural Education in Latin America and its Promises for the Future', in *Phi Delta Kappa*, xiv, Jan. 1964, pp 202–7

Hanson, John W. and Brembeck, Cole S., *Education and the Development of Nations* (New York 1966)

Holmberg, Allan R., 'Changing Community Attitudes and Values in Peru : A Case Study in Guided Change', in *Council on Foreign Relations : Social Change in Latin America Today* (New York 1960)

Hughes, Lloyd, H. 'CREFAL : Training Centre for Community Development for Latin America', in *International Review of Education*, ix, no. 2, 1963–4, pp 226–33

Huiser, Gerrit, 'Community Development and Land Reform, Preliminary Observations on Some Cases in Latin America', in *International Review of Community Development*, no. 15–16, 1966

Jones, Earl, 'An Analysis of Inter-American Adult Education Programs', in *Phi Delta Kappa*, xiv, no. 4, Jan. 1964, pp 189–92

Mathias, R., 'Literacy and Ecuador's National Development', in *School and Society*, 4 Feb. 1967, pp 84–8

Nitsch, M., 'Fundamental Integral Education : Radio Schools in Latin America', in *Comparative Education Review*, iii, Dec. 1964, pp 340–3

AENB S

SOUTH PACIFIC TERRITORIES

Beaglehole, J.C., *The Exploration of the Pacific* (London 1947)

Belshaw, C.S., *Under the Ivi Tree* (Routledge and Kegan Paul 1964)

Berry, Paul C., *Education by Television in American Samoa* (New York 1955)

Cowper, L.T., 'Rural Health Education', in *Community Development*, Dec. 1957, p 6.

Hely, A.S.M., 'The Role of Schools in the Literacy Campaign', in *Journal of Asian and South Pacific Bureau of Adult Education*, Nov. 1966.

Keesing, Felix M., *The South Seas in the Modern World* (New York 1941)

Luke, Sir Harry, *Islands of the South Pacific* (London 1962)

Massal, E., 'Village Hygiene', in *Community Development*, Dec. 1955, p 16

National Assoc. of American Broadcasters, *Education Development in the Trust Territory of the Pacific Islands* (Office of Research and Development NAEB, Washington, D.C., 1967)

Office of the High Commissioner, Trust Territory of the Pacific Islands, *Information Handbook* (Saipan, Mariana Islands, 1967)

Dept. of Public Service Commissioner, Konedobu, Port Moresby, Territory of Papua-New Guinea, *Careers in the Public Service* (Port Moresby 1967)

University of Papua and New Guinea, *Handbook 1967*

Stewart, Marjorie, 'Women in Home and Community', in *Community Development*, June 1963, p 89

Stewart, Marjorie, 'Women's Interests in the Pacific', in *Community Development*, Sept. 1961, p 118

Whiteman, J., 'The Women's Committees of Western Samoa', in *Community Development*, Sept. 1961

Whiteman, J. Annual Reports 1965–6 (Asian and South Pacific Bureau of Adult Education)

Whiteman, J., *Newsletters*, Asian and South Pacific Bureau of Adult Education, no. 1

Whiteman, J., 'Educational Institutions and Adult Literacy – Report of Seminar 1966', in *Journal of Asian and South Pacific Bureau of Adult Education*, no. 5, Dec. 1966

Dept. of Education, TPNG, *Papua and New Guinea Education Gazette*, October 1967, vol. 1, no. 9 (Port Moresby)

Dept. of District Administration, TPNG, *The Welfare Quarterly* no. 18, October 1967

Secretary-General, South Pacific Commission – *Forum, Fourth South Pacific Conference, 1959*, SPC, 1959, p 86

Secretary-General, South Pacific Commission – *Forum, Fifth South Pacific Conference, 1962*, SPC, 1963, p 79

Secretary-General, South Pacific Commission – *Forum, Sixth South Pacific Conference*, 1965, SPC, 1966, p 40

BRITISH SOLOMON ISLANDS PROTECTORATE

Dept of Education Annual Report, 1966 (Honiara, BSIP)

Dept of Island Territories, New Zealand, *Reports on Niue and the Tokelau Islands*, 1965/6 (Wellington, N.Z., 1966)

Careers for Solomon Islanders (Honiara, BSIP)

Legislative Council for Fiji – Council Paper No. 27 of 1966, *Dept of Education Annual Report for Year 1965* (Suva, Fiji)

Legislative Council of Fiji – Council Paper No. 3 of 1967, *Report on the University of the South Pacific* (Suva, Fiji, 1967)

Board of Governors, *Derrick Technical Institute Prospectus, 1967* (Suva)

Ministry of Overseas Development – *Report of the Higher Education Mission to the South Pacific* (HMSO 1966)

Popenoe, Oliver, 'The Importance of Education in National Development', in *International Development Review* (quarterly) Dec. 1966, vol. viii, no. 4

South Pacific Commission, *Adult Education Conference : Report and Recommendations*, July 1968

WEST INDIES

Booth, N., 'West Indian Island', in *Adult Education*, vol. xxx, no. 1, 1958, pp 263–70

Houle, C.O., *Report on Adult Education in the British West Indies* (Chicago 1960)

Kidd, J.R., *Report on Adult Education in the British Caribbean*

Magner, I.L., 'Extra-Mural Work in Trinidad and Tobago', in *Adult Education*, 1960

ZAMBIA

Capricorn Africa Society, *Adult Education in the Federation of Rhodesia and Nyasaland* (London 1959)

Clutton-Brook, G., 'Thoughts on Adult Education in Central Africa', in *Adult Education*, vol. xxx, no. 4, 1958, pp 255–62

Fletcher, B.A., 'Adult Education in Central Africa', in *International Congress of University Adult Education Journal*, vol. 1, no. 1, 1962

Kaunda, K., *Humanism in Africa* (Lusaka 1967)

Kaunda, K., *A Guide to the Implementation of Zambian Humanism* (Lusaka 1967)

Oxenham, J.C.P., 'Literacy and Development in Zambia', in *African Adult Education*, vol. 1, no. 2, March 1968, pp 10–15

Index